“In this groundbreaking w[illegible]ile Nxumalo invites critical thinkers, educators, and activists into a series of unsettling pedagogies of resistance and geographies of radical kinship. Dr. Nxumalo asks us to reimagine the practices of early childhood education and environmental education in historically contextualized, politically demystified, and ethically reflexive ways. Through interrogations of anthropogenic, anti-Black and settler colonial complicities in early childhood education, Dr. Nxumalo opens up new possibilities for ethical living and learning—a radically relational kinship with all of our relations. Situated in a compelling critical analysis of environmental degradation, precariousness, and exploitation, Dr. Nxumalo offers a timely intervention in the field of education. In contrast to preoccupation with psychocentric notions of complex trauma and damage-centered narratives of childhood, Dr. Nxumalo calls educators to take seriously the structural materiality of violence and alterities to it. To chart these unknown futures, Dr. Nxumalo brilliantly theorizes with Black, Indigenous, posthumanist, and feminist studies; and invites us to consider refiguring presence, witnessing, friction, and the super-complexity of ethical entanglements with one another and more-than-human life. This book is nothing short of strong medicine—to affirm Black and Indigenous life, futures and freedoms; and to call us to action toward different ways of being and doing with, and of, land, water, and more than human life. This book should be required reading in studies in education, not only for its incredible theoretical contribution, but for the ways it will enliven radical imagination and movements of resistance.”

—Jeffrey P. Ansloos, Assistant Professor of Indigenous Mental Health and Education, University of Toronto–Ontario Institute for Studies in Education, Canada

“*Decolonizing Place in Early Childhood Education* by Dr. Fikile Nxumalo should be required reading for educators, researchers, and students concerned with the most salient challenges facing early childhood education in the age of the Anthropocene. Dr. Nxumalo builds on decades of experience as an early years scholar, pedagogista, and early years practitioner to offer boldly reimagined theoretical work that disrupts the compromised white anthropocentric anchors of traditional early years education.

The volume draws from Nxumalo’s sustained engagement with early years research sites and practice in settler colonial contexts. A lively transdisciplinary dialogue is enacted through concrete examples that reconfigure children’s messy entanglements with the more than human, including mountains, fallen trees, bees, worms, and gardens. Chapters are anchored around new theoretical and methodological frames, such as refiguring presence, geotheorizing, and testifying-witnessing. Each frame is a call to action to meticulously destabilize the damaging logics of settler colonial anthropocentrism. While holding space for the many promises of posthumanist and more-than-human perspectives, Nxumalo confronts their limitations for resolving the persistent Western appropriation of Indigenous world making and place relations. The standout final chapter proposes an ethico-ontological framework for nuanced, contingent alliances among Black and Indigenous pedagogies that tackles questions of (de)coloniality across transits of empire.

This vibrant volume brings a provocative and resoundingly productive vision to bear on the thick ethical conundrum of early childhood education in settler states."

—Sandrina de Finney, Associate Professor, School of Child and Youth Care, University of Victoria, Canada

# DECOLONIZING PLACE IN EARLY CHILDHOOD EDUCATION

This book draws attention to the urgent need for early childhood education to critically encounter and pedagogically respond to the entanglements of environmentally damaged places, anti-blackness, and settler colonial legacies. Drawing from the author's multi-year participatory action research with educators and children in suburban settings, the book highlights Indigenous presences and land relations within ongoing settler colonialism as necessary, yet often ignored, aspects of environmental education. Chapters discuss topics such as: geotheorizing in a capitalist society, absences of Black place relations, and unsettling unquestioned Western assumptions about nature education. Rather than offer prescriptive solutions, this book works to broaden possibilities and bolster the conversation among teachers and scholars concerned with early years environmental education.

**Fikile Nxumalo** is Assistant Professor of Diversity and Place in Teaching and Teacher Education in the Department of Curriculum, Teaching and Learning at the Ontario Institute for Studies in Education, University of Toronto, Canada.

# INDIGENOUS AND DECOLONIZING STUDIES IN EDUCATION

Series Editors: Eve Tuck and K. Wayne Yang

**Indigenous and Decolonizing Studies in Education**
Mapping the Long View
*edited by Linda Tuhiwai-Smith, Eve Tuck, and K. Wayne Yang*

**Applying Indigenous Research Methods:**
Storying with Peoples and Communities
*edited by Sweeney Windchief and Timothy San Pedro*

**Indigenous Children's Survivance in Public Schools**
*Leilani Sabzalian*

**Decolonizing Place in Early Childhood Education**
*Fikile Nxumalo*

# DECOLONIZING PLACE IN EARLY CHILDHOOD EDUCATION

*Fikile Nxumalo*

Routledge
Taylor & Francis Group
NEW YORK AND LONDON

First published 2019
by Routledge
52 Vanderbilt Avenue, New York, NY 10017

and by Routledge
2 Park Square, Milton Park, Abingdon, Oxon OX14 4RN

*Routledge is an imprint of the Taylor & Francis Group, an informa business*



*Library of Congress Cataloging-in-Publication Data*
Names: Nxumalo, Fikile, 1971- author.
Title: Decolonizing place in early childhood education / Fikile Nxumalo.
Description: New York, NY : Routledge, [2019] |
Includes bibliographical references and index.
Identifiers: LCCN 2018056880| ISBN 9781138384545
(hardback : alk. paper) | ISBN 9781138384538 (pbk. : alk. paper) |
ISBN 9780429427480 (ebook)
Subjects: LCSH: Nature--Study and teaching (Early childhood) |
Early childhood education--Social aspects. | Decolonization--Study and teaching (Early childhood) | Culturally relevant pedagogy.
Classification: LCC LB1139.5.S35 N97 2019 | DDC 372.21--dc23
LC record available at https://lccn.loc.gov/2018056880

ISBN: 978-1-138-38454-5 (hbk)
ISBN: 978-1-138-38453-8 (pbk)
ISBN: 978-0-429-42748-0 (ebk)

Typeset in Bembo
by Taylor & Francis Books

# CONTENTS

# FIGURES

# SERIES EDITORS' INTRODUCTION

*Eve Tuck and K. Wayne Yang*

In the book you are about to read (and likely re-read many times over), Fikile Nxumalo describes what she calls a methodology of refiguring presences, a compelling reimagination of how early childhood educators might engage children differently about relations with place.

In this extraordinary book, early childhood environmental education is opened to a robust set of pedagogies that refigure relations between the human and more-than-human world. It "unsettles the coloniality hidden in the banalities of everyday forest pedagogies with young children," offering instead "a provocation to situate place learning within settler colonial, anti-Black, and anthropogenically damaged lifeworlds" (Chapter 1).

Writing as both a researcher and a pedagogista about early childhood programs in British Columbia, Nxumalo thinks through relating in a good way to place—which encompasses land, waters, persons and nonhuman persons—and to the Indigenous peoples who have taken care of these places since time immemorial. Nxumalo offers "refiguring presences" as an important practice in this work. Presencing is an idea that Leanne Simpson (2011) uses to refer to acts which undo the erasure of Indigenous peoples, histories, ideas, and futurities from land and waters. Refiguring, for Nxumalo, is to "reanimate, rethink, and relate differently to absent presences in everyday place encounters and [to] resist the normative practices and taken-for-granted understandings therein" (Chapter 3). These refiguring pedagogies attend to the knots of relations that have been violently overdetermined in settler colonialism, as well as relations in sore need of regeneration.

In this era of renewed public worry about climate change, all too often are the sovereignty of Indigenous peoples and the sovereignty of nature—in Indigenous worldviews, one and the same sovereignty—supplanted by a colonial concern with protecting the environment as a natural resource. This is how the Standing Rock encampment became popularized among many non-Indigenous allies as a fight for clean water, a fight against oil pipelines. This move made it easy for many to overlook the fundamental fight for Indigenous sovereignty. Nxumalo points out similar colonial moves in early childhood outdoor education, in which "romanticized and decontextualized connections between children and nature" (Chapter 1) become the mainstay of environmental education, supplanting deeper inquiries into the colonization and sovereignty of ecologically damaged places. *Decolonizing Place in Early Childhood Education* disrupts this decontextualization of place, land, and water in environmental pedagogies.

Nxumalo is a scholar who was born and grew up in Swaziland (eSwatini) before moving to unceded Coast Salish territories in what is (for now) called British Columbia, Canada, for university. Thus, when she is considering the ethics of relating to Indigenous land, to unceded land, to the Indigenous peoples who have been in relation to that land, it is as a Black woman scholar who has experienced meaningful relationships to multiple lands in multiple ways. This is a part of how she narrates the emergence of her ethics of attending to Indigenous place stories. She writes that she does not present these stories "as data, but with decolonial intentionality" (Chapter 1). In Chapter 1, Nxumalo elegantly writes:

> Living and staying with unresolved divergences and questions, I have attempted to avoid taking a stance where I can ever fully "know" and define these knowledges, as this "knowability" by others can be seen as a colonizing practice (Battiste & Henderson, 2000). I do not view these lived and living knowledges as fully describable, particularly when writing within the limits of English and from my own situated meaning making of these stories, predominantly from traced audio, video, and written text. Resisting a tendency toward analysis and explanation and the potentially inscriptive and colonizing effects thereof, I have presented these particular situated place stories without analysis—as knowledge making that speaks for itself.

We read these lines and this entire book as a call to attend to questions of which relations research comes from, and which relations research might go toward. The modeling that Nxumalo is providing for engaging Indigenous forms of knowledge making that already speak for themselves is itself game changing. It is just one part of why we are so grateful to publish this book as part of our series.

For educators and researchers looking to disrupt the colonial concepts of wilderness, childhood innocence, and environmental stewardship, this book will be a powerful touchstone. To engage in refiguring presences is "to creatively grapple with, interruptively respond to, and work through the doubts, complicated frictions, discomforts, knots, and silences" (Chapter 3) that abound in thinking about how we teach children and ourselves to be in good relation to stolen land. It is to pause to consider the impacts of programs which position white and wealthy children as "future earth saviors and stewards" (Chapter 1). It is to interrupt how the logics of settler colonialism are taught to children, and to consider how children are not too young, not too removed from understanding the harms of settler colonialism. For all of these reasons, the time for this book, and the many conversations that it inspires, is now. The future generations cannot wait.

# ACKNOWLEDGMENTS

Much of the research from which this book is drawn was conducted on the unceded territories of the Coast Salish peoples, where I lived for over two decades. I express my gratitude for my presence as a guest on these lands, while underlining that a land acknowledgment is one small part of the necessary work of learning to be accountable to, and dismantling, settler colonial legacies.

I thank all the children who have been a part of my research and teaching practice over several years. I have learned and continue to learn so much from your ways of becoming with the world. I am also grateful to the early childhood educators who have so generously shared their everyday practices with me. I feel so privileged to have grappled with doing place pedagogies differently alongside you all.

Thank you, Eve Tuck and K. Wayne Yang for your kindness, patience, and generous feedback through the editing process. I couldn't have asked for better editors and mentors. It is such an honor to be part of this book series.

I am deeply grateful to Veronica Pacini-Ketchabaw, Sandrina de Finney, Pamela Moss, Hans Skott-Mhyre, and Affrica Taylor for your insights, challenging questions, and deep engagement with this work; you have all contributed to my scholarly growth immeasurably.

Tia Madkins, your friendship and encouragement have sustained me in so many ways – thank you! I also extend my thanks to my colleagues in the Common Worlds Research Collective for creating such a nourishing learning community: Thank you Cristina Delgado, Narda Nelson, Nicole Land, Catherine Hamm, Nikki Rotas, and many more. Thank you also to Karin Murris and Vivienne Bozalek who have provided multiple opportunities for me to share the work in this book with audiences in South Africa; I have benefited immensely from the dialogues on decolonizing early childhood education.

I remain always in gratitude to my family, especially Aiyana and Leilani who have given and given up so much toward my still ongoing learning journeys. I dedicate this book to my ancestors: Ngiyabonga boMavuso, Ncele lekhohlwa. Ngiyabonga boNdwandwe, nine base Gudunkomo.

# CREDITS

Chapter 2 is adapted from Nxumalo, F. (2016a). Storying practices of witnessing: Refiguring quality in everyday pedagogical encounters. *Contemporary Issues in Early Childhood, 17*(1), 39–53.

Chapter 3 is adapted from Nxumalo, F. (2016b). Towards "refiguring presences" as an anti-colonial orientation to research in early childhood studies. *International Journal of Qualitative Studies in Education, 29*(5), 640–654.

Chapter 4 is adapted from Nxumalo, F. (2015). Forest stories: Restorying encounters with "natural" places in early childhood education. In V. Pacini-Ketchabaw & A. Taylor (Eds.), *Unsettling the colonial places and spaces of early childhood education* (pp. 21–42). New York, NY: Routledge.

Chapter 5 is adapted from Nxumalo, F. (2016c). Touching place in childhood studies: Situated encounters with a community garden. In H. Skott-Myhre, V. Pacini-Ketchabaw, & K. Skott-Myhre (Eds.), *Youth work, early education, and psychology: Liminal encounters* (pp. 131–158). New York, NY: Palgrave Macmillan.

Chapter 6 is adapted from Nxumalo, F. (2017a). Geotheorizing mountain–child relations within anthropogenic inheritances. *Children's Geographies, 15*(5), 558–569.

Chapter 7 is adapted from Nxumalo, F. (2017b). Stories for living on a damaged planet: Environmental education in a preschool classroom. *Journal of Early Childhood Research.* doi: 10.1177/1476718X17715499

Parts of Chapter 8 are adapted from Nxumalo, F., & Cedillo, S. (2017). Decolonizing "place" in early childhood studies: Thinking with Indigenous onto-epistemologies and Black feminist geographies. *Global Studies of Childhood, 7*(2), 99–112. Other parts are reprinted, in an adapted form, from Nxumalo, F. (2018). Situating Indigenous and Black childhoods in the Anthropocene. In A. Cutter-Mackenzie, K. Malone, & E. Barratt Hacking (Eds.), *International research handbook on childhoodnature: Assemblages of childhood and nature.* New York, NY: Springer.

# 1

# SITUATING ORIENTATIONS

Working from the context of what is currently Canada, the book is intended as an interruption to the erasures and omissions of environmental education with young children. In particular, the premise of this book is that there is an urgent need for early childhood education to critically encounter and pedagogically respond to the entanglements of environmentally damaged places, anti-blackness, and settler colonial legacies. From my perspective, an important part of this decolonizing response is to disrupt romanticized and decontextualized connections between children and nature as part of outdoor pedagogies. As I detail further in Chapter 4, dominant approaches to environmental education for young children in North American contexts recapitulate colonialist and modernist binaries between humans and nature. This is done, for instance, through positioning nature as something that (certain) innocent children need to be returned to, primarily for developmental benefits (see also Taylor, 2013 and Nelson, Pacini-Ketchabaw, & Nxumalo, 2018). I am also interested in the decolonial potentials of disrupting the normalization of the exclusions that occur when predominantly white middle- and upper-class children participate in North American nature or forest schools and become positioned as future earth saviors and stewards. I consider how such disruptions might happen when children and educators learn to relate to settler colonial and anthropogenically damaged lifeworlds in ways that challenge human exceptionalism while attending to their differential situatedness therein. Put another way, I am interested in bringing forward curricular and pedagogical conversations that unsettle undifferentiated and colonizing views of the world in environmental early childhood education. A central aim of the book, then, is to inquire into generative ethical possibilities of politicized, contingent, and place-attuned responses to settler colonial, anti-Black, and anthropogenic inheritances in early childhood education.

In the remainder of this chapter, I introduce the research project from which the book is drawn. I also discuss some key epistemological and ontological orientations of my work. I begin by situating my role as a researcher, pedagogista, and early childhood educator. I include an introduction to pedagogical narrations as key pedagogical and research artifacts in the project. I follow this positioning by laying out the ways in which I understand, use, and frame certain theoretical concepts and ontologies in this book, including my reasons for bringing certain perspectives together and the tensions therein. I discuss how "meeting" certain ontological and theoretical perspectives, alongside my immersion in the assemblage of data, its materialities, and the unsettling effects of certain encounters, led me toward a methodology of refiguring presences. I explain my rationale for the data gathering, analytic, and place (re)storying approaches that I followed as I put this methodology to work. Given that place is central to the pedagogical encounters that are centered in this book, I also discuss some of the ways in which I have come to understand place through my own childhood and youth experiences. Next, I situate the project from which the book emerged, as a response to current dominant discourses and practices in environmental early childhood education for young children in the North American context. Finally, I provide an overview of the book.

## Researcher–Educator–Pedagogista

The particular places that have come to shape the work described in this book are the places in and around a group of early learning and child care centers located in a suburban city in what is now called British Columbia, Canada, on the unceded territories of the Musqueam, Squamish, Stó:lō, and Tsleil-Waututh peoples. I came to be in these places as part of an action research project, the Investigating Quality (IQ) Project, for which ethics approval was obtained from the Human Research Ethics Board at the University of Victoria. Over the course of my four-year involvement in the project, I worked with 23 educators and close to 200 children. This project was intended to disrupt taken-for-granted notions of quality and instead take inspiration from contextualized, dynamic, and politicized conceptions of quality. In Chapter 2, I further discuss this work in relation to the necessity of disruptions of normative conceptions of quality in North American early childhood education.

As a researcher, I spent several hours a week at each of the child care settings making written, video, and photographic observations of everyday moments inside and outside the center. I also participated in practice as an educator. This meant that while I was at the centers, I did more than simply observe and record what was happening. I was also actively involved, alongside educators, in working with children—engaging in planned and unplanned pedagogical provocations and encounters.

My role as a pedagogista was to engage early childhood educators in critically reflective discussions and practices. The role of a pedagogista takes inspiration from the preschools of Reggio Emilia, Italy, where the presence of a pedagogical mentor to support, challenge, and deepen educators' practices and thinking is an embedded part of early childhood education policy and practice (Rinaldi, 2006). My work as a pedagogista involved bringing forward multiple perspectives to educators to facilitate critical approaches and contestations to several areas of pedagogy within each setting (Nxumalo, Delgado, & Nelson, 2018). To do this, I engaged in ongoing written and verbal dialogue with educators, both during and after my prearranged visits to the child care centers. These dialogues included documenting pedagogical encounters in the form of *pedagogical narrations* and raising critical questions on these encounters to educators.

Pedagogical narrations, also referred to as pedagogical documentation in some provinces, have been adopted as policy in early learning contexts across Canada. For example, early learning frameworks from the British Columbia Ministry of Children and Family Development (BC MCFD, 2008) and the Ontario Ministry of Education (2014) both center on narrations or documentation as key parts of early childhood education. Pedagogical narrations are visual and textual documentation of educational encounters which are intended to make children's learning processes visible and to provoke further thought and dialogue on this learning (BC MCFD, 2008; Pacini-Ketchabaw, 2010; Rinaldi, 2006). As Iris Berger (2010) notes, "these narrations provoke us to think anew and to resist normalized habitual conceptions of childhood, education, learning, and assessment" (p. 58). They can include written observations of children, children's work, or photographs that illustrate a process in children's learning. These observations can also be documented as audio and video recordings of children and educators engaged in learning inquiries. However, pedagogical narrations are much more than simply a record of what happened. A critical aspect of pedagogical narrations comprises educators' critical reflections on the moments captured, including, but not limited to, educators' subjective interpretations of these moments and educators' critical reflections on their pedagogical practices. Inspired by the practice of pedagogical documentation, as enacted in Reggio Emilia preschools, pedagogical narrations help to support an inquiry-based curriculum, also referred to as project-based learning (Rinaldi, 2006). Therefore, in addition to educators' interpretations of the learning that occurred, they often include ideas for extending and building on this learning.

Another important part of pedagogical narration is openness to multiple perspectives. Therefore, educators also may invite their colleagues, the children, and the children's families to contribute their ideas, questions, and suggestions for further curriculum making (Pacini-Ketchabaw, Nxumalo, Kocher, Elliot, & Sanchez, 2014). In summary, pedagogical narration is intended to be an ongoing process that includes: observation and documentation of pedagogical encounters; collective and individual critically reflective interpretation, making the narrations public to gain multiple perspectives; adding connections to educators' practices and to early learning areas as described in the BC Early Learning Framework;

and, beginning the process of documentation again (BC MCFD, 2008). In my work with pedagogical narrations, the process and structure prescribed in the BC Early Learning Framework (BC MCFD, 2008), while a useful guide, was not a template to strictly follow. Rather, I worked with educators to hold processes of narration, as provisional and propositional. For example, many of the pedagogical inquiries that are the subject of this book were not adequately captured by the areas of early learning described in the BC Learning Framework. In other words, our pedagogical narrations varied considerably and intentionally disrupted prevalent classroom materializations of pedagogical narrations as 'perfect, aesthetically beautiful' displayed products of early learning that are free of politics, pedagogical tensions, and uncertainty. For further insight into the variation in pedagogical narrations, the book *Journeys: Reconceptualizing early childhood practices through pedagogical narration* (Pacini-Ketchabaw, Nxumalo, Kocher, Elliot, & Sanchez, 2014) contains several examples of pedagogical narrations produced by the Investigating Quality project within the context of British Columbia. These include pedagogical narrations which address topics that are beyond the scope of this book but are critical aspects of pedagogy and curriculum with young children, including gender, disability, and materiality in children's art encounters and provocations.

In this project, we worked extensively with educators' pedagogical narrations to spur discussions on practice, including possibilities for complicating our practices with young children. This book builds on my previous collaborative work on the ways in which pedagogical narrations can be utilized for curriculum development as well as to push and extend educators' practices, particularly in relation to engaging the ethics and politics of everyday practice (Pacini-Ketchabaw & Nxumalo, 2010, 2012, 2013; Pacini-Ketchabaw, Nxumalo, Kocher, Elliot, & Sanchez, 2014). Pedagogical narrations were a key part of the support I provided as a pedagogista, both in sharing narrations that I had prepared from our encounters and in supporting educators in developing their own processes of pedagogical narration and accompanying practices. Many of our pedagogical narrations were also shared with families in several ways, including through email and in documentation panels displayed in the child care centers.

My work with pedagogical narrations in this project also builds on several studies in the early childhood field that have put pedagogical narrations to work as an assessment tool (MacDonald, 2007); to support educators in enacting critically reflective practice (Thompson, 2010); as a research method in inquiry-based early childhood classrooms (Hultman, 2009; Hodgins, 2012; McLellan, 2010); and to support teacher education (Murris, Reynolds, & Peers, 2018). One particular way in which pedagogical narrations emerged in this project was that after a pedagogical encounter, such as a forest walk, which I documented using one or more of photography, video, and field notes, I would prepare a pedagogical narration, including my questions and critical reflections about the encounter. I would then share this pedagogical narration with educators to obtain their perspectives (see Chapter 2 for an example of the email exchanges that often occurred between myself and educators). Some of these collaborative narrations and the accompanying dialogues would then form the basis of our extended inquiries.

Educators in the child care centers also created and shared with me pedagogical narrations, including those from experiences that I may not have been a part of in the center. Part of my feedback, which was both written and verbal, included critical questions that emerged for me, suggestions for extending and deepening their inquiries in practice, and providing educators with related readings and accompanying questions in an effort to invite multiple perspectives. These readings were selected from pertinent work both within and beyond the early childhood field to bring practice into conversation with perspectives such as Indigenous feminist, postcolonial, anti-racist feminist, poststructural feminist, and posthumanist theories, and the environmental humanities. The readings that I provided to educators raised political, pedagogical, and theoretical issues that I wanted to bring to educators' attention, or that we were already thinking about together.[1]

All of the educators from the different participant child care centers also came together for monthly three-hour learning circles that I facilitated. As with the child care setting visits and discussions, the intent in these large group discussions was to deepen, complexify, and critically engage with our pedagogical inquiries. My role in these discussions was to encourage contestations, questions, and multiple critical theoretical and pedagogical perspectives on the pedagogical encounters under discussion. These pedagogical encounters included the inquiries that are included in this book as well as several other areas of practice that are beyond the scope of this book, such as shifting fixed daily routines and schedules and rethinking normative early childhood art practices.

Typically, during the learning circles, we engaged in a detailed collaborative critical reflection of selected pedagogical narrations from one of the child care centers alongside readings that I had selected for the group to read beforehand. As with the readings provided to educators as part of the process of developing pedagogical narrations, I intentionally selected readings for the learning circle discussions that brought forward contextualized perspectives to trouble developmental "readings" of early childhood pedagogies. Euro-Western developmental psychology theories remain foundational to early childhood education practice, and an important aspect of my work was to seek ways to critically encounter, in collaboration with educators, the depoliticized and decontextualized understandings of practice that a predominantly developmental discourse brings (Pacini-Ketchabaw & Nxumalo, 2010, 2013; Pacini-Ketchabaw, Nxumalo, Kocher, Elliot, & Sanchez, 2014). I use the term *Euro-Western* intentionally here and throughout the book to underline the Eurocentric inheritances that continue to influence early childhood education. Euro-Western denotes epistemologies, ontologies, and practices that have originated from what is also referred to as the 'West,' including those from Western Europe, and from white settlers in places such as the United States and Canada (Watts, 2013).

The approaches I worked with toward interrupting practice-as-usual, and the effects thereof, were multiple, emergent, and contingent. That is to say, my role as a pedagogista in supporting and provoking educators to contest, politicize, and disrupt taken-for-granted understandings of childhood and early childhood practices was filled with "tensions, resonances, transformations, resistances, and complicities" (Haraway, 1988, p. 588). One consequence of the inherent tensions in my complex relationship with educators has been that the ways in which I have taken up moments in practice have not necessarily mirrored the interruptive ways that I have taken them up in writing-with the "data" afterwards. For example, in Chapter 4, I write about pedagogical encounters with a forest that I regularly visited with children and educators. In this chapter, the data that I worked with were pedagogical narrations written by educators as well as my field notes and photographic images from these visits to the forest. I also worked with my own research on the settler colonial material and discursive histories of this particular forest and Indigenous relationalities with the Western red cedar trees in it. However, the many discussions with educators that were generated from and helped to generate this data are not fully detailed in this chapter. In relation to unsettling forest pedagogies, these complexities-in-practice have taken a multitude of formations, with varying effects and unresolved tensions (see, for example, Chapter 6; Nxumalo, Delgado, & Nelson, 2018).

My role did not preclude questioning and critically encountering my own practices and situatedness within the pedagogical encounters, particularly in connection with the settler colonial relations that are the predominant focus of this book. Further, while I refer to myself, educators, and children in separate categories, there are no innocent outsider relations implied here. My references to children and educators as separate categories, while perhaps facilitating the clarity of my descriptions of this work, also risk stabilizing some of the very colonizing relations and binaries that this work seeks to unsettle—centering the all-knowing human adult as separate from and above children. It is very important to me that I avoid reenacting colonizing practices with educators and children that "teach that knowers are manipulators who have no reciprocal responsibilities to the things they manipulate" (Battiste & Henderson, 2000, p. 88). Rather than transcending the messiness of that which I aim to unsettle, I am inextricably entangled and implicated in these settler colonial relations.

Foregrounding my implicated situatedness within the encounters also necessitates a telling of the particularities of my positioning within colonialism as an Indigenous African and within settler colonialism as a Black, cis-gendered female immigrant to Canada. As I discuss further in Chapter 3, categories such as this one belie the complexities of the connections between settler colonialism, gender, and anti-blackness, as well as how they come to matter in my everyday place encounters. Within these complexities are structural and everyday violences, complicities, resistances, fluidities, estrangements, and relationalities. Drawing from Chickasaw scholar Jodi Byrd (2011), Eve Tuck (Unangax) and her colleagues Guess and Sultan point to some of the complexities of such categorizations, highlighting how the word *arrivants*, used to refer to people who have come to the Americas through pastpresent histories of slavery and global imperialism:

> is a recognition of the ways in which arrivants both resist and participate as settlers in the historical project of settler colonialism. The word "arrivants" helps to highlight the complicity of all arrivants (including Black people) in Indigenous erasure and dispossession… But "arrivants" may also conceal the unique positioning of Blackness in settler colonialism and the complicity of white people and nonwhite people (including Native people) in antiblackness.
> *(Tuck, Guess, & Sultan, 2014, p. 4)*

My focus in this book is on grappling with possibilities for unsettling encounters with "nature" in settler colonial places and spaces, including possibilities that attend to the entanglements of settler colonialism and anti-blackness.

## Situating Ontological and Epistemological Terrains

Throughout this book I put to work a methodology of refiguring presences (see Chapter 3) and practices of witnessing (see Chapter 2) to attend to settler colonial formations in everyday place encounters in early childhood education. I discuss multiple material and discursive constituents that come together to enact, sediment, or interrupt colonial relations, including, but not limited to, place histories and stories, pedagogical practices, human and more-than-human bodies, things, and affects, and my own situated subjectivities and location within the encounters. In this section, I want to lay out the ways I have taken up and connected specific theoretical, ontological, and epistemological threads in relation to my focus on troubling place encounters with nature in early childhood studies within the context of settler colonialism in what is now British Columbia, Canada. I discuss how these theoretical and onto-epistemological formations are carried through the book by situating my understandings of place, storied place, and place stories. I also situate these formations by discussing some of the ways in which I thought with Indigenous onto-epistemologies and posthumanist theories.

## Place, Storied Place, and Place Stories

In this book, place is engaged not simply as a backdrop for children's learning, but as storied, vibrant, unceded Indigenous land, foregrounding specific Indigenous knowledges and place relations where both human and more-than-human actors participate in the storying of places (Calderón, 2014; Tuck & McKenzie, 2015). I engage with place as storied to discuss specific Indigenous place relations, including Indigenous cosmologies and relationalities with more-than-human others. For example, in Chapter 5, X'muzk'i'um (Camosun Bog) is foregrounded as a storied place of knowledge, life, belonging, spirit, pedagogy, and ceremony for Musqueam peoples (Grant, 2012).

I make no claim to present a complete telling through the place stories contained in this work, but instead, as Anna Tsing (2005) eloquently describes, I attempt to enact an intentional and critical seeking out of "connections rather than seamless generalizations, inclusive tables or comparative grids" (p. xi). In centering multiple place stories, I draw inspiration from recent work that has highlighted the importance of centering storied and more-than-human relationalities in understandings of place in settler colonial contexts. In these understandings, more-than-human bodies, specific stories, ontologies, histories, and humans are all lively and entangled participants in the shaping of place (Calderón, 2014; Jaworski & Thurlow, 2010; Somerville, 2006; Tuck & McKenzie, 2014; Tuck, McKenzie, & McCoy, 2014). However, this active participation occurs within inequitable relations that create certain obscurances and erasures, such as anti-Black and colonial imaginaries that story place as a mute site awaiting settler inscription and property making (Byrd, 2011; Cameron, 2011; Jaworski & Thurlow, 2010; Tuck & Yang, 2012).

While the focus of this book is on places that are typically considered to belong to the realm of nature pedagogies (gardens and forests, for example), I do not consider place to exclude urban or indoor environments, and I work from an understanding of the urban as "storied Indigenous land" (Tuck, McKenzie, & McCoy, 2014, p. 8). In this regard, the urban and suburban child care settings that are storied in this book—including the buildings, the land, the pedagogical materials we worked with (such as paper and paint), the flows of water through pipes, all the human and more-than-human bodies in these places—are intimately entangled with settler colonial and anti-Black relations. These perspectives on place and place relationalities are particularly pertinent to my work because they suggest looking beyond innocent perspectives focused on children's place experiences and instead orienting toward explicitly politicized enactments of and dialogues with place. These dialogues with place critically encounter settler colonialism's ongoing erasures and foreground more-than-human worlds (Simpson, 2011). Importantly, politicizing place also necessitates creating interferences in colonial and neocolonial discourses that figure "humans outside of nature and thus implicitly posit that we are free to control our own destiny within a broader 'natural' world that is devoid of meaning, values, and ethics" (Rose et al., 2012, p. 3).

In this book, I take up this call to politicization through stories that bring contestations of place into view. I am particularly interested in asking how particular places (the places where my research is situated) might be known and experienced differently through stories that highlight marginalized Indigenous stories of place, attend to the vibrant more-than-human relationalities of place, and disrupt erasures of Black relations to nature places. While stories that unsettle colonial and anti-Black relations with place are suggested here as an opening to different and unsettling relations to place, this research orientation is not immune to recent critiques of place-based pedagogies and methodologies. These critiques suggest that this work can act to reinscribe settler connections to Indigenous land and situate non-Indigenous educators as the transmitters of Indigenous knowledges (Calderón, 2014; Korteweg & Russell, 2012; Tuck & McKenzie, 2014; Tuck, McKenzie, & McCoy, 2014). Mistinguette Smith (2013) asks important questions that interrupt the benignity of place stories: "Are there some stories that don't belong in research, stories we should not tell? Which ones? Why?" (para. 4). While staying with these tensions and the limitations of place stories, I nonetheless see them as holding potential to trouble taken-for-granted settler colonial relations and anti-Black encounters in early childhood settings.

I am interested in what unsettling effects might emerge from encountering nature in ways that go beyond an anthropocentric focus on individual children's learning "about" nature. Instead, I bring questions that politicize, unsettle, refigure, reconsider, and (re)story what is considered present in the pedagogical encounters I work with. A question that threads through the book is this: What might attention to Indigenous relational presences, to ongoing colonialisms and anti-blackness, and to more-than-human entanglements in everyday pedagogical encounters with "natural" places in settler colonial British Columbia do toward enacting decolonizing possibilities in early childhood studies?

## Indigenous Knowledges and Posthumanisms: Fractures, Resonances, and Potentialities

In this book, I use the term *Indigenous* in different ways. I use the term broadly to refer to differently located critical Indigenous peoples, methodologies, and knowledges. I also use the term within the specific context of what is now Canada to refer to First Nations, Métis, and Inuit peoples. First Nations, Métis, and Inuit peoples comprise many nations and clans with multiple situated specificities, differences, dynamisms, and interconnections. One such interconnection is an understanding of relationality as not limited to the human, but as encompassing always-already responsible, entangled, and reciprocal relations with land/place and all of its more-than-human inhabitants (Simpson, 2011; Watts, 2013).

An important aspect of how I enact a politicized place methodology in this book is to purposefully bring together different worldviews and theories, particularly perspectives from Indigenous knowledges and posthumanist theories. This complicated bringing together of theories and worldviews is not an attempt to make them the same. It does, however, signal a commitment toward responsible practices of creating interferences, shifting ontologies and epistemologies, and making partial connections (Haraway, 1992; Mol, 2014). Importantly, this bringing into conversation does not seek to minimize the incommensurable foundations of posthumanist and Indigenous perspectives. These foundations include the time and purposes from which these perspectives emerge. Posthuman theories are a Euro-Western response to Euro-Western humanist conceptions of

Euro-Western 'Man' as the ideal of what it means to be human (Braidotti, 2018). My repetition of 'Euro-Western' is intended to underline that the idealization of the human has never been universal. For instance, as Kim TallBear (2015) states, "Indigenous peoples have never forgotten that nonhumans are agential beings engaged in social relations that profoundly shape human lives… 'Objects' and 'forces' such as stones, thunder, or stars are known within our ontologies to be sentient and knowing" (p. 234). In other words, diversely situated Indigenous understandings of what it means to be human that do not maintain human/nonhuman binaries precede the emergence of 'post' theories. In addition, these understandings have not emerged as a critique to Euro-Western modernism and its ontological and epistemological violences; instead, they are intrinsic ways of being, becoming, and knowing in the world.

Highlighting resonances between Indigenous and posthuman perspectives does not imply that they both do not enact particular exclusions, not only of each other, but also of many other ways of knowing. As Elizabeth Povinelli (2014a) notes, "any arrangement of existents/existence builds its own otherwise"—yet these arrangements are not outside the influences of power (such as colonial power effects) and politics that influence the persistence, unity, and dominance of certain arrangements (para. 4). For instance, many Indigenous ontologies enact very precise teachings that are firmly rooted in particular places and bring forward different modes of subjectification than posthuman theorizations of human/more-than-human relations. In Chapter 8, I expand further on this discussion in relation to the complexities brought to the category of the human when situated within pervasive anti-blackness.

I wanted to work with both posthuman and Indigenous knowledges for a number of interconnected reasons. First, a central focus of this book is on center settler colonialism as integral to early childhood pedagogical engagements with "natural" places within the context of what is now British Columbia in Canada. This focus is of particular pertinence given the recent popularity of "nature-based" place pedagogies in the early years. Given my focus then, working with Indigenous perspectives was for me an integral and ethically necessary part of critically engaging with, politicizing, and seeking interruptions to dominant approaches to nature pedagogies in early childhood settings within my current location on Coast Salish territories. Indigenous knowledges enabled me to situate particular pedagogical encounters within the colonial pastpresent and to interrupt what I experienced as absent presences in our human- and Eurocentric pedagogical encounters with nature on stolen land. For instance, in Chapter 4, which focuses on everyday forest encounters at the child care centers where I worked, I set a Stó:lō story of the Western red cedar alongside our everyday encounters with ancient red cedar tree stumps and alongside settler colonial logging histories of this particular mountain forest. I presented this living cedar creation story to interrupt erasures of Indigenous histories, ontologies, and epistemologies from this particular place and our everyday encounters therein. My intention was also to disrupt dominant understandings of the forest as a "wild," empty, and uninscribed space awaiting children's discoveries. Further, when situated within the material–discursive relations of and affectivities enacted by the logged cedar tree stumps, this story brings into view ongoing colonial territorializations.

Working with these stories as someone not indigenous to this place creates many unresolved frictions that I continue to grapple with. For instance, is acknowledging the risks of working with Indigenous knowledges enough within ongoing settler colonialism? What might it mean for non-Indigenous educators to encounter and tell such stories in places where the absences of Indigenous children, families, and educators are intimately connected with ongoing settler colonialism? Who can tell the stories of this place and the more-than-human things in it? Is it possible to conceive of place pedagogies that trouble ongoing settler colonialisms through histories and stories without appropriating and "museumifying" Indigenous knowledges? How can children and educators respectfully learn from stories without coopting them toward settler colonial emplacement and visualities (Tuck, McKenzie, & McCoy, 2014; Tuck & Yang, 2014)? Who can "include" Indigenous knowledges into settler colonial spaces? Does the very act of inclusion reproduce/create marginalization and exclusions? How might inclusion happen while avoiding representational, reified, appropriative, essentialist, and tokenizing colonial relationships? What are the tensions and ethical dilemmas of working with written Indigenous stories as opposed to the living knowledges that reside in Indigenous communities, as well as the resultant frictions that this alternative also presents? Might my attempts to (re)story educators' and children's place relations inadvertently, as Tuck, Guess, and Sultan (2014) suggest, "obscure the fact of Indigenous erasure and resilient, radical relationship to that selfsame land" (p. 9)?

I see my work as neither transcending nor neatly resolving all of these issues and the messy colonial relations in which I, as well as the children and educators, are differentially immersed and implicated. Nonetheless, it is important to pay careful attention to the ethical dilemmas that these questions bring. For instance, in Chapter 4 I explain how the sacred Stó:lō Nation cedar creation story is presented neither as analytic data nor as a knowable, complete representation. The story enacts relational, more-than-human, interruptive, and complicating knowledge making to our situated encounters with ancient cedar tree stumps. In refusing Indigenous erasure and ongoing land relationships (Tuck, Guess, & Sultan, 2014), this story interferes with innocent readings of child–educator–forest encounters.

Living and staying with unresolved divergences and questions, I have attempted to avoid taking a stance where I can ever fully "know" and define these knowledges, as this "knowability" by others can be seen as a colonizing practice (Battiste & Henderson, 2000). I do not view these lived and living knowledges as fully describable, particularly when writing within the limits of English and from my own situated meaning making of these stories, predominantly from traced audio, video, and written text. Resisting a tendency toward analysis and explanation and the potentially inscriptive and colonizing effects thereof, I have presented these particular situated place stories without analysis—as knowledge making that speaks for itself.

I also worked with Indigenous knowledges as a part of my methodology so as to politicize, question, and perhaps shift what typically counts as knowledge both in academic research and in pedagogical practices, where Indigenous ways of knowing and relating to place and the more-than-human relations within it may not be considered as central to ethical ways of knowing and being. In large part due to the labor of Indigenous scholars in the academy over several decades, there is an ongoing shift in the privileged position of Eurocentric academic theories. In my own attempts to support this shift, I draw inspiration from Indigenous scholars in the academy who have called for the centering of marginalized or muted perspectives not considered "academic." For instance, they foreground Indigenous epistemologies and ontologies using methods such as stories, trickster figures, and poetics, among many other approaches (e.g., Chilisa & Ntseane, 2010; Cole, 2006; Elabor-Idemudia, 2002). Alongside calls for the creation of politicized, lived, and embodied approaches to research that unsettle hegemonies of Eurocentric ways of knowing and becoming in academic spaces, there are also several critiques of bringing Indigenous knowledges into academic spaces. For instance, Kwakwaka'wakw scholar Sarah Hunt (2014a, p 31), notes:

> it must also be asked what it means for Indigenous knowledge to be moved from spaces of lived Indigenous governance and culture, such as a potlatch ceremony, to a conference session on ontology with very few Indigenous people and little space for Indigenous methods of teaching and learning… So what does it mean for Indigeneity to be theorized, accounted for, and constructed as a category, within hegemonic geographic systems of knowledge production where only a small number of Indigenous people situate their work?

While I acknowledge and stay with these tensions of knowledge making within neoliberal colonial systems, I do not claim a clear resolution to the ever-present risk of co-optation and simplification of Indigenous perspectives both within everyday education practices and within the hegemonies of academia within which this book is located.

In addition to working with place-specific Indigenous knowledges, I have also referenced Indigenous knowledges throughout this book in a general sense when highlighting the vibrancy of the more-than-human and the entanglements of human/more-than-human relations in everyday place encounters. I have referenced Indigenous relationalities with intention as making meaning of, knowing, and becoming with place and the more than human in ways that disrupt binaries such as subject/object and human/nonhuman. I have done this because an intrinsic part of my work involves paying attention to more-than-human vibrancies, in particular to the material–discursive "force" of things and events. I attend to collisions of matter and meaning in everyday practice in ways that seek connections that might appear, at first, outside of or unconnected to a particular encounter, or even outside of early childhood practice. Referring to Indigenous knowledges in general terms is intended neither to essentialize these knowledges nor to minimize their specificities, differences, dynamisms, and complexities. On the contrary, I also see potentialities in creating openings for resonances and connections between differently located Indigenous knowledges.

Before I engage with some of the resonances between differently located Indigenous knowledges, I want to situate my use of these knowledges within my own learnings as an Indigenous member of the Ndwandwe clan (now primarily dispersed in different countries in Southern Africa, including what is now Swaziland, South Africa, and Zimbabwe). My move to draw on Indigenous knowledges in relation to their resonances with posthumanist theories stems from what I see as strong connections with my own learnings from Ndwandwe clan teachings on my relatedness with my ancestors and place relations as inseparable presences in my life, despite my estrangement from my ancestral home. The praise narratives (*tinanatelo*) of my clan tell of our relationships to specific ancestral places, and tell our interconnected land, human, and more-than-human creation stories. These narratives also tell our genealogies and histories, including shifting pastpresent place relations. Though it is important to convey their diversity, many Indigenous knowledges are rooted in relationalities in which human and more-than-human relationships are situated within the particularities of place (Driskill, Finley, Gilley, & Morgensen, 2011). Many Indigenous peoples in what is now Canada embody relationality such that family is not limited to the human but encompasses an entire cosmology—ancestors, future generations, spiritual beings, animal life, and plant life. These knowledges teach entangled and reciprocal relations with the earth (Watts, 2013). For example, in Stó:lō First Nation teachings, *shxweli* ("spirit or life force") inhabits both human and more-than-human life. *Shxweli* inhabits their territories as living ancestral spirits in the form of land, plant, and animal life, creating an inseparable mutuality (Stó:lō Nation, 2003, p. 1).

These teachings also resonate with many African ontologies. For example, *ubuntu* expressed in Zulu refers to inextricable relatedness between humans and the more human world, all aspects of which are understood as dynamic and as creating effects on the other (Le Grange, 2012a). These dynamic and mutual effects can be described as life forces that place humanity in intrinsically dynamic and ethical ontological relationships with other more-than-human worlds that are active participants in one's life (Le Grange, 2012a). These forces include the Creator, one's ancestors, the elders, family, community, and more-than-human others such as the land and its crops, waters, skies, and animals. Together these forces form active influences and sensed presence in one's everyday life, in constituting the self, and indeed in sustaining life. South African scholar Lesley Le Grange (2012b) has recently discussed how *ubuntu* Indigenous philosophies and ethics among Southern African peoples have been eroded by the multiple ongoing effects of colonialism, neocolonialism, capitalism, and enlightenment humanism.

This brief discussion illustrates that differently located Indigenous onto-epistemologies, which have existed for millennia, figure ethical relationality with the more-than-human as foundational to becoming with the world—teachings that are of critical importance within the current precarious times of planetary destruction. Consequently, as I read posthumanist theories alongside my work with children and educators, I found that they were not enough to critically and productively encounter more-than-human worlds as entangled participants in place relations. I have also found that, together with Indigenous knowledges and situated settler colonial histories, selected understandings and concepts from the posthumanities (including more-than-human geographies, feminist science studies, immanent philosophy, and the environmental humanities) helped me to navigate the multiple connections, complexities, and intricacies that have emerged in everyday place encounters in my work with educators and children. These perspectives allowed me to theorize-with the everyday and mundane as a site of micropolitics, with an emphasis on the multiple more-than-human worlds that assembled therein. These multiplicities included epistemologies, ontologies, biologies, political formations, materialities, and discursivities that emerged from our (children's, educators', and mine) embodied encounters with "natural" places, as detailed in this book.

## Data Assemblages and Interruptions

In this section, I further outline the types of data that I have accumulated as a part of researching this book. I begin with how I encountered data and how I selected data to work with. Together with my focus on decolonizing possibilities grounded in Indigenous knowledges and more-than-human relationalities, this data was integral in coming to a methodology of refiguring presences. Since I give a detailed description of the crafting of my methodology of refiguring presences in Chapter 3, here I will only briefly introduce this methodology, with a focus on methodological connections between everyday place encounters (data), place stories, and more-than-human entanglements.

As the discussion of pedagogical narrations suggests, as key artifacts of our pedagogical encounters and critical collaborative reflective reflections, pedagogical narrations are a key source of the research data that is contained in this book. Many of the visual and textual descriptions of the pedagogical encounters that are described in this book are excerpted from pedagogical narrations—both pedagogical narrations that I initiated as part of our ongoing pedagogical inquiries, and pedagogical narrations that educators initiated and shared with me as part of our collaborative inquiries. In further reflecting on our pedagogical encounters in the preparation of this book, I have also worked with several artifacts that I collected as part of my work with the early childhood centers; some of which did not become a part of our pedagogical narrations. This includes my field notes, recordings and notes from our learning circle discussions, video and photographic images from our pedagogical encounters, and email exchanges with educators.

In addition, several affective more-than-human others (things/objects, plants, animals) also materialized and assembled as data. These active participants are entangled within theoretical and ontological orientations committed to politicizing everyday place encounters and committed to centering the more-than-human. In particular, these emergent data assemblages were not only the mountain, mountain forest, cedar tree stumps, and community garden that I have alluded to previously, but also several multispecies encounters, including with raccoons, deer, rotting tree hollows, earthworms, forest-garden vegetables, a forest trail, garden waste assemblages, and a fence separating the garden from the forest. These more-than-human bodies, and many others, are active participants as data that invited particular place relations for myself, children, and educators. This data resonated with me during the encounters, as I wrote pedagogical narrations of these encounters to share with educators and families, as I sat with these narrations–notes–images–videos (the "conventional" data) that remained as traces of the encounters, and as I made connections with multiple theoretical and ontological perspectives.

Grounded in theoretical and ontological commitments to interrupting colonizing, anti-Black, and anthropocentric place relations, I wanted to find ways to connect cumulative material–discursive resonances and dissonances in my data with place stories, living knowledges, and settler colonial pastpresent histories. I wanted to make these connections between data, stories, knowledges, and pastpresent colonial histories in ways that would bring unsettling, nonanthropocentric perspectives to everyday pedagogical encounters. I reiterate here that I do not present Indigenous place stories and Indigenous knowledges as data, but with decolonial intentionality. As I elaborate in Chapter 3, I wanted to create connections between data, theory, pastpresent histories, and stories in ways that gestured toward the situatedness (Haraway, 1988) of my research practices. In particular, I wanted to situate my research practices as intimately entangled with and productive of the politics, materialities, (power) relations, knowledges/meanings, and socialities that they engage with, make visible, and enact (Haraway, 1988; Mol, 2002). I wanted to find a way, through my writing, to make sense of, respond to, and stay with the troubles (Haraway, 1991) that specific pedagogical encounters brought. Taken together, these desires and the constitutive data led me toward a methodology of refiguring presences. Refiguring presences gestures toward rethinking, politicizing, complicating, and unsettling what is considered present in everyday place encounters in early childhood pedagogies within settler colonialism.

In selecting the everyday moments that I worked with in this book, I purposefully chose everyday moments with children, educators, and, importantly, more-than-human others that affected me and left me feeling troubled and unsettled, moments where I questioned the seemingly innocent and everyday normalization of the encounters and wondered about their connections to unquestioned, silent, and invisible (yet unintended) complicities in settler colonialism. These were also moments where I found myself uncertain of how to respond to what was happening, where I wondered about the human and more-than-human active participants in these encounters, and where, looking back, I found that the usual interruptions that I used in my work with educators—asking critical questions, sending critical readings, making suggestions for different types of relations—didn't "work," were met with resistance, or were taken up in ways that generated further discomfort and uncertainty for me. These are also moments where I struggled with the multiplicities of my role as a researcher, educator, and pedagogista as well as the responses they suggested.

## Kwasuka Sukela

In my first language, Siswati, many folk tales told to children begin with the words *kwasuka sukela*... This phrase is often translated as "once upon a time," but a closer translation is "this is how this story begins..." In situating myself within this work, it is important to me that I include not only my roles in the project as researcher, educator, and pedagogista, but also how my orientations in this project toward place, place learning, and the possibilities for decolonizing early childhood place pedagogies are inseparable from the place learning stories that shaped my childhood and youth. These stories bring into view some of the connections between my own becomings and my orientations toward place, place stories, and the pedagogical possibilities of places.

I was born and spent the first 18 years of my life in what is now known as Swaziland (eSwatini), a postcolonial nation of approximately one million people in Southern Africa that is popularly described as the mountain kingdom for its expansive mountain landscapes. My brother, mother, and I lived in government-subsidized apartment housing in the capital city of Mbabane alongside a busy street. I attended preschool, kindergarten, and my primary schooling at a nearby public school. As I attempt to recollect pedagogies that connected to place learning from my early years of schooling, my most recurrent memories are of required learning of place-as-nation and place-as-created by a Christian God. I particularly recall this learning as enacted through song. In a daily school assembly, our uniformly covered bodies rose in line formation to sing the Swazi national anthem, which, while sung in my first language, Siswati, reminded us of thankfulness to the Lord God for creating our mountains and rivers. We also stood regularly to sing the Anglican hymn "All Things Bright and Beautiful." The chorus and tune remain embedded in me still, with both nostalgic familiarity and a discomfort that comes with its dissonant reverberations. This hymn tells of creatures, rivers, flowers, wind, and the sun as the Lord God's creations. Looking back, I don't think I ever questioned the disconnection of the lyrics of this song from my realities—fruits growing in a garden, tall trees in the greenwood, playing in meadows—all held no resonant connection and meaning to my everyday world. Nonetheless, this song was considered a necessary part of my early childhood education.

Alongside my formal schooling, I spent most weekends and all of my school holidays, right through the end of high school, when I left Swaziland to go to university in Canada, at the rural home of my now passed on grandparents. While I was not always happy at my mother's insistence that we spend time here when we were not in school, I now look back on these times as the most meaningful aspects of my place learning. Here I learned place stories that told of my Indigenous clans' (Ndwandwe and Mavuso) past and present place belongings. I learned the significance of specific Indigenous places, such as the sacred mountain caves where my ancestors, including my father, are buried according to traditional customs.

While many of my relatives are Christians, an inheritance of the British colonial period, most have not discarded their incommensurable traditional beliefs. From them, I also learned creation stories, which spoke of a different God than the Lord God of the hymns and national anthem I sang in school: stories of the Creator, *Mvelinchanti*, who, alongside the *emadloti* (ancestors), was often called upon in times of hardship and thanked for well-being through specific practices and ceremonies. While my increasing affinity for the sciences in my schooling at times created feelings of estrangement from these Indigenous stories and practices, at the same time, they helped me to feel a sense of rooted belonging somewhere.

My childhood place learning in these special rural places was far from an idyllic or romantic nature experience. While I remember the pleasure of hours spent outside far away from adults, I also remember the stomach-tightening combination of fear (of encountering snakes, wild dogs, and other unknowns) and excitement that came with being tasked to walk through the fields to bring the cow herders their meals, just as I also remember the enormous amount of daily work needed to sustain and responsibly nurture land and animals, sometimes without success.

My high school years brought yet more different perspectives of place. I already had a sense of place belongings as intensely contested and political from stories of my Ndwandwe clan's assimilation into nationhood through war and colonial empire building, and from traumatic experiences while visiting relatives in apartheid South Africa as a young child. However, it was during my high school years that I critically encountered politicized understandings of place. Thanks to a targeted scholarship program, I spent seven years in boarding school at the United World College of Southern Africa (Waterford Kamhlaba). This mountain-top international school had been founded on a principle of anti-racism in resistance to neighboring South Africa's segregated schooling policies. Many exiled or imprisoned South African political activists sent their children to this school, and together with a diverse student body and activist teachers, this created a critical place of learning that, while providing a predominantly Euro-Western education, was foundational to developing my anti-racist and decolonial ethics. I remember every June 16 hiking up one of the mountains surrounding the school, where we would noisily dance, chant, and sing freedom songs to commemorate the Soweto youth uprising and remember those who were still imprisoned by the South African regime. These are just a few of the place learnings—place stories, place belongings, place becomings, and place estrangements—that have traveled with and stayed with me as I immigrated to Canada after completing high school in Swaziland. These place learnings have contributed to my critical perspectives as I continue to engage with possibilities for politicized and ethical encounters with so-called natural places in early childhood education.

## Situating Nature in Early Childhood Education

Why decolonize early childhood place-based pedagogies? In this section, I discuss the decolonizing orientation of this book as an intentional response to the current status of nature-based or environmental early childhood education in North America. Environmental or outdoor early childhood education is currently undergoing a marked surge in popularity in North America, as seen by the proliferation of nature kindergartens and preschools. However, many of these approaches, often modeled after European forest schools, can reinscribe settler colonialism through persistently anthropocentric, romanticized apolitical and ahistorical approaches to place (see Chapter 4; also see Taylor, 2013). In these approaches, nature is figured as a mute and untouched site for nurturing individual child development and building individual children's environmental stewardship while erasing Indigenous presences and reinscribing colonizing imaginaries of "pure" Canadian "natures" (see Chapter 4; also see Taylor, 2013). Furthermore, Black people and immigrants of color are often left out of the ECE curriculum on place-based environmental education. This omission assumes Black people to be nongeographic beings who are out of place in "nature," or whose presences in North America are solely understood through the histories of slavery—subject material often deemed too difficult for children. The inclusion of Black and other children from marginalized communities is also often entrenched with deficit developmental perspectives that figure exposure to nature as a "fix" to an already known lack or deprivation. The raced and colonial underpinnings of what constitutes nature (and its separation from human culture) in early childhood educational contexts and what counts as normal childhood experiences of nature also remain largely unquestioned. This is not to suggest that there has not already been important work in this area in early childhood studies. Here I note a few key inspirational examples. Affrica Taylor (2011, 2013), working in the context of settler colonial Australia, has drawn on more-than-human geographies to question what counts as nature and in so doing disrupts dominant romantic views of the child as belonging in nature. Also in Australia, Margaret Somerville (2013) works with "thinking through Country" as an Aboriginal onto-epistemology that disrupts nature/culture binaries in young children's place learning. In Aotearoa New Zealand, Jenny Ritchie (2012) has written on the counter-colonial and ecological possibilities of Indigenous epistemologies in early childhood settings. In Canada, Veronica Pacini-Ketchabaw (2013) has written about the frictions of early childhood forest pedagogies within settler colonialism.

Working from the settler colonial context of North America, this book is intended as an interruptive response to some erasures and omissions in place-based environmental education with young children, with a particular focus on early childhood education. This work feels particularly urgent as we witness increasingly devastating climate-change related events such as extreme flooding and drought throughout the planet. These events are not surprising given the naming of the Anthropocene as the current geological epoch in which humans, as a geophysical force, have irreversibly damaged the earth, as seen in unprecedented species extinctions, climate change, and social turmoil (Crutzen, 2006; Klein, 2014; Rose & van Dooren, 2011). The Anthropocene and its attendant discourses are problematic for many reasons, such as the lack of careful attention to inequality in both contributions to and vulnerability to environmental precarity (Collard, Dempsey, & Sundberg, 2015a). In addition, Western science perspectives on the Anthropocene are only one indicator that it is imperative to find different ways of relating to and living in good relationships with more-than-human others. Indigenous peoples have known and lived these principles of kinship and reciprocity in multiple ways for millennia (Davis & Todd, 2017; TallBear, 2016; Todd, 2015). Nonetheless, while recognizing the insufficiencies and omissions of the Anthropocene, in this book I take the Anthropocene as an urgent provocation to turn away from dominant raced and colonial discourses that reproduce grand narratives of transcendent heroic solutions (Haraway, 2008, 2015) that reinforce a universal human subject of the Anthropocene and that represent the predominantly white middle- and upper-class children that participate in North American nature or forest schools as future earth saviors and stewards (Louv, 2008; Pelo, 2013). Instead, in this book the Anthropocene is engaged with as a provocation to situate place learning within settler colonial, anti-Black, and anthropogenically damaged lifeworlds and to consequently seek ways of responding to environmental precarity that challenge human exceptionalism while attending to differential implicatedness and situatedness within anthropogenically damaged places.

Put another way, this book attempts to mobilize different curricular and pedagogical conversations that unsettle undifferentiated colonizing views of the world. A central aim of the book, then, is to provide examples of and highlight the generative ethical possibilities of politicized, contingent, and place-attuned responses to settler colonial and anti-Black anthropogenic inheritances in early childhood education. I grapple with specific place encounters to politicize and trouble the Indigenous presences, settler colonial relations, and Black geographies that were a part of these everyday place encounters, yet, from my perspective, remained as absent presences. The aims of this book are to draw attention to Black and Indigenous presences and land relations as necessary yet often ignored aspects of environmental education within current anthropogenic, settler colonial, and anti-Black Canadian geographies. My intention is to unsettle innocent and anthropocentric views of specific place encounters and settler colonial child–nature pedagogies more generally.

## Organization of the Book

The following chapters take up the provocation of decolonizing place in early childhood education and early childhood studies. The chapters attend to different yet interconnected ecologies, including a wetland, a mountain forest, and a community garden. While each of these chapters stands alone as a detailed framing of decolonial land education, they are connected by a framework of refiguring presences that focuses on decolonizing place-based early childhood education, pays interruptive attention to social and material pastpresent erasures enacted by settler colonialism and anti-blackness, and is concerned with situating early childhood land education within the real-world, anthropogenically damaged places in which children live.

Chapter 2 investigates the potential for place-attuned pedagogies to expand and unsettle what typically counts as quality in early childhood education. This chapter aims to enact interferences to normative child- and human-centered conceptions of quality in early childhood education. The chapter engages responsive witnessing by paying close, critical, and nonanthropocentric attention to everyday place and multispecies encounters in settler colonial places. Through descriptive visual and textual accounts of encounters with damaged landscapes, urbanized animals, and watery places, the chapter foregrounds implicated, responsive, and messy practices-in-question that bring hopeful possibilities for reimagining quality in early childhood practice. The chapter presents illustrative examples of how land education might refigure dominant questions of quality early childhood education by dwelling on questions related to who and what lives and dies well within particular damaged and colonized lifeworlds.

Chapter 3 conceptualizes refiguring presences as a methodology and a pedagogical orientation with possibilities for restorying contested settler colonial places and foregrounding more-than-human relationalities in land education and research with young children.

Chapter 4 extends refiguring presences as an orientation to research and practice that unsettles taken-for-granted familiarities of outdoor environments as passive and ahistorical objects of human-centered learning. Situated within the place specificities of an urban forest on Coast Salish territories in British Columbia, the chapter draws on children's encounters with the forest and its particularities. The chapter uncouples these encounters from anthropocentric learning narratives through attention to the forest's imbrication in ever-present threads of colonial empire. Juxtaposing tropes of untouched "wild" British Columbia landscapes, situated colonial logging histories, Indigenous presences, and situated immigrant laboring histories, the chapter makes visible and unsettles the coloniality hidden in the banalities of everyday forest pedagogies with young children.

Chapter 5 builds on the theme of resisting simplistic and colonizing couplings of children and nature. Drawing from research on children's pedagogical encounters with a community garden, the chapter is oriented toward noticing the materialities and colonial relations that come together to enact the production of this community garden. It considers the implications of this close noticing for interrupting the enduring modernist child–garden figure. The chapter engages the affective, material, and figurative conceptions of touch (Haraway, 2008) to refigure presences in community garden encounters. Touching historical child gardening pedagogies, political formations of gardens, Indigenous garden spaces, settler colonial worldings of gardening and school gardens, and animated more-than-human garden "things," the chapter aims to open up possibilities for critical and generative engagements with settler childhoods' situatedness within ongoing colonial relations. The chapter gestures toward the ethical implications of paying attention to the entanglements of Indigenous relationalities, colonial replacements (Tuck & Gaztambide-Fernández, 2013), and more-than-human agency in child–garden pedagogies.

Chapter 6 engages with recent work on theorizing Black and Indigenous land relations (Tuck, Smith, Guess, Benjamin, & Jones, 2013), geologic subjectivities (Yusoff, 2015), and geontology in late liberal capitalism (Povinelli, 2014a,b) to consider possibilities for responding to settler colonial fossil-fueled inheritances and accumulations in early childhood education. The chapter focuses on children's entangled, messy, and geopolitical relations with a mountain on unceded Coast Salish territories in British Columbia. This place is a contested site of colonial-capitalist extraction due to a proposal to build a tar sands oil pipeline that would tunnel through the mountain. Drawing inspiration from recent calls for research and pedagogical approaches that center refusals of settler colonialism, this chapter considers the generative possibilities of refusing pedagogies-as-usual that naturalize settler colonialism's extractive structuring. The chapter critically approaches recent colonial extractive events on the mountain as starting points from which to theorize children's subjectivities in relation to the mountain. The chapter creates movements away from an emphasis on children's biopsychological development, a dominant underpinning of curriculum in early childhood education. The reader is invited to consider what refiguring children's subjectivities through geontological relationalities might do as a critical response that refuses dominant developmental and anthropocentric understandings of what is seen as belonging to or appropriate for young children's curricular engagements.

Chapter 7 examines children's encounters with dead and dying bumblebees in their everyday entangled lives. Within the context of child care settings in settler colonial British Columbia, Canada, the chapter stories situated and emergent bee–child worldings to illustrate possibilities for learning with other species in anthropogenically damaged worlds. I pay attention to some of the ways in which children's and educators' practices have shifted away from encountering bees predominantly as objects of scientific knowledge and toward more relational, embodied, and affective immersion in the lives and deaths of bumblebees. Situating these practices within current indigenous western bumblebee vulnerabilities, I consider how children's and educators' inquiries might be viewed as pedagogies that matter for learning to live less destructively with others in current times of anthropogenic change.

Chapter 8 aims to extend the preceding seven chapters by attending to the absenting and essentializing of Black childhoods in dominant nature education for young children. The chapter puts forward propositional articulations of the ways in which Black feminist geographies, Black speculative fictions, and Black geographies offer both conceptual and practical interventions into these erasures. The chapter offers imaginings of what it might look like to foreground Black nature–place relations in early childhood education in settler colonial contexts. The chapter seeks to simultaneously reject deficit images of Black children's relation to land while acknowledging the realities of uneven vulnerabilities to anthropogenic environmental change. The chapter inhabits the question of what gesturing toward Black and Indigenous childhood futurities and relations might mean amid the reality of the increasing unlivability of the earth.

The final chapter provides a synopsis of possibilities for decolonizing place-based early childhood education. This brief conclusion to the book brings together the geo-onto-epistemologically situated approaches discussed in the preceding chapters in relation to potentials to disrupt, destabilize, and subvert taken-for-granted colonial master narratives of knowing particular places in early childhood education. The chapter frames a decolonizing ethic in place-attuned early years education as necessitating political choices, such as which stories, encounters, and histories to make visible, in questioning what knowledge counts in the making of a place, and which pastpresent human and more-than-human inhabitants of place matter. The chapter discusses the significance of politicizing place relations within children's inheritances of settler colonial and anti-Black relations amid increasing environmental precarity.

## Note

1 See the appendix for a listing of some of the readings that educators engaged with over the course of the project.

# 2

# STORYING PRACTICES OF WITNESSING

## Refiguring Quality in Everyday Encounters

As I discussed in the opening chapter, the data that has informed the work described herein was gathered during a project aimed at troubling normative conceptions of quality in early childhood education. Quality remains a powerful signifier in Canadian early childhood education. The term and the notion it refers to are often imbued with universalized, modernist, and deficit constructions of children and articulated through prescriptive "best practices" and "minimum standards" approaches (Moss & Dahlberg, 2008; Pacini-Ketchabaw, Nxumalo, Kocher, Elliot, & Sanchez, 2014). In British Columbia, Canada, where my work is located, understandings of children's school readiness have become increasingly coupled with quality, using technologies of evaluation such as the Early Development Instrument to generate public scholarship that classifies the "vulnerabilities" and "absent qualities" of educational settings and neighborhoods (Guhn, Janus, & Hertzman, 2007).

Pedagogical practices for young children are situated within a problematic context in early childhood education, where developmentalism is the foundation of training in the profession and developmentally appropriate practice is equated with quality practice (Pacini-Ketchabaw & Nxumalo, 2013, 2014; Pacini-Ketchabaw, Nxumalo, Kocher, Elliot, & Sanchez, 2014). As Pacini-Ketchabaw (2008) notes, developmental psychology as a dominant discourse "has taken the position of 'natural' knowledge" (p. 39) in the field, with little critical attention paid to how it is entangled in colonizing histories and to the inequitable structuring impacts on children that are outside its normative formations. My role in the project arose out of an impetus to bring into question inequitable enactments of developmentalism and accompanying governing discourses of appropriate practice, objectivity, and neutrality. This process involved contextualizing, historicizing, and politicizing particular practices underpinned by developmentalism, such as the all-too-common, taken-for-granted, and singular focus on the individual child's progressive learning and meaning making (Pacini-Ketchabaw, Nxumalo, Kocher, Elliot, & Sanchez, 2014). Important aspects of this process of troubling dominant developmental discourses included engaging educators in discussions to bring forward multiple perspectives on practice, provoking disruptions in normative views, interrupting taken-for-granted assumptions about practice, and encouraging experimentations with practices inspired by these provocations (Pacini-Ketchabaw, 2010; Pacini-Ketchabaw & Nxumalo, 2010; Pacini-Ketchabaw, Nxumalo, Kocher, Elliot, & Sanchez, 2014).

The following chapters in this book can be seen as implicitly disrupting what counts as quality in early childhood education and whose knowledges inform these definitions of quality. In this chapter, I am interested in what emerges from paying attention to the sociomaterial contingencies, intricacies, and uncertainties that come together to shape articulations of quality in everyday practice within specific contexts (Dahlberg, Moss, & Pence, 2013; Osgood & Giugni, 2015; Pacini-Ketchabaw & Pence, 2011). One such aspect of the sociomaterial that actively participates in shaping (im)possibilities of quality practice are relations with the more-than-human others that co-inhabit early childhood places. Accordingly, the purpose of this chapter is to contribute to reimaginings of quality through methodological and pedagogical orientations that focus on more-than-human-entanglements in everyday encounters. As it is throughout the book, my emphasis on the more-than-human is inspired by onto-epistemologies of the inseparability of humans from their more-than-human relations and responsibilities (Barad, 2007; Haraway, 2008; Le Grange, 2012a; Martin, 2007; Tuck, 2014).

My intent in this chapter is to contribute reorientations that might spur different kinds of dialogue about meaningful articulations of quality practices, whereby situated quality practices are seen as always in motion. I present a necessarily partial account of everyday practices in inquiries that productively complicate what counts as quality. I present situated sociomaterial visual and textual "small stories" of everyday pedagogical encounters that move away from familiar anthropocentric modes of explanation and away from interpretations of my role as a pedagogista facilitating normative quality practices with young children. Instead, I situate this work as messy, implicated, more-than-human entanglements that refigure quality as ongoing processes of becoming in everyday life (Osgood & Giugni, 2015).

Situated within the intricacies of everyday encounters with the mountain forest that is a part of all the pedagogies described in this book, this chapter stories possibilities for educators to consider what different practices, perspectives, and responses might be provoked "beyond quality" (Dahlberg et al., 2013; Pacini-Ketchabaw, Nxumalo, Kocher, Elliot, & Sanchez, 2014). I story attempts to trouble colonizing developmental enactments of quality by shifting the gaze away from a focus on the individual child's progressive learning. Instead, I foreground creative possibilities for making visible and ethically responding to the entanglements of everyday practice with anthropogenically damaged places.

## Unsettling Quality through Performative Witnessing

In this chapter I emphasize storied descriptions, rather than definitive interpretations of quality early childhood education practices, as a gesture toward a political ontology that seeks to notice the multiplicities present in, and enacted through, different everyday practices (Mol, 2002; Tsing, 2011). This approach echoes what Martin Holbraad and his colleagues (Holbraad, Pedersen, & Viveiros de Castro, 2014) describe as "a technology of description… designed in the optimist (non-skeptical) hope of making the otherwise visible" (para. 5). To help me do this, alongside textual performative stories, visual images, and pedagogical narrations from practice, I place intentionalities, effects, and theoretical aspects of figurations of witnessing (Haraway, 1997; Hunt, 2014b; Tarpley, 1995) that resonate with particular everyday encounters.

The refigured modest witness (Haraway, 1997) helps me to unsettle transcendent unmediated truths (such as the dominant quality truths discussed in the previous section) and to locate pedagogical practices within politically oriented contingencies and contestations that preclude an innocent, self-invisible location (Haraway, 1988, 1997). Working with the contention that practices of figuration do not simply reflect reality, but "'turn' what they figure" (Timeto, 2011, p. 161), the descriptive accounts I present here resonate with the contradictions, leakages, resistances, and hopeful potentialities that have emerged in practice. In other words, witnessing is not put to work to "tidy up" and cleanse what quality practice could or should be. On the contrary, the contention here is that this "figuration is no protection from disorder" (St. Pierre, 1997, p. 281) as it works within and produces places of doubt, tension, and a lack of clarity about meanings and articulations of quality-in-practice.

This understanding of witnessing as firmly situating my own embodied presence, perspectives, and practices as noninnocent also resonates with Kwakwaka'wakw scholar Sarah Hunt's (2014b) crafting of a practice of Kwagiulth witnessing. She situates witnessing within the context of settler colonial violence as that which makes visible what might be otherwise disregarded or marginalized, but with a responsibility to the power relations inherent in acting as a witness and an understanding of witnessing as much more than passively hearing, observing, or seeing. She describes Kwagiulth witnessing as enacting contextualized and embodied relational knowledge making that is "inherently bound up in relations based on responsibility" (p. 39).

I also see resonances, in both Haraway's (1997) and Hunt's (2014b) accounts of witnessing, with the African American tradition of testifying-witnessing, a gathering to bear witness to difficulties and injustices that might otherwise go unnoticed by the dominant society that is at the same time a relational affirmation with the gathered witnesses' hope in the face of injustices (Tarpley, 1995). I see resonances here with my work in bringing focused attention to settler colonial relations as an embedded witness, while at the same time seeking out hopeful and affirmative possibilities. As Tarpley (1995) further explains, testifying, in these understandings, means:

> to *bear witness*, to bring forth, to claim and proclaim oneself as an intrinsic part of the world. The act of testifying or giving testimony has deep roots in African American history, reaching back to slavery (and before), to the places our ancestors created... where they opened themselves up to one another, showed their scars, spoke of their day-to-day life... Testifying... has also performed the function of providing a means by which the slave could make herself visible, in a society which had rendered her invisible; by which she could explore the sound of her own voice when she had been rendered silent. (pp. 2–3, emphasis added)

Working with these multiple understandings of testifying and witnessing, I experiment with the inventive and active concept of witnessing as a situated, messy, implicated, active, and entangled "seeing," where the witnessed and the witnesses are not limited to human storytellers, and where the self-invisibility and innocence of witnesses is not possible (Haraway, 1997; Hunt, 2014b; Tarpley, 1995).

Bringing together Haraway's (1997) modest witness, Hunt's (2014b) methodology of Kwagiulth witnessing, and the African American tradition of testifying-witnessing (e.g., Tarpley, 1995) is not without frictions, and my intent is not to erase their incommensurabilities. These concepts are not intended to "speak" in the same way to the same people. For instance, they have emerged from different specificities: from a need to affirm humanity and spirituality in the face of the dehumanizing violence of slavery in North America (Tarpley, 1995); as a methodology to witness stories of settler colonial violence against Indigenous peoples in British Columbia (Hunt, 2014b); and as a feminist posthumanist resistance to claims to impartial, unlocated objectivity (typically enacted by white males) in Euro-Western scientific research practices (Haraway, 1997). Nonetheless, I see potential in bringing them together as practices that position witnessing as relational, responsive, hopeful, and implicated practices within which I can locate my own practices. I am also committed to finding ways in my citation and knowledge-making practices to unsettle Eurocentrism in the academy.

I inhabit my becomings as a pedagogista through the refigured witness by describing particular entangled interferences of witnessing that orient toward the interruptive meaning making of everyday practices (Haraway, 1997; Hunt, 2014b; Tarpley, 1995). This mode of witnessing, then, is useful as an epistemological and ontological perspective from which to bring a telling, or witnessing, of everyday pedagogical practices whereby I do not sit in transcendence outside of that which I narrate, where I am not the sole (human and more-than-human) narrator of these stories, and where many unpredictable, unsettling, and unresolved questions are thrown up.

Witnessing has within it an element of performativity (Haraway, 1997; Hunt, 2014b; Tarpley, 1995). Practices of witnessing perform worldings that interrupt what is considered important and "present in everyday life" (Hunt, 2014b, p. 6). I present images from everyday practice that might be inhabited as performative imagery that interruptively diffracts (Barad, 2003) everyday pedagogical practices elsewhere, considering what else might be happening, might be noticed, and might be important to think with further, beyond passive representations of educational quality. Typically, in practices of documenting early childhood pedagogies, images are used with a focus on what (individual) children are doing and learning (Rinaldi, 2006). This is not to disregard the importance of making children's learning visible. However, my focus here is to work with images in ways that seek out "otherwise" ways for meaning making beyond the singular focus on the child and quality indicators such as defined learning outcomes (Dahlberg et al., 2013). It is also important to note here that practices of documenting children's learning, such as pedagogical narration, are often captured by dominant quality discourses as signifiers of "quality" early childhood education practices. However, pedagogical narration (also often referred to as pedagogical documentation) can also be a creative force to interrupt those same discourses, such as by inviting multiple perspectives, decentering the individual human learning child-subject, bringing taken-for-granted practice into question, and keeping practices in motion (Hodgins, 2012; Pacini-Ketchabaw, Nxumalo, Kocher, Elliot, & Sanchez, 2014).

Materializing witnessing through performative images brings different kinds of questions and perspectives to our pedagogical practices and complicates meanings of quality. For example, performative images unsettle solely discursive–linguistic–anthropocentric determinations of what counts as quality (Barad, 2003). This imagery brings attention to the performativities of more-than-human assemblages (Barad, 2011) as vibrant participants with children and educators in refiguring quality-practices-in-the-making.

The remainder of the chapter interruptively engages quality practices through "small stories" of encounters between children and more-than-human others articulated as material–discursive practices of witnessing place specificities, cross-species socialities, damaged landscapes, and watery becomings. I conclude on the *mattering* of these stories for refiguring quality practices as always in motion, in question, and in relation with children's immediate more-than-human worlds.

## Attuning to Place Specificities

> The stories we need now are not the big heroic ones, but rather smaller stories that help us rethink our big questions in richer veins.
>
> *(Deborah Bird Rose, 2014, para. 7)*

Witnessing draws attention to place specificity and geopolitical situatedness—a partial and located point of view (Haraway, 1988, 1997; Hunt, 2014b; Tarpley, 1995). This forest and its more-than-human co-inhabitants, which hold pastpresent traces of

**FIGURE 2.1** Forest Encounters: Noticing and Responding to More-than-human Worldings

What do these images from everyday encounters enact/do/unsettle in relating to the forest and to the idea of nature as something "out there," separate, pure, and non-human (Haraway, 2008)? What stories, knowledges, and histories of natural worlds do we privilege? What do we silence?

colonial logging and waste accumulations, are companion witnesses in this chapter; they are "meaning-making figure[s]" (Haraway, 2008, p. 5) that orient my storytelling. Refiguring what is seen as mattering-presences in these forest encounters has been an ongoing experimentation in articulating everyday practice in ways that unsettle the ease with which anthropocentric and child-centered ways of seeing are enacted. As described in Chapter 3, these practices have also sought to unsettle recurring descriptors of everyday forest pedagogies in relation to innocent, anthropocentric, and colonizing understandings that fit neatly into normative quality practice identifiers, such as belonging, ownership, discovery, learning about, and free exploration of an untouched natural environment. For instance, what is unsettled in our pedagogical practices by presencing the forest trail and the ancient tree stumps as witnesses to colonial logging histories? How does English ivy materially and semiotically entangle forest–child–educator–bodies in settler colonial inheritances? How does the mundane yet unexpected presence of an abandoned desk in the forest clearing unsettle nature-pedagogies-as-usual?

Even as I attempt to focus on the specificities of more-than-human worldings and relations in my work with children and educators, I continue to struggle with how I might continually enact "learning to learn without the tools of human exceptionalism" (Haraway, 2014b, n.p.) as foundational to early childhood pedagogies. Many questions emerge in discussions of the forest encounters with educators. These questions bring tensions to our dialogues as we think with place, British Columbia forests, and forest pedagogies as contested and political. Perhaps these questions, alongside the everyday more-than-human encounters that inspired them, might be seen as quality practices-in-motion and quality-practices-in-question: What might it mean to engage in forest pedagogies that entangle ethics and politics, as well as the vibrancies and materialities of the forest? How have we come to understand this place? How might critical attunements to place (Tuck & McKenzie, 2014) become central to early childhood forest pedagogies? For example, how might we make meaning of the forest with children in ways that acknowledge this place as Indigenous Coast Salish territory? How might we attend to our entanglements in colonized worlds with young children? What might it look like to begin to consider the tensions, entanglements, accountabilities, and response-abilities (Haraway, 2008) that Indigenous and settler colonial knowledges of place might bring to our work with young children? What assumptions about place do we bring to our pedagogical encounters?

## Witnessing Cross-Species Socialities

Our location amid a forest inhabited by many plant and animal species, including black bears, moss, mushrooms, English Ivy, deer, raccoons, and coyotes, has offered a rich place in which to apprehend and think with what Donna Haraway (2003) terms noninnocent "co-habitation and embodied cross-species sociality" (p. 4). For example, a family of raccoons that co-inhabit this place have become a regular presence at the child care centers. The raccoons often enter the playgrounds, climbing the trees in the yard, running along the wooden fence that separates the child care centers, and making creative use of toys left outside by the children. Raccoons and children have become attuned to their co-presences, and they watch each other through classroom windows and skylights and from the treetops and playground below. Through attention to everyday raccoon–child encounters and the mutual child–animal curiosities that have emerged, we have begun to consider the ethical potentialities of paying attention to the nuanced ways in which more-than-human species story particular places in relation with humans (Nxumalo, Oh, Hughes, & Bhanji, 2015; van Dooren & Rose, 2012). However, this is not to romanticize raccoon–child relations. Raccoon–child–educator encounters remain frictional, and educator responses to raccoons remain contradictory. An important source of this contradiction is some of the safety measures enacted by educators to maintain "safe" boundaries between children and raccoons (Pacini-Ketchabaw & Nxumalo, 2015). These safety measures are part of adherences to quality standards set by British Columbia child care licensing regulations. However, amid the messy tensions created by regulated quality standards, "uncontrollable" raccoons, and unpredictable raccoon–child encounters, educators have also begun to respond to raccoon–child mutual affectivities in creative ways. We have begun to challenge ourselves to take seriously the effects of our and children's responses to these indigenous animals' presences in this place (Figure 2.2), and to create invitations for children to productively relate to raccoons—both real and imaginary—in multiple ways.

As a part of this work, I shared and discussed with educators scholarly literature from the environmental humanities that offers us questions and perspectives to think with in relation to everyday multispecies relations in early childhood pedagogies. We engaged in ongoing dialogues of questioning what an ethics of living with, responding to, and relating to might mean for the plant and animal species we encounter with children, particularly those such as raccoons that are not easy to live with.

Frictional raccoon–educator encounters, risky raccoon–child connections, affective raccoon–child mutual curiosities, and children's learning with raccoons are impossible to contain within dominant anthropocentric quality measures. Such measures might, for instance, question what children have learned about raccoons, and might focus on normative quality indicators such as children's safety when encountering raccoons. The art encounters shown in Figure 2.3 might be interpreted in terms of children's physical, social, emotional, and cognitive development (Kind, 2010). Such interpretations, while not necessarily wrong, silence the matterings of child–raccoon affectivities or those of children learning to co-inhabit with more-than-human others in more ethical ways. Such interpretations also silence the active participation of raccoons–children–educators–paper–charcoal–light–images–memories–shadows… and more in these matterings. Attention to raccoon–child cross-species socialities entangle us in inequitable arrangements of living and dying

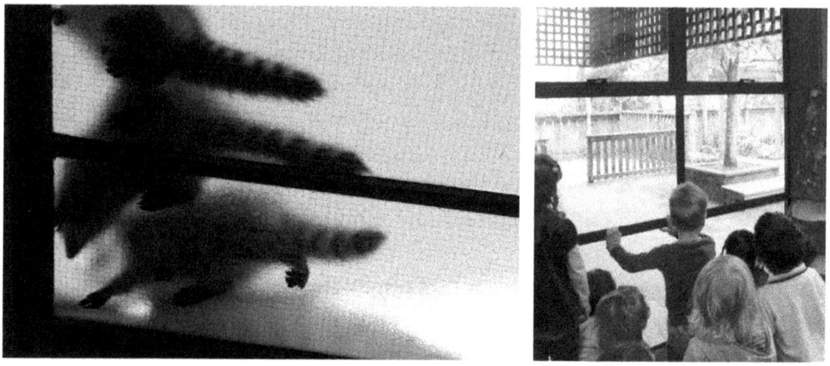

**FIGURE 2.2** Raccoons–Children: Mutual Curiosities at the Childcare Centre

> Touch, regard, looking back, becoming with—all these make us responsible in unpredictable ways for which worlds take shape. In touch and regard, partners willy nilly are in the miscegenous mud that infuses our bodies with all that brought that contact into being. Touch and regard have consequences.
>
> (Haraway, 2008, p. 36)

**FIGURE 2.3** Raccoon–Child Drawing Assemblage

> It is amid the [everyday] practices of 'living with' that accountability, caring for and responsibility come to matter... This way of thinking about ethics [is] partial, particular and rooted in bodies and relations.
>
> (Ginn, 2014, p. 533)

well (Haraway, 2012), bringing important critical questions and ongoing (always imperfect) responses-in-practice.

## Witnessing Damaged Landscapes

As an invitation for children and educators to come to "know forests" in multiple and creative ways, I set out paints and brushes on a drop cloth on the floor and tape a large piece of paper on the wall onto which I projected images of paintings by Coast Salish and Okanagan artist Lawrence Paul Yuxweluptun depicting damaged land and water ("Burying Another Face of Racism on First Nations Soil," 1997 and "Usufruct," 1995). Figure 2.4 shows images and my perspectives from a pedagogical narration I shared with educators.

The shadows on the screen seemed to create another way for the painting and the children to become entangled. Some children experimented with moving their bodies to create different shadows on the painting. I wondered what meanings might be made of these entanglements with the stories told by the

**FIGURE 2.4** Forest Painting Encounters

> The political discourse of my work is involved in environmentalism, globalization, global warming, dealing with capitalism; to analyze where First Nations people are within this planet.
>
> (Yuxweluptun, n.d.)

painting? Multiple meanings emerged as the children painted. Chinese New Year emerged as "dragons," "lions," and "fireworks" became a part of the forest as children painted. Discussions of "a bear coming to eat me up" emerged. I wondered what meanings can be made of these frictional connections? Yuxweluptun's work provides critical perspectives to relating to the forest. For instance, he brings attention to environmental destruction and contested territories. He also engages with Indigenous perspectives of land, such as its inherent vibrancies, cosmologies, histories, socialities, and materialities, rather than as a "mute" landscape or romantic wilderness. What might it mean for us to begin to encounter the forest in some of these ways with children? I also wondered what different, perhaps unfamiliar, ways of relating to the forest the children are already learning about and engaging with in this encounter? For instance, some children noticed that the forest has "eyes," and some children painted faces in the trees, perhaps echoing the vitalities in Yuxweluptun's painting? I wondered what other possibilities might emerge for shifting the familiarity of "nature" or the forest to the unfamiliar? What other possibilities might emerge for multiple ways for us to see and relate to the forest?

Discussions of this pedagogical narration with educators brought multiple contradictory perspectives, interpretations, and questions. Uncertainties emerged as I returned to setting out the painting provocation each day and as the multiplicities of children–educators–paint–paper–forest images and more assembled together and moved apart in different ways each time. In addition to Yuxweluptun's images, we experimented with painting with different "interruptive" forest imagery that the children responded to, such as images of clear-cut British Columbia forests. Each painting experience brought different movements and intensities for the human and more-than-human bodies assembled together, at times in ways that trouble me because they seem disconnected from the provocations of colonized and damaged landscapes posed by Yuxweluptun's images and clear-cut forests. Amid these emergent multiplicities-in-practice and contradictory perspectives of the painting encounters that arise in discussions with educators, I question my intentionalities and remain uncertain of the desired interruptive effects. These moments bear witness to refiguring quality pedagogical practices as what Derrida (1992) refers to as "experience and experiment of the possibility of the impossible" (p. 41). The assemblage of damaged-forest/water-images–paint–projector–children–pedagogista–educators and more is within a place of impossibility—impossibility of predetermined and measurable quality outcomes, and impossibility of transcending colonial relations with the forest. At the same time, amid this impossibility, openings for possibility emerged—such as the possibilities of relating to the forest differently, possibilities enacted by the active material presence of damaged British Columbia forest and waterway imagery in the room. Contested and damaged forests (Figure 2.1) and forest imagery (Figure 2.4), as witnesses, interrupted and complicated our everyday practices beyond quality. Forests as contested settler colonial places came to matter in our pedagogies, spilling over children's learning and educators' practices in ways that cannot be neatly explained by discourses of quality, even as we remained unsure about how to respond to the ethical dilemmas these contestations bring to the anthropogenic colonial worldings inhabited in this particular place.

## Mapping Watery Becomings

Figurative acts of witnessing are creative material-semiotic ways of mapping relations of knowledge, practice, and place in ways that counter monolithic views of the world, such as a singular view of what counts as quality (Haraway, 1992, 1997). Next, I story an illustrative example of pedagogical encounters that might be seen as enacting material, literal, and metaphorical mappings of contested territories. While these encounters—marked by elusiveness—refuse to be neatly represented as quality pedagogical practices, they might be seen as experimental gestures toward refiguring quality practices as lived-affective-performed-productive interferences in colonizing more-than-human relations.

In one child care center, we had been working on an inquiry with children on thinking with water for several months. Educators had been experimenting with possibilities for relating to water and watery places with children in ways that engage with water's liveliness and move away from ways of seeing water solely as a resource. Relating to anthropogenically damaged watery places emerged as a part of this inquiry through encounters with a nearby wetland/waste-dumping ground, named "frog pond" by the children (Nxumalo & Rubin, 2018). Noticing the persistence of plant and animal life amid abandoned waste in this waterway in the forest (Figure 2.5) brought difficult questions and uncertain responses as educators continued to grapple with what interruptive and responsible ways of encountering waste with children might look like beyond neoliberal technologies of waste management (Hird, 2014).

I shared with educators the idea of thinking of our work with children as "re-storying waters," drawing inspiration from Vancouver poet Rita Wong (2011), who challenges us to think with water in ways beyond objectification and commodification, and suggests instead to think with water in ways that are creatively inspired and that focus on ethics and multiple relationalities. The educators and I located a local waterways map and wondered if it might be of interest for children to experiment with creatively mapping "watery places." In the following are excerpts from our email correspondence intermingled with pedagogical experiences, as documented using pedagogical narration, at one of the child care centers:

**FIGURE 2.5** Wetland–Waste–Child Assemblage

> Living and dying in zones of abandonment… beyond the reach of scientific measurement and direct biopolitical regulation.
>
> (Kirksey, 2012, p. 48)

Educator: I think it will be interesting to draw a water map of [the child care setting]. I wonder what children know about water, where it is, and how they are connected… I think this exploration will give our children opportunity to reflect on their image of water and relate to their everyday lives at [the child care center].

Fikile: I think "mapping watery relations to place" has really interesting possibilities—Cecilia Chen (2011, 2013) has interesting ideas in there that we could think with further. I resonate with her idea of creating shifts away from mapping as simply a neutral representational practice and instead recognize that since "maps are never biased, mapping can be thoughtfully revisited as a messy and collective process that helps to negotiate common ground and share common waters" (2011, p. 20). She suggests seeking multiple, creative ways to map our messy "relations to watery places": ways that generate multiple understandings of place, such as mapping practices that incorporate changes over time (e.g., seasonal/history), multiple names, multiple stories, multiple senses (including sound), multiple performative interpretations of place, and maps from different human and more-than-human perspectives.

The educator decides to begin by inviting children to collaboratively draw a map of water-spaces in and around the child care center. Drawings of "a puddle on the grass," "water bottles," "ice in the fridge," and "water going all the way to the forest" emerge. Children are also invited to draw while they are outside. "It's the puddles we jump in" and "our blood is water" are some of the meanings that emerge as children, paper, colored markers, water, educators, sky, and many other more-than-human things come together in these moments.

Revisiting these "mappings" provoked new thinking which I shared with educators:

Fikile: What other possibilities for mapping water and water relations in this place might emerge? I thought children's drawing of their bodies as watery was wonderful to witness as an articulation of our inextricable relationalities/entanglements with water. Are you planning to invite children to map water around the campus, such as in the forest? I wonder if it might be interesting for children not only to "place" where water is, but to begin to "story" these maps as well? For example, I'm wondering about invitations for children to create "water stories" of their water relations in this place. Here are some more ideas from Cecilia Chen's (2013) work that might be interesting for us to think with in connection with these and future practices of mapping: Encouraging experimental "mapping processes that generate collective authorship [and] multiple interpretations" (p. 292)… Generating an evolving community of maps—multiple inter-related maps and multiple maps of the same "watery place" to produce multiple perspectives… Mapping what we

> can't necessarily see (such as the children's "watery" self-portraits)... Disrupting "colonial cartographic practices" (p. 290) by considering the exclusions and inclusions generated by each map.

The children and educators continued drawing water-maps, both individually and collaboratively. After several weeks, the inquiry dissipated as children's and educators' interests shifted away from water and mapping. Despite this dissipation, the tensions brought by interrupting our conventional understandings of children's mapping as representational learning (a common marker of quality) remained. Witnessing interruptive questions and perspectives alongside maps and damaged watery places invited messiness and uncertainty into our pedagogical practices. This messiness is not easily resolved and resists containment by the ending of our mapping experimentations and waste–wetland encounters.

## Living Immanent Quality-in-practice: Aporias and Fissures

This chapter has put more-than-human perspectives to work in refigurings of quality as specifically situated within everyday practices that are always uncertain and in question. I have put performative witnessing to work as a figuration for attending to everyday practices within the particular context of child care settings located in a mountain forest on Coast Salish territories. I have engaged with performative imagery and textual "small stories" of the everyday with a focus on intentionally decentering children's developmentally based learning, which is a typical normative "big story" of quality practices in early childhood education. Instead, I have storied practices of witnessing place specificities, cross-species socialities, damaged landscapes, and watery becomings. These context-specific stories illustrate inescapable aporias and cracks within everyday practices, practices that continuously leak outside of the abstractions and child-centered learning that commonly count as quality early childhood education. The pedagogical encounters presented in this chapter suggest that refiguring quality-in-practice as emergent, more-than-human, and always-in-process requires inhabiting possibility within impossibility (Derrida, 1992). This is illustrated by the unresolved questions and tensions that have emerged and resided alongside hopeful interruptions, imaginaries, possibilities, and relations. My suggestion is that refiguring quality-in-practice might include taking up creative pedagogical and methodological approaches toward noticing our implicated relationalities in a world where humans are not the only actors (Haraway, 2014a; van Dooren, 2014). In this perspective, refiguring quality involves ongoing grapplings with the ethical knots that entangle practice with more-than-human relations. As I have alluded to here, these grapplings might include productively inhabiting questions of who and what lives and dies well within particular damaged and colonized lifeworlds.

Although I worked with the child care centers I describe here for several years, I see this work as only a beginning, as ongoing tentative experimentations in "learning how to be worldly, how to respond" (Haraway, 2008, pp. 281–282) amid uncertainty and complexity. As responsible witnesses, we (more-than-human co-inhabitants, children, and educators) were immersed in ongoing processes of learning to respond to what emerges in the midst of messy quality practices-in-motion. While I bring no smooth resolution to the question of what counts as quality practices in early childhood education, as a modest witness, I remain simultaneously implicated, troubled, and hopeful (Haraway, 1997) about what these unsettling everyday encounters might produce.

# 3

# REFIGURING PRESENCES

Encounters with a nearby mountain forest were part of everyday pedagogies for children and educators at the group of suburban child care centers that are the subject of this book. We (myself and educators) engaged in discussions on these forest encounters and the possibilities for meaningful, non-appropriative presences of Indigenous perspectives in early childhood pedagogies. Amid these discussions, one of the educators composed a pedagogical narration reflecting on the forest encounters and the dialogues that have emerged with children. An excerpt from this pedagogical narration follows:

> So, as the children comfortably continue to explore their forest environment, many questions intrigue me as I wonder more about how we can use the forest as a third learning environment. How can we use what we do inside our classroom and continually bring it out to the forest? What kind of questions will the children have? I also wonder about how to tackle some of the children's questions about who made the forest. And more recently, when we are discussing the First Nations' heritage and culture, what do we discuss? There are some topics that come up in our discussions that make me feel uneasy, such as the ethics of hunting and killing the animals. My eyes have been opened wide to a place that offers so much learning and exploring. There are so many different avenues that this can take us, and wherever we go with it, it will always take us back to nature and to the forest.

## Why Refiguring Presences?

For over 500 years, settler colonialism in Canada has been manifested through ongoing complex, continually shifting processes of control, erasure, and genocidal displacement of Indigenous peoples (Battiste & Henderson, 2000; Morgensen, 2011; Wolfe, 2006). At the center of these processes is the remaking of land into settler property, replacing pedagogical, ancestral, and ontological Indigenous land relations (Tuck & McKenzie, 2014). Early childhood education is not outside of these colonial processes. For example, the increasingly popular forest preschools in North America are one site at which to interrupt colonialist representations of "pure nature" and innocent couplings of settler children and nature (Taylor, 2013).

Situated within the specific context of settler colonial British Columbia, Canada, the purpose of this chapter is to articulate a methodology of *refiguring presences* as a way to creatively grapple with, interruptively respond to, and work through the doubts, complicated frictions, discomforts, knots, and silences that moments such as those narrated in the opening excerpt throw up in research and pedagogical practices. In crafting refiguring presences as an approach to research that interrupts settler colonialism in early childhood studies, I draw inspiration from Anishinaabe scholar Leanne Simpson's (2011) call for *presencing* as decolonial acts that resist the erasures of Indigenous presences from settler colonial places and that politicize engagements with place. I use the concept of *refiguring* to emphasize orientations to research that reanimate, rethink, and relate differently to absent presences in everyday place encounters and that resist the normative practices and taken-for-granted understandings therein.

In this chapter, I develop a methodology of refiguring presences in an effort to create stutters in the innocence of settler children's natural place encounters in Canada. For instance, the opening story raised many questions for me when situated within ongoing settler colonial violence. I wondered what possibilities there might be to interrupt anthropocentric imaginaries of the forest as a separate site of exploration and learning for children? What perspectives might bring into view the material and discursive "liveliness" and political socialities of our forest encounters? How might discussions of traditional Indigenous cultures as a source of unease and of the forest as "belonging" to the children be made visible as entangled within settler colonial relations? What ways of knowing might interrupt static figurations of Indigenous cultures, erasures of complex Indigenous relationalities with more-than-human others, and the assimilation of these relationalities within a normative ethics of "hunting and killing"?

As I began to write about and seek ways to make sense of and respond to these discomforting everyday encounters, I found a number of methodological and ontological orientations invaluable in my inquiries. For instance, affective ethnography helped me to pay close attention to the intensities, embodied affects, and material–discursive textualities of the everyday (Stewart, 2007, 2008). Indigenous methodologies helped me to situate these everyday encounters alongside complicities with the epistemic and ontological erasures of colonialism (Byrd, 2011; Chilisa, 2012; Smith, 2013). Both Indigenous knowledges and posthumanist ontologies helped me to foreground more-than-human others (such as the forest) as active participants in multiple inextricably entangled relations with humans

(Barad, 2007; Haraway, 1988; Le Grange, 2012a; Martin, 2007; TallBear, 2013; Tuck, 2014). Restorying, land education, and place-based methodologies helped me to consider place as intrinsically storied and to find ways to foreground Indigenous place stories (Cameron, 2011; Somerville, 2006; Tuck, McKenzie, & McCoy, 2014). These place-situated methodologies challenged me to seek possibilities for refiguring, politicizing, and materializing everyday place encounters.

These understandings collectively helped me in attuning to the multiple politics, complexities, and contingencies of unsettling moments that have emerged in practice, such as those narrated in the opening of this chapter. These multiplicities include my inextricable situatedness in these moments, as well as the affects, theories, things, situated settler colonial histories, Indigenous knowledges, and more-than-human relationalities that animated these moments, yet often remained seemingly absent or silent. This chapter is an attempt to bring together these multiplicities as an emergent methodology of refiguring presences. I generate and craft refiguring presences by drawing from several methodologies and ontologies in ways that enable me to make visible and create interruptions in everyday early childhood "nature" place encounters that connect to settler colonialisms. I gather and assemble ways of noticing that act toward situating refiguring presences as a methodology that might make a difference to those specters of settler colonialism in everyday place encounters in early childhood education that are not necessarily easily pinned down and might otherwise remain unnoticed.

I position this chapter as resonant with postqualitative research approaches that have illustrated how predominantly discursive and humancentric understandings of difference are inadequate for attending to the material–discursive intensities, contingencies, and contradictions that mark everyday life (Lather, 2013; Law, 2004; MacLure, 2011; St. Pierre, 2011). Taking inspiration from postqualitative approaches and their invitation to attend closely to nature–culture and socio-material entanglements, I engage with research configurations that I see as holding potential to help me generate responsive and responsible modes of inquiry into everyday encounters in early childhood settings. To focus on the more than human, I bring Indigenous relational ontologies and posthuman material feminisms into conversation. I do this as a move toward a research orientation that is interested in the generative possibilities of "holding incompatible things together" (Haraway, 1985, p. 65). These possibilities center on further opening research in early childhood studies to considerations of not only the ethics of more-than-human relationalities, but also a politics that actively resists colonizing formations. While none of the epistemological and ontological formations that I bring together here are unprecedented in early childhood research, it is in their coalescence that I see new decolonial potentialities emerging. In what follows, I outline how I conceptualize refiguring presences as a decolonial methodological orientation in early childhood studies, by articulating integral components of this methodology. I also discuss the implications of this methodology for the messy "doings" of research, that is, implications for thinking with data (such as this chapter's opening story) accumulated from specific place encounters. I begin by situating refiguring presences as a methodology that confronts encounters with settler colonialisms in early childhood education. I discuss how refiguring presences draws critical attention to colonialisms that emerge in everyday life events in early childhood place encounters. Next, I discuss refiguring presences as an approach to research that inquires into the potentialities of engaging with multiple place stories while foregrounding the more than human. Finally, I situate researcher subjectivities as intricately entangled within practices of refiguring presences.

## Refiguring Presences Confronts Everyday Settler Colonialisms

Within the context of my early childhood research and pedagogical practices on unceded Coast Salish territories in what is now known as British Columbia, Canada, settler colonialism is an ongoing presence articulated through a myriad of exclusions, practices, and policies (Battiste & Henderson, 2000; de Finney, 2010; Thobani, 2007). These colonial legacies continue to have impacts on everyday life in multiple, often taken-for-granted ways in the banalities of everyday early childhood pedagogies. Accordingly, I am interested in possibilities for critically and creatively engaging with some of the ways in which the "temporality of empire" (Byrd & Rothberg, 2011, p. 5) emerges as an ongoing material–discursive presence in specific place encounters in early childhood settings. My interest is in seeking possibilities for early childhood scholars and educators to attend to and make visible how settler colonialisms come to matter in the everyday. For example, a methodology of refiguring presences seeks interruptions to the settler norms of ownership of the land and "the banality of settler-colonial forgetting" (Badger, 2013, para. 4) that are illustrated in the narrative that opens this chapter. In this example, decolonial resonances emerge from considering children, educators, and the forest's multiple co-inhabitants as located on Indigenous land, on unceded Coast Salish territories. Refiguring presences, then, takes seriously the challenge of what it might mean to work with early childhood research and pedagogical practices that are explicitly situated in settler colonial places.

A central understanding that shapes my approach to the everyday moments I pay attention to in working with children and educators is that colonialisms do much of their work through erasures, displacements, and exclusions that become normalized in everyday encounters such as the forest encounters described in the opening narrative. Early childhood education is a field permeated by everydayness and seemingly mundane material specificities and normalities—the everyday "banalities" (Horton & Kraftl, 2006; Rautio, 2013) children and educators engage in with, for example, outdoor places and spaces, eating practices, encounters with plants and animal life, and everyday play with objects and materials. My entry point is that these situated everyday practices are one site at which to apprehend colonially ordered relations. Intrinsic to this response is foregrounding both embedded colonial perspectives and possibilities for decolonial ways of seeing.

My focus on the everyday resonates with Elizabeth Povinelli's (2012a) supposition that differences are governed in the taken-for-granted and unquestioned intimate little routines that mark everyday life. Many others have argued that the seemingly "normal," banal, or ordinary is a site of complex political relations and potentials for micropolitical action and resistance (see, for example, Ahmed, 2004; Berlant, 2008; Blaise, 2013; Stewart, 2007, 2012). Taken together, the work of these scholars suggests attunement to the material–discursive political forces within which the situated intricacies, contradictions, and seeming banalities of everyday encounters are composed as both enduring and emergent effects and affects.

Refiguring presences can be thought of, then, as a helpful concept to disrupt the erasures and silences (Simpson, 2011) that mark the ordering of everyday life in child care settings by settler colonial formations. I use the term *concept* to intentionally position refiguring presences as both a way of knowing and as lived ontological acts of reorienting toward specific worlds—as research and knowledge-making practices that reshape everyday events and encounters in an attempt to pull apart their ordering effects (Ahmed, 2014; Deleuze & Guattari, 1987, 1994; Haraway, 1994, 2008). Donna Haraway (1994) eloquently names such practices of knowledge making as simultaneous processes of "description, narration, intervention, inhabiting, conversing, exchanging and building" (p. 62). In this way, I take up research as always in excess of any fact-making intents; the very modes of research, their materialities, and assumptions already create particular effects and stand for specific world-making arrangements (Barad, 2007). I take up refiguring presences as a methodology that is not simply about gathering and then reporting on findings from the work with educators and children, but rather as a form of decolonial interruption.

In the opening narrative, refiguring presences would be put to work to place coloniality at the center of everyday early childhood pedagogical encounters with the forest, its interrelated stories, and animated materialities. For instance, these encounters might be critically apprehended through asking questions such as these:

- What might be set in motion by beginning to notice that which is often taken for granted and normalized in this forest?
- What decolonial relationalities and ethical possibilities might be brought into view from close attention to the situated more-than-human specificities of encounters with the forest?
- What contradictions and ambivalences emerge in each specific encounter that might create new ways of seeing?
- How might close attunement to material and discursive enactments of difference and exclusion as they emerge in everyday pedagogical encounters with the forest be seen as micropolitical acts?
- What new or different perspectives and affects emerge from considering the words *comfort* and *unease* in frictional connection with forest encounters, settler colonialism, and Indigenous cultures?

These questions are posed as invitations to respond interruptively and creatively to everyday pedagogical encounters with settler colonial places. They are an illustration of possibilities for responding in ways that politicize, unsettle, refigure, reconsider, and (re)story what is considered present in these encounters. Taken together, these interrelated questions suggest that everyday banalities might be a site at which to notice and thereby create interruptions in (neo)colonial relations and their accompanying "physicalities, fabricated habitudes, habituated visions… [and] habituated materialities" (Povinelli, 2012b, p. 374). As these questions illustrate, refiguring presences is centered on possibilities for interrupting everyday material–discursive colonial *place* relations in both research and practice. This emphasis on place is intentional—refiguring presences is concerned with reorienting settler relations to specific places (and the more-than-human life therein) in decolonizing ways. Accordingly, I now turn to the methodological implications of decolonizing place relations.

## Refiguring Presences as Restorying Place

Refiguring presences is specifically situated and located in particular place encounters within the geopolitical and geohistorical (Mignolo, 2002) specificities of settler colonialism. Refiguring presences requires politicized attention to the settler colonial places that early childhood educators inhabit and encounter with children. Consequently, this methodology generates material–discursive stories of place, where both the stories and the "storytellers" are more than human and where mapping marginalized stories and generating different stories requires experimentation with diverse methods. I want to emphasize here that place refers not only to territorial physicalities or materialities of place, but also to the specific stories, worldviews, and human and more-than-human relations therein (Calderón, 2014). That is to say, place is conceptualized as a gathering of things, human and nonhuman bodies, and stories that require attention beyond the individual child's experiences. Place is also seen as enacted through colonial and neocolonial assemblages, including knowledges, practices, and other social forces that come together to compose a politicized conception and "doing of place" (Anderson, 2012; Stewart, 2008). This orientation toward "alternative, repressed and contradictory stories of place" (Somerville, 2006, para. 9) is a mode of critical encounter with settler colonialism. Attending to place stories creates an opening for grappling with the ethical potentialities of plural more-than-human worldings where both the human and more than human "shape and are shaped by political, economic, and cultural forces" (Kirksey & Helmreich, 2010, p. 545). Refiguring presences, then, is an intentional experimentation with how to notice the material–discursive boundaries and hierarchical orderings that come to matter in encounters with particular settler colonial places. This is an approach to inquiry that escapes a neat description because it is contingent and emergent knowledge making (Haraway, 1988, 1991, 2006) that attempts to attend to some of the complexities in an intentionally chosen moment of encounter with place.

Refiguring presences materializes place stories in diverse ways, encompassing critical narratives generated from situated place-based historical fragments, written non-Indigenous and Indigenous stories of particular places, visual images, and stories of specific plant and animal species encountered with children. For example, in a methodology of refiguring presences, the opening narrative could be juxtaposed with situated settler colonial historical fragments and Indigenous stories of the particular place in which this work is located. The narrative would also be set alongside visual images of the specific active materialities of the forest encounters. Figure 3.1 illustrates one possibility of (re)storying visualities through the image of children's and educators' encounters with a human-made forest trail that is a remnant of the colonial logging histories of this particular place. Chapter 4 includes further discussion of these logging histories.

In addition to (re)storying place, refiguring presences generates detailed, critically descriptive accounts of everyday encounters. These descriptions are situated articulations of what Kathleen Stewart (2014) calls a "critical stance of curiosity and responsibility that attempts to approach... diverging practices, materialities, and events" (p. 550) in ways that attend to more-than-human and settler colonial relations. For instance, the opening narrative might be refigured as a critical description through an interweaving of questions that emerged for myself and educators in discussions of this pedagogical narration. I see potential for refiguring presences as a research methodology that maps place stories and sets them alongside critically descriptive accounts of everyday encounters to see what they produce and unsettle. In this regard, refiguring presences works with selected everyday moments

**FIGURE 3.1** Forest Trail Encounters

as data to juxtapose and connect these narrated moments with interruptive place stories.

This way of working with data and place stories emphasizes what I see as active presences in these encounters: assemblages of situated Indigenous stories; children's and educators' embodied embeddedness in settler colonial pastpresent histories; and more-than-human worlds. Importantly, while I have listed these integral presences separately, inherent to this method are their complex interconnections. Refiguring presences intentionally resists a conventional analysis or interpretation of the data-place-stories assemblages. This inventive and experimental approach to "meeting" data, theory, and knowledge perhaps shares affinities with what Elizabeth St. Pierre and Alecia Jackson (2014) refer to as *postcoding analysis*—research practices that:

> borrow concepts, invent approaches, and create new assemblages that demonstrate a range of analytic practices... Post-coding analysis, then, can be thought as non-technique and non-method that is always in a process of becoming... [It] cannot be neat, tidy, and contained. Furthermore, it cannot be easily explained either during or after analysis. It certainly cannot be replicated because it is emergent and experimental. In addition, its space–time cannot be secured in the traditional linear "process" trajectory of data collection> analysis> representation. (p. 717)

In resonance with postcoding analysis, refiguring presences intentionally intermingles data (such as textual and visual descriptions of encounters) and place stories with theoretical and Indigenous ontological perspectives, creating movement away from a clean separation of data, place stories, Indigenous knowledges, and posthumanist theories. Instead, staying with the messiness and complexities enacted by these everyday encounters, I engage these juxtapositions and frictional connections as interruptive, and highlight the difficult questions that they bring to situated research and practice.

## Refiguring More-than-human Presences

As the preceding discussion of interruptive visual images suggests, an important aspect of refiguring presences is shifting attention from the child as the subject of research and practice to children's entanglements within multiple human and more-than-human relations (Hultman & Lenz Taguchi, 2010; Taylor, 2013). In the opening narrative, child-centered pedagogies create occlusions and silences—such as in creating the forest as a passive environment subject to children's actions and imaginaries. By seeking shifts away from anthropocentrism, refiguring presences is an approach to research that pays close attention to matter—the things and places that actively participate in our (children's and educators') everyday encounters. In making this shift, I take inspiration from Indigenous knowledges, which are rooted in more-than-human reciprocal relationalities that are situated in place (Le Grange, 2009, 2012a; Martin, 2007).

For many Indigenous knowledges, the more than human is an active, vital force that is entangled in complex nonhierarchical relationalities with the human (e.g., see Dei, 2002; Martin, 2007; Sundberg, 2014; TallBear, 2013). Here, humans and nonhumans are active and relational participants in world making, rather than passive or inactive objects of human knowledge (Four Arrows, Jacobs, & Ryan, 2010; Le Grange, 2009, 2012a; Tuck, 2014). Drawing from Indigenous ontologies and epistemologies in conceptualizing refiguring presences is a risky, tension-filled move. As Tuck, McKenzie, and McCoy (2014) note:

> mindfulness of non-Indigenous desires to access assumed Indigenous knowledge also needs to extend to a mindfulness of non-Indigenous desires to adopt or use such knowledge… This is difficult terrain in working both with Indigenous and non-Indigenous learners: to acknowledge and include Indigenous knowledge and perspectives but in non-determined ways that do not stereotype Indigenous knowledge or identities. (pp. 10–11)

In addition to acknowledging the risks and tensions in working with Indigenous knowledges, it is important for me to emphasize here that while I use the term *Indigenous* to refer broadly to North American, Australian, and African contexts and, more specifically, in relation to my location on Coast Salish territories, this is not intended to imply that there are not important irreducible and place-specific differences both within and across these vastly diverse locations. Indigenous knowledges are multiple, complex, and dynamic (Driskill, Finley, Gilley, & Morgensen, 2011). As Kwakwaka'wakw scholar Sarah Hunt (2014a) notes, "the heterogeneity of Indigenous voices and worldviews can easily become lost in efforts to understand Indigeneity in ways that fix Indigenous knowledge, suppressing its dynamic nature" (p. 29). My intents in the move to reference Indigenous knowledge to frame more-than-human active presences (Simpson, 2011) are multiple, interrelated, and intentional, and next I attempt to explicate them.

Refiguring presences is a political orientation to research that intentionally seeks to unsettle Eurocentrism (Battiste, Bell, Findlay, Findlay, & Henderson, 2005). As Sara Ahmed (2010) notes, "orientations matter. Those who are 'out of place' have to secure a place that is not already given" (p. 254). Refiguring presences, then, engages with Indigenous relationalities to counter (neo)colonial erasures in connection with knowledge production in the academy. I also work with Indigenous relationalities to make visible possibilities for more ethical relationships with the more-than-human presences I encounter with children and educators.

Drawing on Indigenous knowledges to orient research practices toward the mutual constitution and entanglements of the human and more than human does not disappear relations that are marked by inequity and tensions that connect with settler colonialism. Indigenous knowledges provide an entry into inquiring into and making visible power asymmetries by locating this research within the context of a settler colonial location. That is to say, refiguring presences pays attention to the "*unequal* organization of social life" (Povinelli, 2012a, p. 77, emphasis added).

These knowledges make possible important questions that create interruptions to the opening narrative. Some of the questions that emerged for me in returning to critically reflect on our encounters with the forest were: What might specific Indigenous stories teach us about the specific, vibrant, and relational participation of the forest in the making of this particular place on Coast Salish territories? How might we come to encounter the forest, not as a mute, benign, or empty space, but as a vibrant, active, social space in which we (children and educators) are all entangled? For instance, in learning circle discussions with educators, I wondered how we might contest taken-for-granted assumptions that positioned the forest as simply a learning environment for children. Drawing from our reading discussions, I also questioned what we might notice differently if we considered pedagogies of learning with the forest and moved away from learning about the forest (Pacini-Ketchabaw, 2013). I wondered: What does the forest know of us? What happens when we think of this forest and its animated materialities, including logged ancient tree stumps, invasive ivy, a human-made forest (logging) trail, and rotting tree hollows as storied witnesses to colonial pastpresent histories? How might we think with the things that the children encounter in the forest as not simply awaiting children's discoveries, but as participants that are always already in relation with other humans and nonhumans? What other ways of relating to the forest and the more-than-human things in it might be possible? How can we pay attention to our entanglement within colonized places?

Indigenous relational ontologies, while not reducible to the same, share an affinity with Euro-Western material feminist conceptualizations of the mutually coconstitutive entanglements of human and nonhuman worlds (Jackson, 2013; Tuck, 2014). These materialist perspectives also highlight more-than-human relational becomings and disrupt taken-for-granted anthropocentric ways of knowing and relating. For instance, recent materialist research practices interrupt the primacy of human-centered discursive representation and challenge an inanimate view of nonhuman worlds (Barad, 2007; Jackson, 2013; Saldanha, 2006; Sundberg, 2014; Whatmore, 2006). In these methodologies, attention to the materiality of encounters foregrounds the active force, relational, and disconnective effects, as well as the gestural expressions of human and more-than-human bodies (Bennett, 2004; Saldanha, 2006). Both the human and nonhuman are seen as active, coconstitutive participants, and the human, as Sarah Whatmore (2006) asserts, is "no less a subject of ongoing cofabrication than any other socio-material assemblage" (p. 603).

Taking inspiration from this focus on materiality and more-than-human relationalities, a methodology of refiguring presences asks questions such as: What emerges from paying attention to the "materializing effects" created by the ways in which boundaries are drawn between the human/more-than-human and between nature/culture (Barad, 2011)? What ethical relationalities between children and more-than-human life might an ethics of "responsive attentiveness" (Rose, 2004, p. 5) to material–discursive and nature–culture entanglements bring into view? For instance, performative image assemblages can be put to work to bring a critical focus to more-than-human presences and human/more-than-human entanglements. The visual of an ivy-entangled tree, shown in Figure 3.2, is an illustrative example of a critical responsiveness to more-than-human presences that complicates the opening narrative. This image was taken during encounters that I, children, and educators had with invasive and colonizing English ivy in the forest. This image decenters the child and instead brings attention to the intensities of more-than-human materialities and points to the noninnocence of human/more-than-human entanglements. Children's and educators' encounters with ivy perhaps unsettle relating to the forest and to the idea of nature as pure, as "something out there" awaiting children's discovery, as exclusively nonhuman. English ivy knotted around trees and on the forest floor—it caught children's feet and tripped them up as they walked and ran through the area. What might thinking with the invasive ivy, such as how it materially and

**FIGURE 3.2** English-ivy–Forest Entanglements

metaphorically entangles us and the forest, in colonial pastpresent histories do? What might acts of pulling ivy and working with pulled ivy and ivy leaves with children enact and interrupt?

Refiguring presences, then, are noninnocent research and pedagogical practices that are materially and discursively consequential; they creatively unsettle what is seen to matter (Figure 3.2). They are unsettling processes of "materialized refiguration" (Haraway, 1994, p. 62). In this regard, a methodology of refiguring presences is particularly curious about presences and absences (Law, 2004; Simpson, 2011) in everyday early childhood pedagogical place encounters that connect to colonialism. This orientation toward research engages with the potentialities of material–discursive stories situated within particular encounters between children, educators, and their more-than-human worlds as a politicized bringing together of particular "forms of presence and absence" (Law, 2004, p. 85). Resisting a focus on simply representing reality, this is a political orientation that is concerned with what forms of reality are made visible, including what and who participates in making that reality (Blaser, 2014). In Figure 3.2, what is made present that might otherwise be rendered invisible or absent? What human/more-than-human relationalities are always present (Law, 2004; Simpson, 2011)? Importantly, refiguring presences is not simply about making present that which is absent—for example, Indigenous relationalities are always already there, even as they remain as absent presences due to the erasures manifested through colonial worldings (Simpson, 2011; Spivak, 1990).

My troubling of the binary of presence and absence is important and intentional. There is a danger that refiguring presences might reproduce colonial representational practices, such as in creating an idealized "looking back" to a reified authentic Indigenous identity—another form of erasure through silencing contemporary Indigenous presences and current lived colonial realities (Byrd, 2011; Fawaz, 2012). This politicized attention to human and more-than-human presences and absences foregrounds complexity, uncertainty, contingency, and partiality as central to the ways in which becoming with the world is envisaged, including the ways in which researcher subjectivities come to matter in anticolonial knowledge-making practices.

## (Dis)entangling Researcher Subjectivities

One way in which I have taken up the challenge of articulating a location that is resolutely accountable to the more than human in a methodology of refiguring presences is to intentionally shift the focus away from humanistic subjectivities (Haraway, 2006; Le Grange, 2012a). To enact this practice, as I have discussed throughout the chapter, I experiment with refiguring presences as a methodology that decenters the individual human subject and instead attends to human/more-than-human relational entanglements—the vibrant force and material–discursive socialities—of things, plants, and animals (Bennett, 2010; Four Arrows et al.,

2010; Tsing, 2013). Important questions emerge from this shift to the more than human. For instance, how might early childhood scholars and educators engage with place-focused research and pedagogies in ways that resist a disembodied neutral positioning, while also complicating their situatedness—situatedness that might be marked contingently by alterity, relationality, and complicity in the everyday encounters that they bring into view? How might refiguring presences, as ways of relating to complex material–discursive and more-than-human worlds, also point to the specificities of researchers' and educators' implicated locations within settler colonialism?

Here I want to turn toward what might seem to be in tension with the focus on the more than human that I have assembled in this chapter. Refiguring presences by foregrounding the more than human does not erase the effects of human bodies (including their embodied and material differences) and their differential situatedness in a place—human difference matters (Ahmed, 2010). While remaining aware of the danger of slippage toward the anthropocentric centering of myself that I wish to avoid, I think it is important to illustrate what I mean here by briefly narrating a necessarily partial view of my own locations-in-the-making.

Refiguring presences as a centering of more-than-human relationality is an intentional resistance to orienting myself simply in relation to fixed locations—Black cis female, Indigenous Ndwandwe clan member, "postcolonial" Swazi citizen, Canadian citizen, African immigrant–settler… among many others. When understood within geopolitical and historical specificities, these locations can be an important place from which to critically encounter systemic oppressions and everyday marginalizations (Mohanty, 2003). However, some of these categories emerge and reemerge through ongoing racialized, neoliberal, and colonial formations to become material–discursive processes of governing difference. Haraway (1997) foregrounds the complexity of a situated and partial location:

> Location is not the listing of adjectives or assigning of labels such as race, sex, and class. Location is not the concrete abstract of decontextualization. Location is the always partial, always finite, always fraught play of foreground and background, text and context, that constitutes critical inquiry. Above all location is not self-evident or transparent. Location is also partial in the sense of being for some worlds and not others. (p. 37)

My subjectivities have been and are continually negotiated within the inequities produced by complex neocolonial, racial, and globalized neoliberal relations. I cannot, however, as an immigrant to what is now Canada, claim an innocent relationship to settler colonialism and ongoing territorial dispossession. My multiple belongings to and estrangements from the places I call home suggest that the locations that I have named above are much more than what they represent; they are just some of the rooted yet rootless material–discursive marks of difference that render my self-invisibility (Haraway, 1997) in my research and pedagogical work an impossibility. I also resonate with Haraway's figure of the reconfigured modest witness to describe immersion in practices of noninnocent, entangled, and implicated knowledge making (Haraway, 1997). This immersion necessitates continually being accountable to and vulnerable to the situated and always partial ways in which I encounter and make meaning of the world. In other words, my particular perspectives, histories, and experiences always already create a propensity toward particular ways of seeing, noticing, and contesting colonialisms.

My becomings are always already entangled with my research and pedagogical practices. At the same time, these marks of difference bring no guarantee of a simplified subaltern positioning (Spivak, 2010). For example, it is important for me to resist conflating and simplifying the specificities and effects of racial and colonial formations of difference, particularly within the context of "multicultural" settler colonial Canada, where complicity in the "colonial racial-spatial order" (Opondo, 2008, p. 61) of things cannot be evenly assigned to all bodies. I also intentionally resist attempting to translate (Spivak, 2000) those unrepresentable subjectivities that are a part of my becomings, because I remain wary of reproducing colonial tropes of the "authentic African" made knowable through (self)representation (Opondo, 2008).

Povinelli (2012a) also helps me think through the tensions, complexities, and ambivalences of researcher subjectivities as "immanent modes of obligation" (p. 83) filled with both fixed and emergent ethical responsibilities. She suggests that reflexivity is insufficient in its centering of the individual and the personal, since "no one is merely the given-form of identity. Every identity is shot through with unnamable networks of deep unspecifiable, unnamable obligation" (p. 83). She suggests that a difficult but necessary task is to figure out how to remain situated in and responsive to our relational obligations, while, at the same time, critically engaging with the relations of power that "act to disrupt and contain and redirect these immanent modes of obligation" (p. 83).

As a researcher and educator, I have found that negotiating the entanglements of relational subjectivities while maintaining a focus on the more than human is a challenging task. As a beginning, I have attempted to make visible the partial perspectives afforded by particular locations (Haraway, 1988) by situating myself as an implicated participant within the specific ongoing everyday settler colonial relations that emerge and entangle everyday encounters in this research. In the opening story, while I have included only a partial perspective from one educator (and at the same time risked representing a singular view of "the educator"), making meaning of this encounter in a methodology of refiguring presences necessitates an engagement with the noninnocent affects and silences this story generated in me. It also requires attention to be paid to my embodied presence in the forest pedagogies described by the educator, and the tensions, challenges, and divergences that emerged from attempted responses to this encounter.

What I have tried to outline in this discussion of my location within settler colonial relations is that, rather than privileging a predefined universal researcher subjectivity that seeks a definitive complete truth, a methodology of refiguring presences enacts situated, implicated, and politicized acts of connecting with what comes into view in a particular encounter. These acts are always entangled with subjective and always partial perspectives (Haraway, 1988) that create particular orientations toward interfering in colonizing relations in everyday early childhood pedagogical encounters. As Haraway (1988) notes, one's location, even while neither singular nor unchanging, provides a "view from a body, always a complex, contradictory, structuring, and structured body, versus the view from above, from nowhere, from simplicity" (p. 589). In a methodology of refiguring presences, the embodied presence and the partial "view[s] from somewhere" (Haraway, 1988, p. 590) enacted by shifting researcher or educator subjectivities are always already entangled within the everyday place encounters described.

## Toward Refiguring Presences

In this chapter, I have gathered together concepts, ontologies, methods, and research practices to propose refiguring presences as an anticolonial methodological orientation to place-based research in early childhood education settings. I have situated refiguring presences by conceiving it as a methodology that unsettles taken-for-granted ways of seeing and noticing connections to settler colonialisms. I have suggested that refiguring presences needs to draw attention to the intricacies of everyday moments in ways that have an interruptive intentionality in seeking to make visible the colonial resonances and flows of power that circulate through everyday life. I have also discussed how refiguring presences is attuned to ordering effects, as well as to the ethical potentialities of more-than-human relations. In this understanding, seeking situated stories of place is of critical importance in refiguring presences as an anticolonial orientation to early childhood research, where place is a site of asymmetrical relations that require close attention (Somerville, 2006). In taking seriously the vibrancies of places and their more-than-human presences, a methodology of refiguring presences interrupts anthropocentric and colonial perspectives that privilege humans as the central actors. At the same time, affective, embodied, entangled, and implicated researcher subjectivities are also active material–discursive participants in refiguring presences. While oriented toward interruptive attention to settler colonialism and its ongoing resonances in the practices of everyday life, refiguring presences is also a messy, provisional, and imperfect research practice. That is to say, the elements that I bring together in this chapter are not exhaustive in informing a methodology of refiguring presences. While I have discussed what I consider to be important elements of refiguring presences, I want to avoid the suggestion of certainty and fixed borders around this methodology. Following Lather (2013), I consider this methodology as "non-totalizable, sometimes fugitive, also aggregate, innumerable, resisting stasis and capture, hierarchy and totality" (p. 635). Situating everyday (neo)colonialisms in early childhood pedagogical encounters as continually emerging, cunningly inventive, and entangled with multiple material–discursive assemblages (Alfred & Corntassel, 2005; Pacini-Ketchabaw, Nxumalo, & Rowan, 2011; Povinelli, 2012a) means that there will be other elements that aggregate in refiguring presences that I have not considered here. In this chapter, I have articulated refiguring presences as emergent entanglements of researcher subjectivities—data—more-than-human presences—place stories—analysis—Indigenous knowledges—theories. However, refiguring presences requires opening to the emergent, unforeseen, and unexpected, while acknowledging the impossibility of mapping all the constituent parts of the stories or histories that animate a particular place encounter. Rather than a totalizing account, this research orientation is an implicated, intentional, politicized, and selective noticing, a partial beginning toward interrupting settler colonialisms and anthropocentrisms in everyday early childhood place encounters. However, this is without the promise of a final resolution of the contradictions, frictions, and troubles that abound. Finally, refiguring presences is not without important limitations in enacting decolonizing possibilities. To actively enact decolonizing early childhood studies, much more is required than what I have begun to gather here. Refiguring presences might perhaps be seen, then, as beginning to engage with the situated messiness of decolonizing early childhood studies.

# 4

# UNSETTLING FOREST ENCOUNTERS

> We often walked to the forest close by to the child care center with the children. Each encounter with the forest invited different curiosities—hollowed-out tree stumps, shiny green moss clinging to the trees and tree stumps, mushrooms, sticks… looking down to the ocean inlet and across it to snow-capped mountains, salmonberries in the summer, fallen leaves in the fall—these are just some of the things that came together to create particular wonderings and curiosities in encounters with this place. One morning before our walk, the educator told the children, "Today we will use our senses to discover the forest." She asked them, "What will we hear? What will we see? What will we touch? What will we discover today?" The children answered: "lions"; "bears"; "tigers"; "trees and clouds"; "flowers, sticks, and berries."

There is a now a significant body of scholarship in early childhood studies that has sought to trouble developmental psychology as the dominant way of understanding young children and their modes of learning. In disrupting dominant truths of the young child, early childhood studies scholars have drawn on theories including poststructural, feminist, anti-racist, postcolonial, and posthumanist theories. Despite important critiques of the dominance of Global North theoretical perspectives in early childhood studies, this body of work has brought needed critical lenses to understandings of early childhood and early childhood education (Pérez & Saavedra, 2017). More recently, as part of this ongoing effort to contextualize early childhood and trouble the individualistic fixations of developmental psychology, work in early childhood studies has turned to considerations of place. For instance, some of this work has centered children's more-than-human place relations, drawing primarily on posthuman theories, feminist geographies, and the environmental humanities. This focus on human/more-than-human entanglements has been put to work to disrupt anthropocentric viewpoints in environmental education for young children

(Taylor & Giugni, 2012). Such normative viewpoints position the individual developing child as learning through direct experiences with nature—where nature is positioned as a pure space, separate from the child, keeping the nature–culture binary intact (Murris, Reynolds, & Peers, 2018; Pacini-Ketchabaw, 2012; Nelson, Pacini-Ketchabaw, & Nxumalo, 2018; Taylor, 2013).

Building on this work, this chapter seeks to unsettle taken-for-granted familiarities of nature as a site to enhance children's learning experiences. This inquiry is situated within the current high level of interest in nature early childhood pedagogies in British Columbia (BC), Canada, where my work is located. Recent calls for children to spend time in nature are marked by several normative assumptions and omissions. For instance, pastpresent colonial histories, assumptions of nature–culture separation, discourses of childhood innocence, privileging of a "scientific" approach to nature education, and classed and racialized assumptions of what constitutes "normal" childhood experiences of nature remain, for the most part, unquestioned (see Dickinson, 2013; Pacini-Ketchabaw, 2013; Taylor, 2013 for work that engages critically with some of these gaps in nature education). As the opening story illustrates, unquestioned assumptions of nature education are apparent in easy moves to representations of a static nature in everyday pedagogies and conceptualizations of nature as separate from children and simply awaiting their discoveries.

In this chapter, my specific focus is on everyday encounters that children, early childhood educators, and I had with particular things (the forest trail, tree stumps, and tree hollows) in a specific socially, materially, and historically situated mountain forest. An intrinsic part of situating this place is attending to the ever-present threads of empire (Tsing, 2012a). The mountain forest we visited regularly lies on unceded Musqueam, Squamish, Stó:lō, and Tsleil-Waututh territories amid ongoing settler colonial conditions. Settler colonial conditions include material and discursive erasures, as well as dispossessions, displacements, and appropriations that shape everyday relations, often in taken-for-granted ways (Barker, 2009). These erasures and displacements include the underpinning of understandings and encounters with nature, where dominant tropes of BC's untouched wild landscapes are intimately entangled with ongoing colonial legacies (Braun, 2002; Oliver, 2010). Settler colonialism is deeply entangled within taken-for-granted banalities of everyday early childhood nature pedagogies in BC. At the same time, colonialisms are shifting, malleable, and articulated differently in different places at different times—often in contradictory and contingent ways (Alfred & Corntassel, 2005; Kothari & Wilkinson, 2010). Colonialisms have been and continue to be enacted through "greatly varied forms of engagement and encounter, political purposes, local complexities and distinct geographies" (Kothari & Wilkinson, 2010, p. 1398). Colonialism is implicated in ruptures to Indigenous relationalities with place. Colonial encounters imposed hierarchical humanisms, racializing and dichotomizing human/nonhuman and wild-nature/civilized-culture, and placing the colonized along a linear trajectory to "civility" and "humanity"—albeit with contextually contingent intents, effects, and affects in differently situated colonial encounters (Anderson, 2007). In this way, colonial authority attempts to bind the colonized within the "limits of their presupposed ontological difference" (Mbembe, 2002, p. 246), figured in hierarchical order to the colonizers.

I inhabit the forest encounters described herein as noninnocent "everyday worldings that matter in many ways beyond their status as representations" (K. Stewart, 2012, p. 519). I consider how restorying (Cameron, 2011) this particular place and the "things" in it, through material–discursive relations (Barad, 2007) and Indigenous relationalities, might be a productive move toward refiguring presences and countering the "continual colonial mapping and erasing of Indigenous presence" (Simpson, 2011, p. 96) in encounters with so-called natural places.

As described more fully in Chapter 3, refiguring presences is inspired by Anishinaabe scholar Leanne Simpson's (2011) call for presencing as anticolonial acts by Indigenous peoples through which reconnections are created with colonized places in multiple ways, including stories that presence Indigenous relationships within occupied territories. Refiguring presences through stories seeks to interrupt normative assumptions of place and to create openings toward engaging in politicized dialogues with places such as the mountain forest. I use the concept of refiguring to highlight that these are acts of resistance that are not simply about making present that which is absent—these relationalities are "always already" there despite the erasures manifested through colonial worldings (Spivak, 1990). Refiguring gestures toward rethinking and relating differently to absent presences and the normative practices and taken-for-granted understandings therein. These relationalities include a consideration of not only the more-than-human—including matter, relations, meanings, and understandings—but also the wider historical geopolitics within which the more-than-human is located and entangled, most notably settler colonialism.

My intent then, is to center refiguring presences as an anticolonial practice aimed at provoking educators' attention toward the things, practices, relations, and historical and social forces through which nature is enacted (Braun, 2002; Instone, 2004). By attending to colonial erasures, I am interested in relating differently to the question of "whose stories come to matter" (van Dooren & Rose, 2012, p. 3) in the making of this particular forest that we visit with the children. The stories I choose to tell are deliberate interruptions to (the seemingly) innocent stories of early childhood places and nature pedagogies within a settler location. What disparate gatherings might be enacted through material and figurative encounters with this forest and its particularities? What connections might be made with colonial imaginaries (Said, 1978) of other forests in BC? What possibilities might emerge for troubling the "social and spatial, material and discursive" (Instone, 2010a, p. 360) boundaries and borders enacted through nature as benign sites for "discovery"? What anticolonial possibilities might emerge from stories that unsettle "dualistic constructions and hierarchical relations with the natural world" (Instone, 1998, p. 457)? What might inhabiting the historical politics of this particular place do (Instone, 2010a, b)? With these questions, as with other questions I ask throughout the chapter, I do not necessarily provide answers, but rather pose them as invitations to early childhood educators to engage with an ethics of "responsive attentiveness" (Rose, 2004, p. 5) to everyday encounters and the complexities, relationalities, and tensions they bring into view.

I began this chapter by locating my work within BC as a place in which representations of nature are intimately connected with ongoing colonialisms. I then introduced refiguring presences as a form of responsive, accountable attention that makes visible and interrupts connections to colonialisms in everyday nature encounters that might otherwise remain unnoticed. I explored how refiguring presences might be useful as relational, situated, and non-innocent storying practices that unsettle taken-for-granted ways of seeing and provoke different ways of relating to everyday encounters with the forest. For the remainder of the chapter, I enact a series of interruptive stories of forest encounters. I put refiguring presences to work through the noninnocent tales of walking the forest trail, lingering at tree stumps, and touching tree hollows. I consider how interruptive stories, such as these, which attend to the inherent vibrancies, tensions, and contestations of place, might be put to work as an anticolonial practice.

## Forest Encounters

> For every one of your questions there is a story hidden in the skin of the forest.
>
> *(Simpson, 2013b, p. 132)*

The stories I tell of my encounters with the forest with children and educators emerged from my work with three child care centers located atop a mountain and surrounded by a forest. I worked as a pedagogical facilitator, supporting educators in their pedagogical practices. The forest encounters took place at different times during the academic year. From the pedagogical narrations that myself and educators used to document and reflect on our forest encounters, I have selected particular moments that spoke to me, troubled me, and left me with questions about what remained invisible. I want to note here that I am intimately implicated and entangled in these pedagogical encounters; I situate myself alongside the educators as a noninnocent participant in these practices. My primary interest in this chapter is in complicating and interrupting these enactments of nature and children in nature, as well as in considering what refiguring more-than-human (Whatmore, 2006) and Indigenous presences might provide toward anticolonial pedagogical possibilities in encounters with the forest. In other words, my intent is not to critique educators but to unsettle this mountain forest as simply a place for children's real and imaginary discoveries.

I experiment with what Stacy Alaimo (2010) refers to as "modes of inquiry and analysis that do not diminish the significance of the very stuff of the more-than-human world" (p. 73), while simultaneously attending to material and discursive neocolonial relations and presences within the geopolitical context of what is now BC. Throughout the chapter, I write about the settler colonial histories that are ever-present in the opening story by attending to how they are enacted through the idea of wild and empty lands and discourses of protecting nature, while simultaneously undergoing erasure by the same imaginaries of a wild, empty forest awaiting discovery and protection (Cattelino, 2011; Willems-Braun, 1997).

Following Haraway (2008), I explore how knowledge making, through foregrounding more-than-human worlds, might bring into view multiple stories of this particular situated mountain forest: stories that act toward relational and anticolonial early childhood nature pedagogies. I am interested in the anticolonial possibilities of restorying (Cameron, 2011) a particular so-called natural place and the human/more-than-human relations therein. I wish to put restorying place to work through stories of relationalities that create interferences (Haraway, 1992) in images of innocence in children's relations with nature within the specific settler colonial context of BC. I attempt to refigure the multiple presences, tensions, and complexities that are always already entangled prior to and within these encounters.

It is important to emphasize here that foregrounding Indigenous presences through stories and histories of place cannot alone dismantle structural and systemic colonial and racial formations nor "the 'educated ignorance' enabled by hegemonic narratives" (Cameron, 2012, p. 190). Drawing inspiration from Indigenous knowledges as a non-Indigenous (to here) immigrant also brings with it the serious problematics of representation and appropriation. For instance, the printed sources of the stories that I present (rather than consulting directly with First Nations communities) could be read as Western representations and romanticizations of Indigenous oral storytelling cultures. Furthermore, as Keith Carlson (2009) notes, "Indigenous knowledge, as Skagitt Coast Salish Elder Vi Hilbert so often and forcefully reminded people, cannot be learned from a book. It can only be learned through long-term face-to-face human interaction" (p. 11). This work does not transcend or neatly resolve these issues and the messy colonial relations in which I am immersed and implicated. I tell these stories to bring educators' attention to taken-for-granted silences and erasures in everyday early childhood pedagogies in settler colonial spaces.

## Walking the Forest Trail

The child care centers are built atop a mountain and are one part of several building developments surrounded by close to 600 hectares of second-growth forest that is inhabited by black bears, cougars, deer, coyote, and many other animal and plant species (City of Burnaby, 2013a). The mountain is named after a prominent settler who surveyed the area for colonial settlement and economic pursuits on behalf of the

British Empire (Wolfenden, 2000). The "untouched," "wild," and "pristine" nature of this mountain forest is a common narrative used in its description. A brochure I came across on the city's website reads: "As you reach the top, pause for a breath and consider how the preservation of this environment ensures that generations to come will enjoy and appreciate our natural heritage" (City of Burnaby, 2013b, n. p.). Much of the mountain forest has been demarcated as a designated protected conservation park area, administered by the local municipality (City of Burnaby, 2013b).

**FIGURES 4.1 and 4.2** Encountering the Forest Trail

Our walks with the children into the forest are along part of an extensive hiking trail system that has been constructed through the mountain forest. Encountering this partly paved trail is to walk literally and figuratively amid tensions. The disruptions enacted challenge the dominant imaginaries of an untouched wilderness and suggest that it might be a site at which to pause and "lookout for movements beneath the apparent order" (Instone, 2010a, p. 373) to seek out unexpected material and discursive connections. Perhaps we might begin to think of walking as an embodied and affective practice, where walking along the trail might be seen as, in Lesley Instone's (2010a) words, "not a linear journey, but rhizomatic voyaging of hesitant beginnings, doubtful meanders, indistinct side tracks and unlikely alliances" (p. 362).

This forest trail is materially and discursively connected to colonial past and present histories. Many of the hiking trails on the mountain incorporate earlier logging roads (skid roads) that were cut into the forest as part of the extensive commercial logging that began in 1903 and accompanied colonial settlement in the area. With the opening of a lumber mill close to the foot of the mountain, the mountain was quickly cleared of its trees (Crampton, 1980; Heritage Burnaby, 2013). As M. E. Borkwood (1980) explains, "any small trees or trees not wanted had simply been felled and left to rot" (p. 13). Steam-powered logging engines (also known as donkey engines) were used to haul the logs down the mountain along the logging roads and over to the mill, where, after processing, the lumber was loaded onto ships and trains adjacent to the mill (Green, 1947). The lumber processed at the saw mill (at the time, one of the largest in the British Empire until it ceased operation 30 years later) was exported to destinations in the British colonies, such as Australia, as well as to other export markets, such as South America. This lumber was used for many purposes, including shingles, railway ties, and spars for sailing ships (Borkwood, 1980; Braches, 2009).

Much of the Douglas fir, Western hemlock, and Western red cedar trees that covered the mountain were removed or destroyed by fires during the logging period (Heritage Burnaby, 2013). The extensive commercial logging resulted in the current second-growth trees that have grown and recolonized most areas. These trees range in age from 50 to 100 years old and primarily consist of red alder, with some broadleaf maple, vine maple, and balsam poplar trees (City of Burnaby, 2000; Crampton, 1980). Note that while I purposefully name the species of trees that populate this forest prior to and after colonial logging practices to unsettle the timelessness of the forest and to point to the destruction of the red cedar tree, the very naming and classification of the trees according to Euro-Western taxonomies is itself not an innocent practice, and is entangled in specific colonial worlding histories and practices that privilege particular ways of knowing the world while intentionally or unintentionally ignoring others (Dickinson, 2013; Pacini-Ketchabaw, 2013).

Walking through the forest along the partly human-made trail traversing the wooded landscape is a compelling way through which educators might begin to refigure presences in this particular place by unsettling the separation of past/

**FIGURE 4.3** "A Good Size Log," 1912
Photo from City of Vancouver Archives

present, constructed/natural, human/nonhuman, nature/culture. As Haraway (2008) reminds me, critical attention to these entangled relationalities through the embodied act of walking holds ethical world-making potentialities because "actual encounters are what make beings" (p. 67).

What histories, demarcations, and boundaries are either enacted or obscured, or perhaps both, by the forest trail and the apparent timelessness of the forest when we walk with children? Instone (2010a) provides a helpful shift in this timelessness in reconfiguring walking as a literal and metaphoric journey, providing openings to the affectivities in the "mobile and contested meanings" of a place (p. 362). Thinking of our walks through the trail as encountering a contested place, what stories might educators think with to "destabilize notions of fixed national space and stable identity" and foreground the inherent contestations that pervade this place (Instone, 2010a, p. 360)?

Leanne Simpson (2013a) tells a story of colonialism and its entanglements with extraction that highlights these contestations, particularly when placed alongside the preceding story of the mountain forest's logging history:

> Extraction and assimilation go together. Colonialism and capitalism are based on extracting and assimilating. My land is seen as a resource. My relatives in the plant and animal worlds are seen as resources. My culture and knowledge is a resource... The act of extraction removes all of the relationships that give whatever is being extracted meaning... Colonialism has always extracted the indigenous—extraction of indigenous knowledge, indigenous women, indigenous peoples. (para. 11)

What does this story do to the act of walking through the forest trail? What might educators learn by following extractive settler colonial logging histories in this forest as a past that is not closed but remains as an active presence in the fabric of the forest, the forest trail, and its vibrant materialities (Barad, 2011) and in the *Shxwelí*, "the life force that exists in all things" (Stó:lō Nation Lalems ye Stó:lō Si: ya:m, 2003, p. 5)? Perhaps this might create interferences (Haraway, 1992) in the authority of colonial imaginaries (Said, 1978) that represent this place as unspoiled pure nature, obscuring its contestations and territorial appropriations. As Lisa Korteweg and Connie Russell (2012) suggest, "we cannot skip ahead to some neutralized ahistorical, guilt-free, pain-free, 'romanticized' version of environmental education" (p. 8). In the encounter described in the opening to this chapter, nature is framed as awaiting human inscription through children's discoveries, rather than in always-already-present entangled yet noninnocent and asymmetrical power relations (Taylor, 2013).

Foregrounding entanglements between time and place, then, might act as a means to interrupt the representational, decontextualized colonial gaze that most early childhood nature pedagogies embed, including conceptions of this land/place as natural territory that is discoverable, unoccupied, mute, a commodity, and static (Clare, 2011; Ritskes, 2012; Taylor, 2013). These interruptions might also create openings toward inhabiting the multiplicities of place, engaging in politicized dialogues with place—for refiguring presences. For educators, this might include experimenting with being in relation with a particular place, and its specificities, through material stories, myth, more-than-human vibrancies, colonial pastpresent histories, and other disparate connections (Instone, 2010a). In these understandings, as we (the educators and I) walk through the mountain forest with children, perhaps we might see this place as neither simply physical nor easily categorized, but rather as a place of complex mutual encounters.

## Lingering at Tree Stumps

The children stop to climb atop the old tree stumps and touch the deeply lined crevices. Atop some of the decaying tree stumps, young trees and new shoots have emerged.

Red cedar tree stumps might teach us different stories as witnesses (Haraway, 1997) to colonial histories and Indigenous relationalities with the land. Perhaps anticolonial "worlding stories of accountability" (Haraway, 2011, n.p.) and responsibility to this place and its histories might be enacted through these stories. Perhaps bringing these stories to nature pedagogies might create movement toward what Jessica Cattelino (2013) refers to as "the hard work of unsettling nature as it is imagined and engaged in settler societies" (para. 16). While the old-growth red cedar trees of this mountain were mostly destroyed by commercial logging (Heritage Burnaby, 2013), the cedar tree stump is also a site at which to

**FIGURES 4.4 and 4.5** Encountering an Old Tree Stump

disrupt imaginaries of an empty and untouched landscape prior to the colonial project. Ethnobotanists Ann Garibaldi and Nancy Turner (2004) explain:

> Traditional use of cedar has changed over roughly the past hundred years. Its prominence in Northwest Coast culture is still very high, but many of its uses have notably diminished. Coupled with an escalating demand for western red cedar as a timber species, the quantity of cedar available to First Peoples is only a fraction of its former amount. Alienation from their former land base because of factors such as tree farm licenses and the creation of parks and protected areas has further reduced the availability and accessibility of cedar… In ongoing treaty and land rights negotiations between First Nations and federal and provincial governments, the availability of cedar features prominently. (p. 5)
>
> There was a real good man who was always helping others. Whatever they needed, he had; when they wanted, he gave them food and clothing. When the Great Spirit [Xá:ls] saw this, he said, "That man has done his work; when he dies and where he is buried, a cedar tree will grow and be useful to the people—the roots for baskets, the bark for clothing, the wood for shelter."
>
> *(Stó:lō elder Bertha Peters, as cited in H. Stewart, 1995, p. 22)*

In a publication in a local tourism website that encourages visitors to "discover" this mountain and its forests and trails, there is one reference to First Nations, referring to past villages along one of the rivers in the area (Tourism Burnaby, 2013). On the city's heritage site, the city's history is divided into "early," "pioneer," "boom," and "modern" periods. First Nations are mentioned only in the early period, in a reference to the significant reduction in the population due to disease and smallpox brought by Europeans (Heritage Burnaby, 2013). In other words, First Nations are relegated to the past and to the edges of the forest (Oliver, 2007). This particular shaping of nature "discovery" and "heritage conservation" might be seen as neither a simple nor an innocent act, but as a part of practices that create particular ordering imaginaries as, in Cattelino's (2013) words, "a process not only of acquisition and dispossession, but also of cultural production and forgetting" (para. 8).

As we walk through the forest with children and enact representational practices that frame "the 'natural' as an entity separate from the 'cultural'" (Willems-Braun, 1997, p. 7), we, as early childhood educators, are also implicated in reproducing settler colonial imaginaries and practices of dispossession and forgetting (Cattelino, 2013). Imaginaries of untouched nature devoid of Indigenous material, social, and cultural presences are part of "colonial perceptions [that] have worked to de-humanize the landscape" (Oliver, 2007, p. 8) in BC through erasures of Indigenous presences—Indigenous peoples' interactions with, relating to, and transformations of the forest landscape in different ways. As Jeff Oliver (2010) notes, these erasures have become a dominant, normalized way of seeing BC:

> A myriad of popular websites, glossy coffee-table books, and tourist memorabilia reproduce the idea of the Northwest Coast as forever primeval and untouched… References to past or present Indigenous inhabitation beyond the water's edge are relegated to the media's margin… a convoluted history entangled with the agendas of different interest groups has influenced these perceptions… Over the last few decades this landscape has been as much a contested background for the forestry lobby and environmental activists as a source of artistic inspiration or recreational playground. Nevertheless if we accept the grand narrative of first contact and European colonialism, the marginality of the landscape and its lack of human agency—in short, its domination by nature not culture—represent the region's most salient plotline. (p. 26)

What might pausing at the tree stumps to honor both this land on unceded Coast Salish territories and Stó:lō stories of this place, as witnesses to Indigenous active presences, refigure and unsettle for us (children, educators, and myself)? Perhaps doing so might enact a situated politics of interference (Haraway, 1997), refiguring presences by unsettling the boundaries and relations between what is present and absent or rendered absent/invisible (Law, 2004). What might it mean for us to pause at the tree stumps, not to "discover" nature, but to refigure what is already there? What might this do toward creating openings for different and unexpected affectivities, connections, relations, and pedagogical responses/reorientations that might unsettle the relegation of Indigenous peoples and relationalities to "absence"—to what Emilie Cameron (2008) refers to as "the immaterial and spectral past" (p. 388)?

## Touching Tree Hollows

The tree cavities carved into the trees in the forest we visit invite the children's curiosities. Some tree hollows are close enough to the ground that the children can peer closely and reach in, touching the depths and edges of the holes. Another hollowed-out tree trunk is large enough for the children to step inside its depths. Encounters with these tree hollows enact many "real" and "imaginary" inhabitants for the children: "acorns"; "a bath for dinosaurs and bears"; "a rabbit-hole"; "bear-prints"; "a bear-hole"; "a giant's prints"; "a special bird"…

Educators might wonder what other ways of storying tree hollows in this particular place might emerge by looking beyond their familiarity. It might be possible to bring into view some of the multiple figurative and material relationalities that are enacted when children "touch" tree hollows (Haraway, 2008). For instance, perhaps different histories and stories of this forest and the tree hollows that we touch might emerge—stories that connect to land and place. These tree hollows can be seen as world making: not inert or passive, but as lively actants (Latour, 2004a) that participate in creating particular material and social worlds. These worlds are not "exclusively human achievement[s]" but "are co-fabricated between more-than-human bodies and a lively earth" in which the human is but

**FIGURES 4.6 and 4.7** Encountering Tree Hollows

one aspect (Whatmore, 2006, p. 603). As Indigenous knowledges teach us, relationality encompasses complex relations to the earth, cosmologies, living and nonliving beings, and all other matter: "a powerful force beyond the immediate and more physically observable culture, one that directs social action beyond the perspective of human control in terms of what can be counted, evaluated, and physically grasped" (Dei, 2002, as cited in Ritskes, 2012, p. 38). The complex ecologies of the life inhabited in tree hollows—from the microorganisms that coat the cavities, to fungi, insects, squirrels, birds, bears, and many others (Cockle, Martin, & Wesołowski, 2011)—might have much to teach early childhood educators about the interdependencies, contradictions, and relations of life and death as co-inhabitants of tree hollows. The more-than-human inhabitants of this forest reciprocally change each other as active participants in the storying of this place (van Dooren & Rose, 2012). Thom van Dooren and Deborah Bird Rose (2012) suggest that "attentiveness to nonhuman storying of places… [has the] ability to provide new perspectives on the world, and in so doing to draw us into deeper and more demanding accountabilities for nonhuman others" (pp. 1–2).

What histories of the tree hollow as an active participant in this encounter might be told, if we contend, as van Dooren and Rose (2012) suggest, that "places are materialized as historical and meaningful, and no place is produced by a singular vision of how it is or might be" (p. 2)? In other words, tree hollows can be seen as more than benign sites for children's discoveries and imaginaries of nature; tree hollows "inhabit their own richly meaningful and storied worlds" (van Dooren & Rose, 2012, p. 10). Different possibilities might be enacted by refiguring this place as a landscape that is inextricably materially and discursively linked to settler colonial histories and Indigenous relationalities with this place (a place where tree hollows hold the traces of colonial histories). As Instone (2010a) notes:

> territory is always an assemblage made up of many elements, many perspectives, many stories—and at times the lines shift, sprout connections, move in unpredictable ways, edges open out and territories change, possibility blossoms… It is possible to choose to sing other refrains, ones attuned to the multiplicity and multivocality. (p. 373)

What might it mean for educators to look out for the entanglements and vibrancies suggested by tree hollows? What might doing so enact and bring into view in terms of new possibilities for anticolonial scientific nature pedagogies? Perhaps educators might wonder about tree hollows and their inhabitants and how they are a part of mutually constitutive "human-plant-place relations, colonial dispossession, and other modes of connection between humans and nonhumans" (Instone, 2010b, p. 96)? For instance, it typically takes over a century for decay holes to begin to form in dying trees, and often several centuries for a large tree hollow to form (Cockle et al., 2011). Touching the old tree hollow, then, is also touching colonial histories and wondering about the human and more-than-human pastpresent histories of this place that have been captured through the shaping of the tree hollows themselves over time. Put another way, touching tree hollows could be a pedagogical opportunity to critically encounter the entanglement of human-more-than human relations, scientific processes, and colonial histories in this particular place. In resonance with this proposition on embodied multispecies encounters as holding potential for decolonial nature–culture pedagogies is Barajas-López and Megan Bang's (2018) important work with Indigenous youth learning with tidal pools and the multispecies inhabitants therein. Their work is drawn from an Indigenous Science, Technology, Engineering, Arts, and Mathematics (STEAM) summer program, where youth participated in making, storytelling, and walking pedagogies that foregrounded Indigenous ways of knowing critical dialogues with Western science. This work has shown how culturally constructed relational epistemologies and ontologies are an intrinsic part of scientific learning with the natural world. Importantly, Barajas-López and Bang (2018) demonstrate how cultivating situated nature–culture relations for young Indigenous people brings the potential to disrupt pedagogies based on extractive, human-centered relations with the natural world.

Returning to the tree hollow example; it is important to note that tree hollows are not only interesting because their interdependent inhabitants illustrate how more-than-human worlds entail "multispecies knots" (Haraway, 2011) that are active participants in shaping and storying the forest. Tree hollows also offer possibilities for disrupting "the fixed territory of Cartesian linearity" (Instone, 2010a, p. 374) implied by viewing the forest from an anthropocentric perspective. Trees and tree hollows, in other words, are "too social and too narrated to be truly natural" (Latour, 1993, p. 6). I see this perspective as one possible invitation for early childhood educators to simultaneously grapple with material and discursive relationalities in inhabiting and narrating particular "webs" (Haraway, 2011) that animate the forest. The materiality of the tree hollows that the children touch cannot be thought apart from their signification or narration, and the tensions and connections thereof (Latour, 1993).

What might it mean and do for educators to inhabit tree hollows figuratively through ongoing worldings of colonialism? How might seeing tree hollows as figurative for the rot and devastation created by settler colonialism unsettle our (myself and educators') pedagogical practices and their unintentional "imagining, representing, and purifying [of] 'natural' landscapes" (Willems-Braun, 1997, p. 11)? As Anishinaabe scholar Damien Lee (2011) describes, "over 500 years of colonial attacks have ripped holes in the fabric of our relationships within our places" (para. 2). Thinking with the tree hollow as a figure for the effects of colonialism might also be helpful in considering the complexities of colonialism: that the Indigenous cannot be relegated to an absence. Complex relationships and relationalities abound, persist, and continually shift amid the rot. Tree hollows perhaps have much to teach us about living with what Donna Haraway (2011) refers to as "ontological, ethical, and ecological knots in multispecies contact zones" (n.p.).

A tree hollow in a different forest in what is now BC also illustrates ethical knots and colonial entanglements. An iconic 700-year-old Western red cedar tree hollow is located in Stanley Park in Vancouver; it was the subject of intense public efforts to save it after it was extensively damaged by windstorms. Stanley Park is a world-famous tourist attraction named after the man who was governor general of Canada in 1888, when the park was first opened (Barman, 2006). The

Stanley Park tree hollow remains standing today, supported by steel beams (CTV News, 2011). The immense public effort to save this tree is interesting in itself in relation to the effort to maintain settler imaginaries of pristine wilderness in park spaces—park spaces created through human acts (Barman, 2006; Kheraj, 2007).

> No park is virginal, nor does it remain so... The pastoral settings of parks obscure their fractured histories legitimizing elements of the story that those in control choose to share with visitors... despite the rhetoric, and there is a lot of it, Stanley Park was not pristine. It was not even first growth forest. Much of it had been logged... Trees grow back but there was a greater, ongoing challenge to Stanley Park's virginity. The park was imposed on existing ways of life... It took over two-thirds of a century from the imposition of Stanley Park in 1887, for the last of its families to be removed... The park was imposed on existing ways of life... its creation was a consummately colonial enterprise.
>
> *(Barman, 2006, p. 13)*

Jean Barman (2006) writes about the history, tensions, and colonial relations entangled within Stanley Park and the effort to save the old tree hollow. In mentioning this story, I highlight another account that can be placed alongside the tree hollows we touch in our walks through the mountain forest. Touching the old tree hollow in Stanley Park is to touch the colonial histories of the park,

**FIGURE 4.8** Touring Car in Front of Hollow Tree at Stanley Park, 1915
Photo Credit: Stanley Park Photographers, City of Vancouver Archives

which includes the removal of Indigenous peoples who lived there for thousands of years in material, spiritual, and ceremonial relationship with the red cedar trees before the last dwellings of the Squamish peoples that inhabited this place were burned down (Barman, 2006).

## Towards Unsettling Place Relations

In this chapter, I have engaged with interruptive situated stories of walking forest trails, lingering at tree stumps and touching tree hollows as anticolonial ways of seeing and relating to a place in early childhood nature encounters. I used the notion of refiguring presences through stories that attend to settler colonial tensions and Indigenous relationalities that inhabit this particular place. I have intentionally brought forward stories that create possibilities for ways of relating that unsettle anthropocentric and colonial enactments of nature education and the erasures therein. My intent has been to experiment with possibilities that unsettle innocent and romantic visions of children's relations with nature (Taylor, 2013), to foreground the decolonial potential of Indigenous relational epistemologies and ontologies in place learning (Bang & Marin, 2015; Bang & Medin, 2010; Barajas-López & Bang, 2018) and to take seriously the implications of inheriting settler colonial histories (Haraway, 2011) in the particular situated localities where I live and practice. I have attempted to resist a singular master narrative—by posing questions rather than definitive answers alongside the stories, and by attempting, as Kathleen Stewart (2011) says, to "write theory through stories" in which "things matter not because of how they are represented but because they have qualities, rhythms, forces, relations, and movements" (p. 445).

While restorying places might create possibilities toward more equitable orientations and ethical relationalities, it is important to note that this does not present a resolution to the messiness of ongoing colonialisms. Indigenous people's displacements from the places I describe in this chapter remain, as Eve Tuck and Wayne Yang (2012) remind us, as unresolved "epistemic, ontological, cosmological violence" (p. 5). Here I have just begun to suggest possibilities for early childhood educators to attend closely, to borrow Karen Barad's (2007) words, to "how differences get made, what gets excluded, and how these exclusions matter" (p. 30) in everyday encounters with "natural" places. I have also suggested possibilities for experimentation with tracing the multiplicities of place through storied encounters—where place and the things that inhabit it are seen as active, contingent, and situated witnesses to colonial worldings (Haraway, 2011; Spivak, 1990). As a beginning to anticolonial practices in early childhood education, I suggest that relating to the mountain forest trail, to tree hollows, and to tree stumps in this particular place though multiple material–discursive stories and histories might trouble views of this particular mountain forest as an uninscribed place, and might create openings toward difficult conversations, disruptive understandings, and different unsettled place relations.

# 5

# RESTORYING GARDEN RELATIONS

I situate this chapter alongside recent work in early childhood studies that has used more-than-human epistemologies and ontologies to consider nature pedagogies in relation to Indigenous knowledges, human/more-than-human relationalities, natureculture entanglements, and anticolonial possibilities (Duhn, 2012; Pacini-Ketchabaw, 2013; Ritchie, 2012; Somerville, 2006; Taylor, 2013). Inspired by this work and its commitment to resisting simplistic and romantic couplings of children and nature, I seek to notice the practices, sociomaterialities, and colonial histories and relations that come together to enact the production of a community garden that I visit with children and early childhood educators in the child care centers where my research is situated. My specific localities in the Greater Vancouver area are unceded Musqueam, Squamish, Stó:lō, and Tsleil-Waututh territories. Putting to work an emergent methodology that I refer to as refiguring presences (see Chapter 3), I rethink, refigure, and complicate what is considered present in everyday child–educator–community-garden encounters by paying particular attention to Indigenous relationalities, colonial displacements, garden histories, sociomaterial encounters, and more-than-human vibrancies (Massey, 2005; Pratt, 1992; Simpson, 2011). I intentionally write the garden encounters in the present tense as a mode of engaging the reader in the embodied and affective resonances of these encounters, and my implicatedness therein. These encounters were documented in the form of pedagogical narrations and field notes (see Chapter 1 for a detailed description of data collection methods). By pedagogical narrations I am referring to the processes by which myself and educators observed, documented, reflected on, and shared everyday pedagogical encounters with the children (British Columbia Ministry of Education 2008). By field notes, I am referring to the documentation and reflection processes that I engaged in during and after our pedagogical encounters; some of which were used to develop pedagogical narrations with educators, and some of which I returned to later in my individual writing about and meaning making of these encounters. In returning to these visual and textual pedagogical narrations and field notes, I pay particular attention to the unruly propensities of more-than-human actors (Ginn, 2008) and the possibilities this noticing might bring as knowledge making that complicates the boundaries enacted in this place. My intent here is to see what anticolonial resonances might emerge through these practices of refiguring presences. I view these resonances as having the potential to unsettle everyday taken-for-granted relations.

I begin the chapter by discussing how and why I use "touch" to refigure presences in community-garden encounters. For the remainder of the chapter, I engage in literal and metaphorical practices of refiguring presences in the garden assemblage (Deleuze & Guattari, 1987) through entangled histories, socio-materialities, and more-than-human actors. More specifically, I refigure presences in the garden through touching historical children–garden pedagogies, political formations of gardens, and settler colonial worldings of gardens. I then map and experiment with touching and unsettling garden lines and line making, attending closely to the complexities and disruptive potentials of the lively yet messy assemblages of garden things and child–garden–worm encounters. I conclude the chapter by revisiting the anticolonial resonances that might be enacted through this work.

## Refiguring Presences in Community Garden Encounters

Donna Haraway (2006) inspires close attention to the political and ethical potentialities set in motion through human/more-than-human encounters, asking: "Which worldings and which sorts of temporalities and materialities erupt into this touch" (p. 145)? Taking up her invitation to think with, respond to, and become accountable to the worldings enacted through specific encounters, I experiment with refiguring what is considered present in a community garden through research practices that restory (Cameron, 2011) this place. In so doing, I am placed within multiple connecting "temporalities and materialities" (Haraway, 2006, p. 145). I intentionally use touch in restorying this place to emphasize that the practices of refiguring presences that I enact in this chapter are particularly attentive to material and affective relations with the garden assemblage. I affect and am affected (Deleuze & Guattari, 1987) by more-than-human relationalities, entanglements with pastpresent histories, and the tensions that are thrown up by encounters with the community garden. In other words, by touching, I mean more than my physical presence in the garden with children and educators: I touch through affective modes that allow me to restory place in politically disruptive ways. I touch with particular politicized curiosities, as well as with openings to my own unsettling. Refiguring presences is also a creative knowledge-making (Haraway, 1997) process. As I engage with making connections, I also experiment with hopeful yet risky possibilities for refiguring what is seen as present in this garden and the garden encounters. Through both the relationalities and dissonances that emerge from actual and metaphorical acts of touching, I seek out responsive and responsible interruptions of colonial, anthropocentric, and innocent worldings of gardens and gardening practices. However, touching does not come without dangers. As Maria Puig de la Bellacasa (2009) says, "there is a risk of idealizing the paradigmatic 'other' of vision, for instance, as a signifier of embodied unmediated knowing and relating. Thinking with touch does not assure resolution; it opens new questions" (p. 299). The hopeful possibilities that I enact point to ways of knowing and relating that elude easy resolution and are always partial. As Haraway (2008) reminds me:

> Touch ramifies and shapes accountability. Accountability, caring for, being affected, and entering into responsibility are not ethical abstractions; these mundane, prosaic things are the result of having truck with each other. Touch does not make one small; it peppers its partners with attachment sites for world making. Touch, regard, looking back, becoming with—all these make us responsible in unpredictable ways for which worlds take shape... Touch and regard have consequences. (p. 36)

Importantly, refiguring presences through generative human/more-than-human comminglings, mutualities, and relationalities assumes neither the absence of human difference nor the presence of equal relations between humans. In other words, the sociomaterial asymmetries enacted through presences of settler colonialism, racialization, whiteness, gender, and class are never erased from gardens and are an intrinsic part of my own situated, contingent, and embodied location as a racialized settler immigrant in colonial gardens and colonial garden histories. In this chapter I intentionally attempt to decenter the human by foregrounding human/more-than-human entanglements and more-than-human vibrancies. I do this in ways that engage gardens in both their dampening and transformative effects within ongoing sociomaterial formations of empire. I engage touch through art images of gardens, historical imageries of gardening, and specific sociomaterialities of everyday child–educator–garden encounters. I engage touch with images, not to represent place but rather to enact a politicized (re)storying of place within a settler colonial context—a noninnocent, entangled, and implicated worlding. Puig de la Bellacasa (2009) refers to this as "touching vision" (p. 308), where "refusing the distinction between vision and touch troubles the ground of objectivity" (p. 308). What might these practices of refiguring presences do? What interruptions might be created to practice-as-usual? What connections might emerge and enact disruptions to visions of already demarcated, categorized, "settled," and defined colonial place? How might inhabiting multiple and differential place relations as a site for early childhood inquiry open up lines for engaging with complexity? As I discuss in the next section, situating gardens within Euro-Western early childhood pedagogies is one place to begin to encounter these complexities.

## Cultivating Nature's Children: Gardening Pedagogy Histories

The university-based child care centers where I work are located alongside a second-growth forest, a large part of which is a designated protected conservation area that is home to several animal species, including deer, raccoons, black bears, and coyotes. The forest has become an important part of the children's pedagogical experiences. A community garden that lies at the edge of a part of this forest has also recently become a place of interest for educators and children.[1] The garden was started by students living on campus in the 1970s, and now provides produce to people on campus and in the local community. The community garden's stated purpose is to engage in "healthy recreational activity while growing nutritious food, benefiting from the connection to nature, and social interaction." The space has been divided into garden plots, separated by wooden planks available for rental to grow organic vegetables in numbered assigned plots subject to adherence to the policies and procedures in the gardening agreement.

Gardening is already a part of the children's experiences at the child care center. Each of the centers has a garden area in its outdoor play space, where educators and children tend and grow flowers and vegetables. These practices have a long history in Euro-Western early childhood education. Eighteenth-century Swiss philosopher Jean-Jacques Rousseau inspired generations of romantic nature-based early childhood pedagogies with his belief in "'Nature' as the child's best teacher" (Taylor & Giugni, 2012, p. 114). For instance, in 1840 Friedrich Fröebel began gardens specifically designed to prepare kindergarten children "for living in a perfectly ordered civil society" (Taylor, 2013, p. 41). Rudolf Steiner, Maria Montessori, and Loris Malaguzzi are other notable early childhood educational philosophers inspired by Rousseau's emphasis on connecting children with nature (Taylor & Giugni, 2012). In early-twentieth-century North American schools, gardens were part of the nature study movement and were designed to give children opportunities to learn about nature through the garden (Frost, 2009). School gardens were also widely introduced as tools to teach desired moral and social attributes, such as pride in community and individual responsibility for public property (Lawson, 2005). They were also used to teach the respectability of labor. Children, under close adult supervision, were trained to work efficiently in the belief that this training could be transferred to factory work (Lawson, 2005). This role of the adult figure in leading or shaping children followers is apparent in the wartime propaganda poster depicted in Figure 5.1. Here, children are depicted joining the "school garden army" using the famed children's tale figure of the Pied Piper, now remade into America's nation-building and patriarchal Uncle Sam character. These histories remain an active presence in Euro-Western early childhood garden pedagogies, continuing to do the work of maintaining nature/culture divisions, enacting romantic discourses of a special relationship between children and nature, and structuring childhood (and education) as a preparatory site toward normative adulthood (Taylor, 2013; Williamson, 2002).

**FIGURE 5.1** "Follow the Pied Piper"
(Barney, 1919)

## Situating Community Gardens in Political Formations

As children and educators engage in "everyday" gardening practices—planting, tending, weeding, and learning about healthy foods—I am unsettled as I consider the seeming innocence of these practices. I wonder what looking into the entanglements of gardening with empire building and settler colonialism might do. Community gardens in urban environments have been introduced with different purposes in a multitude of spaces and places, including, but not limited to, providing food to poor urban families, targeting immigrant families to inculcate "civic duty, health and sanitation, and middle-class aesthetic values" (Lawson, 2005, p. 8), building a sense of community, beautifying city neighborhoods, supporting war efforts materially and discursively, revitalizing depressed neighborhoods, and as a source for local business development (Lawson, 2005).

In North America, community gardens flourished during the Great Depression as relief gardens, during World War I as liberty gardens, and during World War II as victory gardens or war gardens (Williamson, 2002). In British Columbia, there were over 1,400 victory gardens in 1943, prompting a headline in the *Vancouver News Herald* stating that "if all the Victory Gardens in British Columbia were lumped together, they would occupy a space approximately three times the size of Vancouver's great Stanley Park" (Buswell, 1980, para. 11). As illustrated in Figure 5.2, through government propaganda in Canada, the United States, and Britain, gardening during wartime became permeated with nationalist idealism and figured as a weapon of war. As Ginn (2012) notes, "The garden, a place where craft, soil and blood mingled, was doubly inscribed not only as a place from which the war might be won, but also as a reason why the war should be won" (p. 297). During this time, these community gardens were also referred to as "food gardens for defense" (Buswell, 1980). More recent community garden movements have arisen from the resistance movements generated during the 1960s civil rights and counterculture eras (French, 2008; Warner, 1987). These community gardens, while typically not conceptualized by the government, require governmental support to provide land for gardening. Other reasons behind the recent rise in community gardens have been a concern with climate change and an accompanying interest in organic gardening (Ministry of Community Development & Union of British Columbia Municipalities, 2009). An in-depth discussion of all of the diverse and entangled reasons for the current emergence of community gardens and their many formations is beyond the scope of this chapter, and it is not my purpose to minimize the beneficial effects of community gardens. With this very brief historical overview, my primary purpose is to restory community gardens in ways that disrupt innocence. These are intensely political and ideological places.

The community garden I encounter with children and educators is not outside of these political formations. This organic-only garden, while a place where healthy food might become more accessible, is still located within a locus of sociomaterial stratification, racialized class privilege, and individualized neoliberal relations to food access (see Nxumalo, Pacini-Ketchabaw, & Rowan, 2011, for an in-depth illustration of connections between neoliberal formations and food/eating practices in early childhood education). These asymmetries are, as Franklin Ginn (2014) asserts, continually "made, marked and re-made" (p. 536), such as through practices of plot rental fees and contracts, garden rules, and individual allotment plots. They are also continually articulated through affective materializations, such as the fence that borders the garden and the accompanying signage marking the garden as patrolled private property. As the following section suggests, the asymmetries of gardens also need to be considered within their presence in settler colonial logics (Casteel, 2003; Longhurst, 2006; Plumwood, 2005).

**FIGURE 5.2** "Plant a Victory Garden" (circa 1944)
Source: Library and Archives Canada Harry Mayerovitch Fonds, c115716

> Food is no less a weapon than tanks, guns, and planes... the duty of every loyal citizen [is] to do everything possible, to accept any sacrifice, so that there shall be plentiful supplies of food for the fighting forces and facilities for delivering them.
> (Bassett, 1981, p 7, as cited in Williamson, 2002, p. 13)

## Digging Deeper: Community Gardens in Worldings of Settler Colonialism

As I dig into colonial worldings in gardens of North America, I notice an idyllic vision of nature (Casteel, 2007) materialized and enacted in paintings such as the one shown in Figure 5.3. This painting depicts romanticized visions of a Garden of Eden-like paradise in North America figured as representative of the innocence and normative whiteness of childhood. While this particular painting was an American-commissioned work, many of the nineteenth-century landscape paintings emerged when artists were commissioned to produce paintings from colonial excursions to the Americas, bringing back representations of the "discovered" world to Europeans (Clark, Pacini-Ketchabaw, & Hodgins, 2015). These depictions of idyllic garden-like landscapes stand in stark contrast to the violences enacted during and after these voyages of "discovery" and conquest (Battiste, Bell, Findlay, Findlay, & Henderson, 2005; Povinelli, 2011; Simpson, 2011).

I also unearth colonial imaginaries of terra nullius that attempted to erase Indigenous presences and set about "improving" "empty, wild" land into property used for "productive" farms and gardens (Ginn, 2008, 2009). As the late ecofeminist philosopher Val Plumwood (2005) noted, today's gardens continue to be imbued with settler colonial practices of "domestication and Eurocentric ideals of beauty" (para. 5), imposing order through various flora and fauna. Eurocentric ideals of gardens emerge and are enacted in gardening books, magazines, clubs, and shows that situate gardens within commodifying practices, privilege particular aesthetics, and "idolize the gardens of the Euro-centre" (Plumwood, 2005, para. 6; also see "Highlights for the armchair gardener," 2002). These imaginaries and gardening practices come together to help shape what belongs, lives, and grows inside certain gardens and what becomes classified

**FIGURE 5.3** "The Voyage of Life: Childhood" (Cole, 1842)

as a weed or an "invasive pest." I do not want to suggest an uncomplicated, fixed division between "alien" and "Indigenous" species. For instance, my use of the term *Indigenous* carries with it omissions that mask the complexities, nuances, politics, and situatedness of Indigeneity—such as specific cosmologies, ceremonies, living knowledges, and many human and more-than-human relations (Sandrina de Finney, personal communication, May 1, 2014). Further, within the limits of this chapter, I am not discussing in depth the historical contingencies and situated contradictions in how divisions between alien and Indigenous have been and continue to be viewed and taken up in gardening practices of killing and "saving" certain plant species (Braun, 2002; Ginn, 2008, 2009). Some of these include practices of preserving or saving certain places as "wild" nature; forest conservation; neoliberal natures; and "native species" gardening trends, among several techniques of contingent and contradictory stratifications of land (Braun, 2002; Ginn, 2009; Langford, 2012; Lorimer, 2012). What I am more interested in here is beginning to untangle some of the sociomaterial workings of plant, animal, and land domestication as active presences in establishing settler colonialism. Also, as I discuss later in the chapter, I am interested in the slippages, resistances, and mutualities that create stutters to colonial ways of seeing and doing garden encounters with young children.

As I continue to dig into settler colonial practices that introduced imported species that have diminished or destroyed indigenous species (Plumwood, 2005), I find an example that illustrates that domestication relationships are complex and are neither inherently exploitative nor solely human directed (Haraway, 2008). I find this example in camas,[2] a starchy flowering vegetable that the Coast Salish peoples domesticated for many generations, using multiple and complex practices (Kwiáht, 2014). Some of the entangled human and more-than-human participants in empire building that led to the decline of both wild camas fields and domesticated camas gardens include increased potato cultivation that effectively displaced camas, appropriation of lands for settler agriculture, the spread of invasive grasses that accompanied sheep grazing, and colonial restrictions on traditional food cultivation and gathering (Corntassel & Bryce, 2012; Deur & Turner, 2005; Kwiáht, 2014).

The lands on which we stand—gardens, plants, organisms, soil, and many unseen presences—all "hold the memory of all traces" (Barad, 2011, p. 146) of their intimate entanglements with violent empire building in settler colonial places. As Shelley Saguaro (2006) notes, there are many variations of gardens in settler colonial places, but they are all imbued with colonial histories, including displacements of people, plants, and animals. To illustrate this, I turn to the story of X'muzk'i'um (Camosun Bog), a place on Musqueam territories, and wonder about both the traces of empire and the Indigenous relational presences that are alive in this place, which has been a part of Musqueam First Nation stories, food, medicine, and ceremony for thousands of years (Point, 2012). I pause here and let the following words speak for themselves:

> [X'muzk'i'um / Camosun Bog] is also a place that I take my grandchildren. It's a place that has been here for thousands of years. And there are very few people within the city of Vancouver that even know of this place.
>
> *(Susan Point, Musqueam artist, as cited in Point, 2012)*

> This was our garden, our people's garden, where they had picked the berries, picked the medicinal plants… We have to save this for our children and our children's children.
>
> *(Rose Point, Musqueam elder, as cited in Point, 2012)*

> When the bog shrinks, that means people have drained the bog for urbanization, for uses of land, removing what Western culture calls unusable land or unusable space… If it is allowed to shrink anymore that actually erases all of the corroborating evidence of the story of Musqueam… it removes all traces of any of the stories that we are able to tell… We can still tell the story, but we won't be able to say this is where it originates.
>
> *(Larry Grant, Musqueam elder, as cited in David Suzuki Foundation, 2012)*

What memories do places like X'muzk'i'um hold of past and present Indigenous relationalities? What might we (myself, educators, and children) learn from the story of this place as a Musqueam people's garden for medicine and ceremony, from its near destruction from construction site dumping and intentional draining, from its ongoing partial restoration by Indigenous and non-Indigenous people (see Camosun Bog Restoration Group, n.d.), and from ongoing colonial dispossession from this place? These stories, while necessarily incomplete, hold and enact a "revolutionary force" (Deleuze & Guattari, 1986, p. 19) that disrupts taken-for-granted settler understandings of what gardens are and can be. I see this as what Donna Haraway (1991) refers to as "knowledge potent for constructing worlds less organized by axes of domination" (p. 192). Camas and X'muzk'i'um stories resonate and stay with me as I reconsider the community garden I encounter with children and educators in connection to seen and unseen presences. If we take seriously Karen Barad's (2012) idea that "touch is never pure or innocent… [and is] inseparable from the field of differential relations that constitute it" (p. 215), how then might touching place in early childhood education be refigured to interrupt the violent banality of disregard for these presences?

## Unsettling Forest/Garden Lines

A fence encloses the community garden we visit with children, separating it from the surrounding forest. The fence seems to struggle to separate the "wild" forest from the "domesticated" garden. The deer we sometimes encounter in the garden feeding on the vegetables also seem out of place, yet they highlight the tenuousness of this separation. The possibility of an encounter with the coyotes and bears that inhabit the forest is another unsettling affective presence. "Wild" vegetables also seem to contest this separation by growing outside of garden row formation beyond the boundaries of the forest–garden-fence–line. A pile of uprooted weeds sits at the entrance to the garden; while some plots appear neat and carefully tended with rows of vegetables, others are overgrown with weeds (field notes).

The creation of lines around what counts as nature is intimately entangled with setter colonial pastpresent histories. As previously discussed, I consider certain acts of domesticating, demarcation, and controlled planting of landscapes as part of the making of colonial projects within imaginaries "of a pristine, purified and timeless precolonial nature" (Instone, 2010b, p. 97). What emerges from paying attention to the "materializing effects" (Barad, 2011, pp. 123–124) created by the ways in which boundaries are drawn between the human/more-than-human and between nature/culture? Here I want to touch and be touched by lines such as the fence that struggles to contain the garden and forest boundaries (see Figure 5.4), the lines that separate each garden plot, and the gate to the garden with the sign marking this place as "private property." These lines are enacting colonizing orderings, management, and mastery over the cultivated plants and the wild forest. As Linda Smith (2012) notes, "the line is important, because it was used to map territory, to survey land, [and] to establish boundaries" (p. 53). I witness the lines separating the individual garden plots and separating the forest from the garden as connected with the colonial mapping of territories. I become curious about how certain demarcating lines are made and decided.

Gilles Deleuze (2009) suggests, "Some lines are segments, or segmented; some lines get caught in a rut, or disappear into 'black holes'; some are destructive, sketching death; and some lines are vital and creative" (p. 1). What if we (myself and educators) consider both the productive and oppressive forces of the lines in the relations that come together in the forest–garden assemblage? How do the vibrancies of place restoried through multispecies relations sit alongside the

**FIGURE 5.4** Encountering Community Garden Lines

borderlines of the garden? What might we learn by paying attention, not only to colonial framing enacted by lines, but also to leaks, cracks, and ruptures in these lines? How do these lines escape their intended effects as acts of containment, representation, and visibility (Holmes, 2012)?

What is set into motion as children notice and touch the vegetables growing in the forest beyond the fence line (see Figure 5.5), and as they encounter deer feeding on the vegetables in the garden? These "escapes" of plants and animals across forest and garden line are not without danger, including possible harm to the forest floor. However, before I consider pulling up the "wild forest vegetables," I want to engage with the potentials of the presence of unruly assemblages. Perhaps these moments might also be seen as encounters with the active presences and queer performativities of the more-than-human world (Barad, 2011; Ginn, 2014). Such unexpected encounters might also bring into view potentialities for alternative relations to this place beyond an already-known, defined, and separate "domesticated community garden" and "wild forest." Perhaps common worlds (Latour, 2004a; Taylor, 2013) emerge here through such unpredictable assemblages, where, as Ginn (2014) suggests, the composers of these entangled worlds "are certainly not all human, nor are they evenly empowered or equally interested in the composing" (p. 533). How might touching these messy and continually shifting common worlds of forest/vegetable garden/human/animal co-presences be a place to relate differently to nature as natureculture (Haraway, 2008)? These different relations might include what Lesley Instone (2010b) refers to as "a dissonance, a provocation to re-think and to walk

**FIGURE 5.5** Vegetables Growing on the Forest Floor

differently… [and consider] human–plant–place relations, colonial dispossession, and other modes of connection between humans and nonhumans" (p. 96). I pause in this place to consider the possibilities suggested by nonconformity, by coimplication, by becoming with (Haraway, 2011). I wonder about the disruptive potentialities enacted by the forest and the garden vegetables in interrupting and unsettling colonial ordering practices that are embedded in the domesticated garden. Encountering this garden as a place of liminality may create pedagogical openings for destabilizing Eurocentric colonial rootedness (Head & Muir, 2006). Perhaps this unsettles the dualities between nonhuman nature and human culture, and between the wild and domesticated, which have acted to erase Indigenous presences.

These dualisms can be traced back to the Enlightenment-era centering of the thinking human subject (Potter & Hawkins, 2009). Perhaps, as Anna Tsing (2013) suggests, close attention to the vitality and assemblages of plant worlds might be a way to begin to bring into view some of the ways in which more-than-human worlds are made, where humans are not the central participants. Tsing notes that "to even begin to tell these stories offers a reminder of the entangling of multiple scales and trajectories in the making of social landscapes" (p. 36). While both the community garden and the adjacent forest have emerged from human disruptions to the landscape (see Chapter 3 on the logging histories of this forest), such as logging, cultivation, weeding, and composting practices, the active relations among the multiple plant and animal species that inhabit the forest have created assemblages beyond human control (Tsing, 2013). I witness these interruptions as creating openings toward inhabiting messiness and for generating politicized dialogues with this place. Touching this forest garden and its lines and boundaries in this way is about much more than exposing children to learning about a pure and separate nature (Taylor, 2013). Instead, it restories this forest and its boundaries as a place where early childhood educators and children might begin, as Haraway (2006) suggests, "to live the consequences of nonstop curiosity inside mortal, situated, relentlessly relational worlding" (p. 143). In these understandings then, places such as this forest garden are neither simply physical nor easily categorized, but are places of complex mutual encounter. Joseph Weakland (2012) explains that "ethics then emerges not from a transcendant interpretation of nature, but from our always imperfect and never innocent responses to the specific naturalcultural entanglements through which we come to be in the world" (p. 129). Apprehending the emergent interactions between the forest and garden highlights the tenuousness of boundaries around what counts as pure nature (Ginn, 2009; Haraway, 1997). The garden, perhaps then, is never, as Ginn (2009) states, "simply the product of settler's imaginations, but [is] a much more contested material landscape, where trees, [plants, worms] and weeds 'push back' to alter the nature of the project" (p. 40). In other words, more-than-human socialities (Tsing, 2013) disrupt and subvert colonial impositions of control, belonging, and order.

## Relating to More-than-human Assemblages

This garden has invited multiple possibilities for engaging with "the otherwise." This particular community garden, its location on the edge of the forest, the shifting "disorderly" assemblages of things in it—have become a site of curiosity for children and educators. These things include chairs, carefully tended plots alongside overgrown untended plots, giant-sized vegetables and flowers, a pile of uprooted weeds, a concrete shed, worms, a makeshift "no stealing" sign—and more... A small tire is picked up and briefly carried along, then put down on a log as it becomes too heavy for the child to carry.

I intentionally want to refigure these materialities by considering ways of relating that go beyond seeing and responding to these things (see Figure 5.6) as garbage, clutter, out of place, and ugly. The "things" that are in the garden (chairs, vegetables, a sign, etc.) and the different ways they beckon to and affect the children (provoking questions, curiosity, and touch/carrying) are perhaps disruptive of the romanticization of the child in the pristine garden in normative garden pedagogies, as seen in the "New World" painting in Figure 5.3. Perhaps attending to and responding to children's relations with the more-than-human vibrancies of the "queer" things in this place might enact anticolonial ways of seeing—ways of seeing that begin to appreciate the complex liveliness of this garden and its resistances to a simple categorization as an organic-only community garden, or as an enclosed, pure, romantic natural place awaiting children's

**FIGURE 5.6** Garden Assemblage

learning about nature. These messy relations are, as Jamie Lorimer (2012) suggests, "characterized by lively processes and impure forms, co-existing in inhabited landscapes" (p. 595) that elude categorization within the borders of community gardening. Disruptions of purity are important in a settler colonial society where purificationist resonances in delineations of belonging for plants and animals are entangled in complex ways with settler constructions of belonging (Head & Muir, 2006).

In touching this assemblage of images and seeking out other practices/ways of becoming with these seemingly disparate things, my hope is to create interruptive affects. I wonder if attending to these affective resonances might interfere with the technologies and histories of control that permeate gardening practices in this settler colonial place? What new realities and knowledges might be enacted through attention to the human and more-than-human "transformative mutualism" (Tsing, 2012a, p. 515) enacted through the garden, the forest, the things in it, and the assemblages that come together therein? More-than-human assemblages in this place perhaps point to the instability and leakiness of the boundaries created by anthropomorphic colonizing conceptions of place, such as the domesticated garden and the wild forest.

## Touching Garden Worms

A noninnocent relational ethics (Simpson, 2011; Whatmore, 2006) of caring and protection seems to emerge in children's embodied encounters with the worms that are abundant in the garden's soil. The educator and I witness relations marked by mutual attentiveness, curiosity, and touch: Children name the worms, imagine worm families, and are closely attentive to the worms' various actions and movements, including their movements on the children's hands, which they describe as, for example, "tickling me," "looking at me," "thinking," and "giggling." I see potential in these mundane encounters between children and worms for an ethical becoming with through mutual touch, responsiveness, and curiosity, rather than through a predefined "learning" experience (Haraway, 2008; Pacini-Ketchabaw & Taylor, 2013; Taylor & Pacini-Ketchabaw, 2015). Here, ethical caring relations are seen as emerging in the middle of everyday life through immanent materialized connections (Puig de la Bellacasa, 2009). That is to say, *seemingly* mundane and unimportant things and places can be a site for caring ethical relations involving tasks that, as Puig de la Bellacasa (2011) argues, "make living better in interdependence, but which are often considered petty and unimportant, however vital they are for liveable relations" (p. 9). I emphasize the word seemingly here to underline that, as I have attempted to illustrate throughout this chapter, the garden is far from a mundane place. For example, camas fields and X'muzk'i'um (Camosun Bog) speak as complex, sacred, and pedagogical places in Indigenous ontologies.

Even the playfulness of children's encounters with gardens and garden worms (see Figure 5.7) is a site from which to consider how touching worms holds

FIGURE 5.7 Touching Garden Worms

consequential possibilities for children to learn how to get along with and care for more-than-human others in these messy inherited histories (Pacini-Ketchabaw & Taylor, 2013). If we take seriously John Law's (2011) contention that "different practices enact different realities" (p. 3), we might ask how nature is enacted by paying attention to the kind of worm that emerges through these embodied practices. Perhaps then we might encourage relations that foreground the worm as responsive—as evoking care, attention, and responsibility. Here worms evoke affective responses through the specific mutual sociomaterial compositions they take in these encounters (Bertoni, 2012).

The worms in this encounter emerge through complex human/more-than-human interrelationships, including the worms' movements on children's bodies and through the soil, in relation with children's and educators' words and actions. Through these situated encounters, the assemblages of worms, children, and their relations that emerge suggest enactments of worms through mutual interaction between humans and nonhuman species. In paying attention to disruptive presences in these encounters, I want to highlight the political potentiality of the ordinary (Ahmed, 2004; Berlant, 2008; Blaise, 2013; Stewart, 2007, 2011, 2012; Tsing, 2005). Perhaps these ordinary encounters might be seen as holding potential to seek less anthropomorphic ways of relating to this place—as a vibrant assemblage (Bennett, 2010) rather than a mute site awaiting children's meaning making.

In this particular situated settler colonial place, the ethical animal–place–body resonances I am tentatively suggesting here are always already partial; relationality does not aim to erase or transcend difference (Haraway, 2011). As Lorimer (2012) states, "the coming into being of humans and nonhumans involves immanent processes, not the revelation of universal and transcendent forms" (p. 596). Attention to reciprocal encounters between children and the more-than-human plants, animals, and objects in this garden neither erases nor resolves difficult ethical questions, such as "what counts as a livable life and a grievable death" (Butler, 2004, p. xv) in the making of the forest garden and its entanglements with pastpresent colonialisms? In other words, perhaps educators might also begin to consider how touching earthworms in this garden is also to touch colonial histories.

The colonial "temporalities and materialities" (Haraway, 2006, p. 145) that emerge from touching earthworms in this community garden are complex, and here I just briefly engage with where they might take us (myself, educators, and children). Touching worms takes us to glaciers during a Pleistocene Ice Age that brought indigenous worms in North America close to extinction; it takes us to colonial ships that carried most of the earthworm species currently in North America (Smithsonian Environmental Research Center, 2013). As the Smithsonian Environmental Research Center (2013) explains:

> new earthworms began entering North America as early as the 1600s, with the first European settlers. They crossed over in root balls or the dry ballast of ships. As the British, French, Spanish and Dutch colonized the American continent, they were largely oblivious to another colonization going on under their feet. European earthworms thrived in the upper soils of forests and gardens. Native earthworms, if there were any, remained deeper underground. In the end Europe's earthworms established an empire. (para. 2)

In British Columbia, these introduced worms quickly spread through the land, outpacing the few remaining indigenous earthworms. Known as "ancient earthworms," these indigenous worms inhabit British Columbia's forest soils (Marshall & Fender, 1998, 2007). While worms' benefits to the earth's ecosystems are well known, recent work also points to the destructive effects of the spread of introduced worms to Canadian forests (Addison, 2009). This story illustrates the contingencies, complexities, and contradictions of domestication relationships. As I discussed earlier, more-than-human socialities are active and unruly participants in domestication relationships (Cassidy, 2007; Haraway, 2008; Tsing, 2013). Children's relations with garden worms, the forest, the community garden, and the boundaries and porosities therein become even more complicated, noninnocent, and unsettling.

## Conclusions: Opening up to Anticolonial Resonances

In this chapter, I have intentionally focused my attention toward knowledge-making practices that trouble the enduring innocence of the child–garden and child-in-nature figures. I have attempted to critically engage with the socio-materialities, tensions, and situated histories that emerge from refiguring presences in everyday encounters with a particular community garden. I have made no attempts to tidy up this place, and I have resisted avoiding the mess that emerges from making visible connections among histories of community gardens, children in gardens, and settler colonialism. Instead, I have experimented with literal and figurative touch as a way to refigure presences by foregrounding colonial territorialities and multiple place stories. I have also noticed and become unsettled by everyday encounters with unexpected and unruly performativities of more-than-human assemblages. I see this unsettling as an important part of enacting anticolonial resonances and possibilities—possibilities that disrupt normative, orderly gardening pedagogies. While I suggest that educators and children actively seek out the histories and Indigenous ontologies of the places they inhabit, and consider what an "interspecies garden ethics" (Plumwood, 2005, para. 23) might look like in their particular contexts, I also wonder what other effects these moments of unsettling (which cannot necessarily be known in advance) might have for practice with children. I remain hopeful that noticing with children unexpected garden assemblages and more-than-human relations might enact a beginning toward unsettling the "colonial order of things" (Stoler, 2008, p. 193) embedded in the romantic visualities of gardens and gardening in early childhood environmental education.

## Note

1 Community garden reference omitted to maintain anonymity.
2 Thank you to Dr. Sandrina de Finney and Vanessa Clark for pointing me toward the Camas example.

# 6

# GEOTHEORIZING PLACE RELATIONS

It is early in the fall of 2014. Alongside a large media presence, there is a growing group of protestors camped out at the top of Burnaby Mountain on the unceded territories of the Musqueam, Squamish, Stó:lō, and Tsleil-Waututh Indigenous peoples in what is now British Columbia, Canada, close to a site where a pipeline company has recently received approval to access Burnaby Mountain Conservation Area to begin their drilling assessments in support of a pipeline proposal. This proposal to expand pipeline capacity to transport unrefined oil from Alberta's tar sands would include tunneling under the mountain forest in a protected conservation area close to the child care center where I work with educators and children several days a week as a researcher and pedagogical mentor. Several groups of people with convergent and divergent interests have emerged in opposition to the pipeline. These include Indigenous peoples on whose unceded territories the mountain stands, who, alongside environmental activists and the local municipal government, are concerned about the potential environmental damage of an oil spill, both along the pipeline route and at an ocean inlet that would see a large increase in tanker traffic (Burgmann, 2014). The pipeline would also traverse through a wealthy suburb at the bottom of the mountain, and many local residents who do not want the pipeline to pass near their homes have joined the protests. An elder from the Squamish First Nation has been allowed past the protest injunction line to light a sacred fire near the initial drilling site. She tends the fire over the period of the pipeline company's presence at the site. The protest site is located in an area that is not visible on my almost daily bus trip up the winding mountain road. On this particular day, a lone sign at the bottom of the mountain reminds me of the ongoing turmoil on the mountain where I work: NO PIPELINES. The sign stands in juxtaposition to the vista of green forest on either side of the mountain road, including the parts of the forest I encounter regularly with children and educators. The protest and the imminent drilling have not entered into our curriculum yet. Later that day, I send an email to the educators with links to media news coverage about the ongoing protest events and ask for their perspectives.

## Geotheorizing Mountain–Child Relations

As the opening retrospective narrative illustrates, ongoing settler colonialism and its intimate entanglements with capitalist extraction have come together as active presences on Burnaby Mountain, a forested mountain on the west coast of Canada. Despite growing protests and increasing numbers of people intentionally crossing the injunction line and subsequently being arrested, the pipeline company was able to complete the drilling of one test borehole through the mountain-rock strata and extract core samples from the mountain for study as part of a submission of evidence toward the pipeline application (Crawford, 2014). As I write this, several years after the initial protests, the application has received conditional approval from the National Energy Board amid an ongoing court challenge from the Tsleil-Waututh First Nation (Prystupa, 2015; Tsleil-Waututh Sacred Trust, 2016). This chapter is my attempt to think through, in interruptive ways, separations of the protest and extractive events on the mountain from our childhood pedagogies on this selfsame mountain. In seeking possibilities for unsettling children's separation from these ongoing mountain contestations, the Anthropocene, despite its contentions, is used as an opportunity to geotheorize children's relations and encounters with the mountain. A term crafted by Allison Guess (Tuck, Guess, & Sultan, 2014), "geotheorizing" refers to a reconceptualization of Black relations to land in ways that refuse discourses of Black life in North America as ungeographic and in ways that refuse to dwell only in tales of damage-centered relations to land (Tuck, Guess, & Sultan, 2014; Tuck, Smith, Guess, Benjamin, & Jones, 2013). In this work, Black relationships to land are theorized as a political stance that resists the reduction of land relationships to extractive property making while simultaneously tracing land histories that have dispossessed Black and Indigenous people. Learning from that use of the term, geotheorizing captures the interrelated onto-epistemic moves I make in this chapter. My purpose is to consider how children's relations within this particular mountain place might be reconceptualized and rematerialized as refusals of the separation of children from meaning making about events such as those described in the opening excerpt, events that entangle settler colonial governance and anthropogenic extractivism.

Inspired by Tuck, Guess, and Sultan (2014), I want to consider possibilities for thinking through children's relations to this place in ways that might act not only as a refusal of their separation from colonial possession and dispossession on Burnaby Mountain, but also as a refusal to dwell only in these extractive relations. I also see this refusal as part of a necessary interruption to modern humanist views of the world, including those reinforced by the dominant individually focused and child-centered developmental approach to early childhood education. If we take seriously the contention that such humanist and divisive views are implicated in the urgent environmental challenges of the Anthropocene, then it is an ethical and political necessity to seek "otherwise" possibilities (Plumwood, 1993; Yusoff, 2013). Alongside other scholars, I view the Anthropocene as necessitating a radical change toward education that emphasizes relationality rather than domination of and separation from the more-than-human world (Lloro-Bidart, 2015; Rautio, 2013; Taylor, 2013). I am interested in grappling with mountain and mountain–child relations as routes toward modes of subjectification that acknowledge children as a geologic force. In this perspective, children are inextricably materially and discursively co-constituted within fossil-fueled genealogies in both anthropogenic and potentially interruptive ways. This mode of geotheorizing acknowledges that all human genealogies are entangled with fossil fuels, yet it also refuses an uncritical and undifferentiated inheritance of colonial extractive relations. That is to say, geotheorizing children's relations might bring forth new ways of relating beyond those already determined by viewing the mountain as a passive object of geologic knowledge and fossil-fueled relations. In particular, as I discuss later in the chapter, I am on the lookout for relations that bring more generative modes of inheritance and that entangle children in more inclusive connections with the more-than-human world. Here, inheritance refers to the hard work of learning how to become responsively accountable to the pastpresent material, affective, and discursive messy worlds in which children live (Haraway, 2008; Instone, 2014).

A critical examination of the imbrications of children and more-than-human lifeworlds is pertinent to the context from which I am writing in British Columbia, where nature/forest kindergartens are undergoing proliferative growth, yet are often marked by an absence of a deeper engagement with difficult questions surrounding the assumptions about nature, place, and childhood that underpin these pedagogies. Particularly pertinent to my inquiry here, young children's environmental pedagogies are rarely situated within the interconnected effects of settler colonialism's Indigenous displacements and anthropogenic ecological damage (Pacini-Ketchabaw, 2013). My turn toward geotheorizing is also resonant with recent work in early childhood studies and children's geographies that has suggested rethinking children's multispecies pedagogical relationships in ways that pay close attention to the real situated common worlds that children co-inhabit with human and more-than-human others (Hodgins, 2015; Taylor, 2013; Taylor & Pacini-Ketchabaw, 2015). This chapter is resonant with this work in assembling connections that bring critical attention to humancentric pedagogies and that enter into the interruptive potentials of ordinary encounters between children and more-than-human worlds. The stories in this chapter are intended to decenter children as the central actors in these relations by situating the mountain itself as a figure that reveals extractive settler colonial relations, yet also exceeds and refuses these relations.

For the remainder of the chapter, I put the concept of geotheorizing to work by engaging with orientations toward children's mountain encounters. These encounters were documented through my field notes developed during and after these pedagogical encounters. They were also documented through pedagogical narrations prepared by both myself and educators as modes of making children's learning visible and to facilitate our critical reflections on our pedagogical practices and our planning on ways to extend and deepen our inquiries (see Chapter 1 for an in-depth discussion of pedagogical narrations and the data collection methods in this work). The data, as presented herein, represents an assemblage of excerpts of pedagogical narrations and field notes. In addition, the data includes my retrospective theorizing and analytic engagements with these field notes and narrations, alongside Indigenous relational knowledges, situated mountain geohistories and geomaterialities, and specific extractive mountain events and protest actions. Taking seriously the contention of Collard, Dempsey, and Sundberg (2015a) that "different stories perform different yet interconnected worlds" (p. 328), this data assemblage comes together as an attempt to figure the mountain as inextricably entangled with children, a critical and generative response that interrupts dominant developmental understandings of what is seen as belonging to young children's curricular engagements.

## Situating Children's Geo-colonial Inheritances in British Columbia

Burnaby Mountain is located in a suburban city in Greater Vancouver. Much of the mountain is second-growth forest that has been designated protected conservation land under the management of the local municipality. This designation is itself entangled within violent and ongoing settler colonial dispossession of Indigenous lands. This is always already contested territory: The remaking of land into property, including the transfer of land to the domain of government conservation protection, is intrinsic to settler colonialism (Tuck & Yang, 2012). In this particular place, as Rosemary-Claire Collard and her colleagues (2015a) assert, "nature is steeped in colonial patterns of power and knowledge" (p. 326).

Mountains, as common figures used to represent British Columbia's topography and idyllic "natures," have long loomed large in settler imaginaries. The mountain remains a dominant representative figure of the "great wild outdoors" in British Columbia. As Bruce Braun (2000) notes, within settler colonial British Columbia, mountains are circulated through multiple "practices of *representation*—deeply cultural and historical in character—[that] are both central to and necessary for nature's *material* transformation in circuits of capital" (p. 27, emphasis in original). British colonial explorers such as James Cook and George Vancouver generated detailed descriptions of western Canadian mountain landscapes as a part of the colonial project's processes of calculation. Not only was the outer structure of mountains subject to measurement and calculation, the emergence of geology as a particular way of visualizing and knowing British Columbia mountains made the innermost

**FIGURE 6.1** Walking in the Mountain Forest

parts of landscapes objects of knowledge open to extraction. British Columbia, through these practices, emerged as a quantifiable vertical territory (Braun, 2000).

These colonial spatializing practices and their accompanying material artifacts, including maps, travel logs, engravings, newspapers, almanacs, and many other forms of colonial writings, "formed a systematic practice of confining and defining" Indigenous land (Goeman, 2008, p. 296). These representational practices are intimately entangled with colonial anthropogenic inheritances that have seen Burnaby Mountain become the site of the drilling of test boreholes and the removal of core rock samples to be studied as quantifiable evidence toward the pipeline application, an example of humans as a geologic, mineralogical (Yusoff, 2013) force irreversibly altering mountain strata. As the next section illustrates, contemporary children in British Columbia are also materially and discursively entangled in these pastpresent "geologic logics" of mountains and mountain matter, including through pedagogies, such as those described next, which are already structured within geo-colonial inheritances.

## Child–Mountain–Rock Geologic Pedagogies

On our regular walks on Burnaby Mountain, children have become interested in rocks. Rocks fill pockets and are carried back to the child care center. Rocks are piled, sorted, measured, and accumulated inside and outside the classroom. The individualistic developmental (human) child-subject is reiterated as rocks become geologic objects of children's study. Geology books are brought out for the children so they can classify the rocks they have chosen. The sink or float experiment, a mainstay of North American early childhood classrooms, becomes another way to know and study rocks and implement already-known learning goals rooted in developmental psychology, such as classification, motor skill development, categorization, observation, prediction, scientific thinking, and language development (see Figure 6.2). Several field trips to a nearby geology lab are organized. Inside, children peer at carefully labeled and arranged rock specimens, often with magnifying glasses. On some visits to the lab, paper and pencils are brought out as invitations for children to draw the rocks. Some fossilized rocks are displayed behind glass, and children peer curiously at the museumified

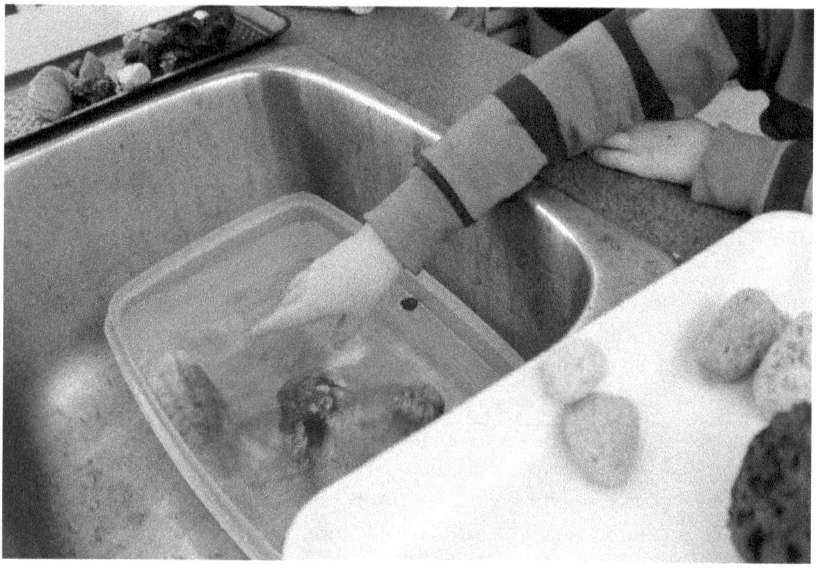

**FIGURE 6.2** Child–Mountain–Rock Geologies

> Burnaby Mountain is underlain by layers of conglomerate, sandstone, siltstone and shale deposited in the Georgia Basin during the Eocene (39–45 million years ago)... The south side is mantled by glacial till (11,000–13,000 years old) as well as shell-bearing, silty and stony glaciomarine sediments. Large boulders called 'erratics' are found on the surface. They were transported from the Coast Mountains glacial ice, and remained after the ice melted. On the steep north side, sedimentary rocks have broken off in blocks of million tonnes and slumped downhill. Construction of the railway and Barnet Highway along the base of the caused new slumps in the unstable deposits.
>
> (Armstrong, 1990, pp. 77–78)

specimens. Some of the fossil specimens and volcano models are brought out for the children to examine. Stories about ancient dinosaur histories emerge from children, intermingled with references from popular culture. Children express an interest in creating a rock museum with the growing collection of rocks, and a discussion emerges among the educators on what labels to attach to the rocks—the children have given their own descriptive names to some of the found rocks.

Alongside the familiar, sedimented repetitions of anthropocentric scientific/geologic study in early childhood classrooms described above, I am also interested in children's becomings with this mountain that potentially interrupt its materialities as a part of the lifeblood of settler colonial governance (Yusoff, 2015). I am on the lookout for ways of knowing, seeing, and encountering that create movements away from an emphasis on the biopsychological development of children, as seen, for instance, in only learning about the geologies and scientific properties of rocks. I am on the lookout for everyday encounters between children and more-than-human worlds that might be a place to foreground relations that bring forward a nonpredetermined "something else" beyond child-centeredness. Such encounters might create openings that unhinge the humanistic learning child as the sole center of early childhood pedagogy. It is these possibilities that I turn to in the next section.

## Geontological Interruptions and Resonances

During our almost daily walks in the mountain forest, in addition to the small rocks that children can easily pick up, we also encounter large rocks of many textures and shapes. Some of the boulders we encounter invite children to look closely... touch... climb... slip... jump on/off... slide... draw... and more. Over several weeks, children engage in embodied dialogues with the liveliness of rocks and the rocks' entangled becomings with moss and other more-than-human life. "Eating dirt," "feeding," "drinking rain," "growing," "walking," "nocturnal," "helping," "thinking," and "hibernating" emerge as some descriptors of the rocks' liveliness among the children. Children–rock–moss encounters seem to be disrupting the separations of mind–body–spirit in life/nonlife dualistic ontologies. Families are also invited to share their perspectives on whether rocks are alive or not, and multiple perspectives emerge. As children learn with rocks and rock–moss entanglements and affectivities, tensions emerge among educators in relation to whether children should be provided with information that conflicts with their theories that rocks are alive. As we (educators) discuss children's theory making on whether rocks are alive or not, some want to explain to children, from a scientific/biological perspective, why rocks are not alive. These tensions and disagreements invigorate rather than close down the inquiry as educators engage in lively discussions that touch on questions such as the roles of teaching, learning, and pedagogical conflict.

On the surface, children's theorizing on the liveliness of rocks in the preceding dialogues might be viewed, from a developmental perspective, as a lack of

**FIGURE 6.3** Mountain–Rock–Child Encounters

"This rock is alive!"
"No, it is not alive!"
"Yes, it is alive; see it has green moss living on it."
"No way! Rocks don't move."
"The moss will take care of the rocks and teeny tiny bugs live there."
"That rock is so huge that a lot of moss feed on it."
"I think it is a hundred and forty million years old."

understanding. However, these mountain–rock–child encounters challenged educators' views on human life/geologic nonlife separations. This mountain and its rocks refused to remain an inert object of children's pedagogy; it also refused to be known only within colonial logics and geologic science logics. Instead, child–mountain–rock relations can be seen as enacting geontological world making (Haraway, 2008; Povinelli, 2014a,b).

Geontology is an orientation that provides an opening toward a rethinking of dualistic bio/geo and life/nonlife divides (Povinelli, 2013, 2014a,b). Geontology is in dialectical opposition to colonial bio-ontologies that have maintained hierarchical relationships between life and nonlife and served as justification for human exploitation of those places and spaces deemed nonlife, such as seen in the dominance of environmentally damaging extractive relations with land in the Anthropocene. On the contrary, biographic, biological, geographic, and geologic obligations are seen as co-constituted and inseparable (Povinelli, 2014b). This perspective is resonant with many Indigenous ontologies, where "biography and geography are in a relation of extimacy (extimité) [where]… there is not biography (life descriptions) on the one side and geography (nonlife-descriptions) on the other… Their very natures are internal and external to each other simultaneously and thus their distinction essentially without meaning" (Povinelli, 2014b, para. 9).

Geontology, as an alternative to extractive place relations, might be useful in thinking with the rock–child encounters described above in relation to the geomaterialities of settler colonialism. Geontology might be thought with as a form of contestation of this mountain as simply a site of colonial-capitalist rule, as a place reduced within late liberal capitalist governance and its accompanying extractive industries to a geographic geologic place. Importantly, geontology as contestation is inseparable from the complex, multiple, storied, lived, and specific Indigenous Coast Salish relationships with, and obligations to, this particular mountain. This geontological shift might then act as an interruption to what Povinelli (2013) calls geontopower, a current form of colonial governance that places what is determined as nonlife (land) as subject to extraction and extinguishment, erasing Indigenous geontological obligations to specific places (Povinelli, 2013). In this perspective, the extractive events on the mountain can be viewed as an expression of geontopower, the governance of life/nonlife dualisms (Povinelli, 2013, 2014a,b). In this "speaking back" to colonizing dualisms, geontological formations of children–rocks as lively entanglements might be seen as creating movements toward otherwise forms of existence that do not rely on the reproduction of bio/geo binaries.

When set alongside Indigenous ways of knowing and relating to more-than-human life, children's learnings—and becomings—with moss and rocks, as illustrated in the dialogues and drawing in Figure 6.4, are not easily contained within one way of knowing:

> The rocks are full of intention, a deep presence attracting life… The rocks are beyond slow, beyond strong, and yet yielding to a soft green breath as powerful as a glacier, the mosses wearing away their surfaces, grain by grain bringing them slowly back to sand. There is an ancient conversation going on between mosses and rocks, poetry to be sure. About light and shadow and the drift of continents.
>
> *(Potawatomi scholar Robin Wall Kimmerer, 2003, p. 5)*

> Stones carry earth histories, stories, songs, prayers, so their stone faces hold memories of existence of other eras.
>
> *(Anishinaabe poet and novelist GordonHenry, 1994, p. 41)*

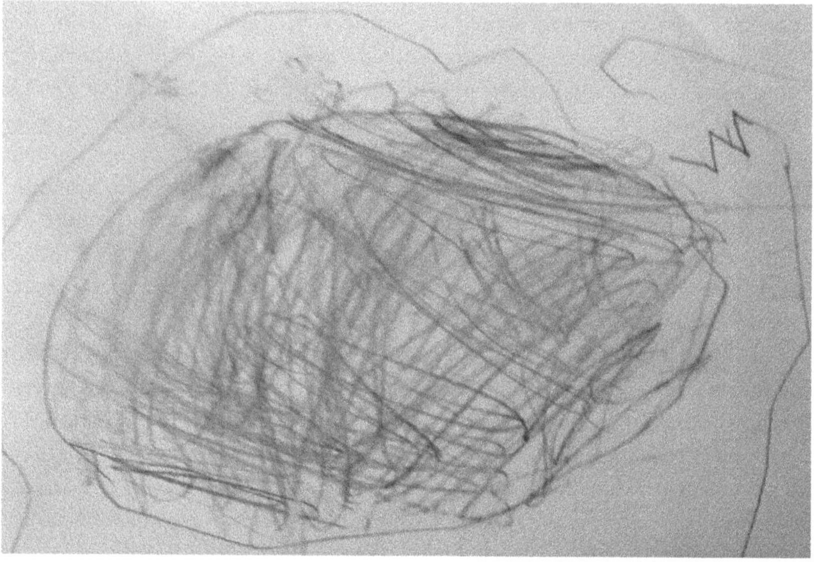

FIGURE 6.4 Mossy-rock Drawings and Children's Dialogues

"This rock is alive and growing. Soon it will have moss all over it."
"Rocks keep teeny tiny ants warm."
"The moss will take care of the rocks and teeny tiny bugs live there."
"This moss is growing on the rocks. I think the rocks feel warm with it."

The assemblages of small rocks–child-bodies–pockets, as rocks were carried back to the child care center, while small everyday encounters, are themselves important as moments in which the particular materialities and liveliness of rocks (TallBear, 2011, 2013) bring children into affective bodily relations that momentarily escape capture as individual children learning about rocks. However, the generative potentiality of these moments was made more fleeting as they came up against property-making practices of collecting, sorting, museumifying, and geologic study. This is not to say that these geologic/scientific ways of knowing rocks are wrong, but that perhaps, as Robin Wall Kimmerer (2003) so eloquently states, "rocks' ways of being in the world cannot be told by data alone… attentiveness alone can rival the most powerful magnifying lens" (p. 8). Perhaps the type of embodied affectivity that emerges in everyday encounters as children touch and respond to mossy rocks and as they collaboratively theorize multiple stories and histories of the interconnectedness and liveliness of earth matter might be seen as opening possibilities toward more responsible geontological relations to this mountain.

The differences between the worlds enacted by geologic study (classification, collection, and scientific experimentation) and those that emerge through affectively responding to the liveliness of rocks and moss seem to hinge on the affective and material resonances of the latter. Rocks seem to come to matter differently in these affective encounters, in both material and imaginary "qualities, rhythms, forces, relations and movements" (Stewart, 2011, p. 445); perhaps in ways that at least temporarily resist humancentric colonial logics. However, these geontological becomings do not erase children's material inheritances of the colonizing, geologically informed epistemologies of this mountain. That is to say that I think it is important to resist reading these everyday moments within a lens that views nature, in Affrica Taylor's (2013) words, as a "perfect safe haven for pure and innocent children" (pp. 114–115). Next, I discuss further the frictions of these relational encounters amid ongoing settler colonial conditions.

## Unresolved Frictions

From a geologic perspective, frictional forces are intrinsic material participants in how mountains grow, helping to create distinct mountain structure, topography, and sedimentation patterns (Peng & Thompson, 2003; Pinter & Brandon, 1997). Frictions are also important discursive formations in thinking childhoods through the geologic within the era of the Anthropocene. First, important unresolved frictions remain amid children's affective encounters with this mountain. Our ways of relating to the mountain always already perform and reinforce erasures. In particular, Indigenous geontological obligations to this particular place remain for the most part as unacknowledged presences in our mountain pedagogies, propagating erasures of Indigenous knowledges that have never limited life and vitality to the biological. Furthermore, while no one remains outside of the vulnerabilities and benefits accruing from fossil fuel extraction, these extractive relations are entangled in differentiated, situated, racialized (neo)colonial and neoliberal inequities. Despite this observation, critical examination of the highly differentiated effects of and complicities in current times of anthropogenic change along racial, Indigenous, gender, and class lines has been relatively lacking (Baldwin, 2013; Collard, Dempsey, & Sundberg, 2015b). This is a potential effect of the universalizing of the human as a geologic force underpinning the naming of the Anthropocene. It is important then to continue to seek out ways to rethink and rearticulate geontological relations in ways that do not erase the differential accumulation of anthropogenic inheritances, yet provide interruptive, hopeful, and more sustainable relations with more-than-human life. For instance, in this chapter, I have worked with geotheorizing, an analytic of the complexities of Indigenous and Black geographies within the interconnected worlds of anti-blackness and settler colonialism (Tuck, Guess, & Sultan, 2014) by bringing it to think with predominantly white settler children's place relations. This move risks reproducing the settler emplacements and visualities that I have argued need to be continuously unsettled. In bringing this theoretical perspective to settler children's place relations, I have not engaged with the intricacies and contingencies of the children's gendered–classed–raced–immigrant–settler subjectivities within this particular place. However, rather than assuming a universal child or educator of the Anthropocene that is equally situated within settler colonial relations, I acknowledge that uneven human responsibilities for and exposures to the vulnerabilities of extractivism within neocolonial capitalist natures continue to haunt childhood studies in the Anthropocene. While remaining attuned to the increasing inequity of life in the Anthropocene, I see possibilities in consideration of geological and geontological lives as immanent to children's modes of subjectification in these current times.

Perhaps, the critical and generative perspectives brought in this chapter to children's mundane mountain encounters amid the absent presences of ongoing Indigenous displacements in this place might be seen as imperfect and always partial practices of response-ability (Haraway, 1997) toward settler colonial anthropogenic inheritances. I also see potential in pointing to children's situatedness within the ruins of settler colonialism and extractivist capitalism, while simultaneously seeking possibilities for place relations that might in some small way generate more livable worlds. This chapter, then, is a beginning toward orientations that situate children within real unequal worlds, and toward seeking possibilities for learning how to unsettle, rather than sustain, what is inherited.

## A Return to Extractive Events on Burnaby Mountain

While the main protest area on Burnaby Mountain is at a site that is not visible to the children when we are in the forest, during this time, during our everyday encounters with the mountain, we notice that we encounter many more people walking on the trail, because it is one route to the main protest area. On one day, we encounter a handwritten sign that reads: "enter at your own risk." While we wonder about the meaning of this sign and its origins and, on that particular day, we turn around, we decide to continue the mountain forest encounters with the children. At the same time, we (educators and myself) continue to discuss how or whether to broach the question of the pipeline events with the children. However, the entanglements of biopsychological discourses of childhood innocence, the intense politics surrounding the pipeline protest events, multiple divergent perspectives on the pipeline, the colonizing absent presence of this land as Indigenous land, the affective material discomforting presence of this sign on the ground, the presence of protest signs and human presences apprehended as "strange" and "unsafe" along the roads leading to the child care center… and much more all assemble to figure this event as an issue that should remain outside of the curriculum. However, events, things, and bodies such as the "do not enter" sign, cut trees, garbage along the trail, and other unexpected human and more-than-human encounters on the mountain trail spill over and leak into the curriculum and interrupt the innocence of our mountain forest pedagogies. While we do not reach a consensus on how to navigate the tensions and divergent views surrounding the pipeline with families and children, in subsequent dialogues with the educators, one educator notes:

> I've changed my mind from when you were emailing us those questions around the protests happening on the mountain. I started thinking about that and what we do with children. I thought, well it's not our job to make our opinions theirs, but to see what they believe or what they think about it [the protests] as well.

The educator decides to send an email to the families in her child care center asking if they have had conversations with their children about the pipeline and possible responses if questions emerge from the children. As expected, there are divergent perspectives from families on pipeline and related protest events entering children's curriculum, and we do not engage further with pedagogical intention.

## Toward Geontological Pedagogies

This chapter has been an attempt to respond to extractive events on a mountain and the ways in which they have remained absent presences in our pedagogies with young children. I have used the concept of geotheorizing to think through the ways in which children are in complex relations with this mountain, its lively materialities, and its inherited pastpresent histories. These relations include ways of knowing and becoming that can be seen as normalizing settler colonialism's extractive and humancentric formations. However, alongside these relations, I have attempted to make visible small encounters that I view as consequential in enacting geontological relations. These geontologies unsettle humancentric modes of learning that preassume what counts as life and nonlife. I see geotheorizing as more than a mode of rethinking children's place relations; it is also an opening to experimenting with new, more relational early childhood pedagogies. My modest proposal is that children's everyday affective encounters with the more-than-human world, rather than being seen as moments at which to provide the "correct" knowledge, might be taken as openings through which to try out pedagogies that build on the relational perspectives that children are often already embodying and contemplating. These new pedagogies can be seen as emergent practices of inheritance. Here, learning to inherit requires movements away from divisive and objectifying ways of knowing, toward geontological pedagogies that nourish children's relational knowledge making. Importantly, geontological pedagogies not only unsettle anthropocentric and instrumentalist orientations toward young children's learning; they also do the important work of situating children in the world rather than separating them from it. That is to say, these geontologies bring important insight for rethinking early childhood pedagogy beyond the developmental logics that would structure extractive pipeline logics as separate from children's worlds. In dominant developmental discourses, young children are seen as not able to engage in discussions about fraught social issues, and instead, as innocent beings, require protection. Consequently, issues such as the pipeline contestations are positioned as outside of children's curriculum making. However, geontological orientations in refusing both human/more-than-human binaries and the divided (subject/object) disciplinary logics of geology make possible more relational and situated pedagogies. I see these pedagogies as a necessary response to the interconnected legacies of settler colonialism and anthropogenically damaged places which rely on violent nature/culture and human/nonhuman divisions. Rather than separation and human centeredness, geontological pedagogies require modes of attending to the ways in which children are always already entangled with the more-than-human-world. Such a shift toward geontological orientations might bring new questions for educators, such as these: What pedagogical possibilities open up in these moments of embodied encounter? What other stories of mountains, rocks, rock–moss–animal relations might emerge through creative and embodied pedagogical practices? What always already present Indigenous knowledges of mountain, mountain-rock, and rock–animal–moss worlds in this particular place might be brought to children? For example, what might be unsettled by bringing the knowledge that "rocks hold the earth's stories" (Kimmerer, 2003, p. 5) to children to cohabit alongside scientific ways of knowing rocks? How might these stories and embodied encounters interrupt the mountain and mountain-rocks as sites of colonial extraction? It seems to me that there are rich potentials for responsive yet implicated geontological early childhood pedagogies that mobilize new curricular conversations, while unsettling and refusing a colonizing view of the world.

# 7

# LIVING WITH BEE DEATH

## Western Bumblebees: A Matter of Concern in the Anthropocene

Indigenous western bumblebee populations are just one of many more-than-human others that have become vulnerable in the Anthropocene to what environmental humanities scholar Deborah Bird Rose (2014) terms *double death*: "the death of temporal, fleshy, metabolic relationships across generations and species… [and] cascades of death that curtail the future and unmake the living presence of the past" (n.p.). The far-reaching implications of the Anthropocene include the imperative for current and future generations to learn to live in less destructive and more ethical ways with more-than-human life.

Picking up on recent insights into the problematics of taking up the concept of the Anthropocene to posit the human-as-savior, in this chapter the naming of the Anthropocene is a provocation to turn away from dominant discourses that reproduce grand narratives of transcendent heroic solutions that reinforce a universal human subject of the Anthropocene and represent children as the "solution" for the future (Haraway, 2008, 2015; Taylor, 2013). Instead, the Anthropocene is engaged as a provocation to examine, in situated encounters and specific ways, young children's responses to multispecies death and to inquire into the partially recuperative (Haraway, 2015) actions and small interruptions enacted by embodied and affective learning with more-than-human others. Current times of anthropogenic loss are taken as a provocation to consider how children and educators might learn to relate to lifeworlds in ways that challenge human exceptionalism while attending to their particular situatedness within specific places. The specific place discussed in this chapter is a suburban preschool located on unceded Coast Salish territories in Greater Vancouver, British Columbia, Canada. The situated example of western bumblebee vulnerability in this location presented an impetus to contemplate responding with young children to the ever-increasing presences of unlivability in the Anthropocene (Tsing, 2015). Considerations of these pedagogical responses are situated within specific theoretical and ontological orientations, which I introduce next, prior to thinking with them in relation to children's and educators' encounters with bees.

I draw inspiration from work in the environmental humanities and Indigenous knowledges on the importance of modes of attention to the interconnectedness of human and more-than-human lives, as a becoming-with that matters for contemplating situated modes of responding (Haraway, 2008; TallBear, 2013; van Dooren, 2010). One such mode of responding is to tell stories of living on a damaged planet that center learning within entangled multispecies social worlds (Haraway, 2015). Inspired by this call to story more-than-human modes of relating and learning, I engage children's everyday pedagogical encounters in relation to their potentialities for attuning and responding to messy anthropogenic inheritances, including grappling with encounters and questions that unsettle discourses of innocent childhoods. An important part of this unsettling is to consider how emergent bee–child pedagogies might be situated within a relational and affective ethics of caring that does not distance children from anthropogenic death and that engages with difficult questions regarding the mattering of certain deaths.

## Methodological Considerations: Bee–Child Worlding Stories

In storying the relations and curiosities that have emerged between educators, children, and western bumblebees, I craft and put to work a methodology of worlding as a mode of storying, attuning to, and responding to bee–child encounters and bee pedagogies in ways that bring close attentiveness to the impacts of more-than-human worlds and to the mutually affective relations between children and bees. Here, worldings are emergent forms of human and more-than-human relating that are grounded in the details of everyday life yet filled with frictions, tensions, and ethical potentials: a form of micropolitics that takes place, as Kathleen Stewart (2012) suggests, "as intensities of all kinds and in various registers" (n.p.). I refer to these encounters as worldings for a number of interconnected reasons. First, worlding highlights child–bee relations as emergent relations that immerse children within the world in multiple and at times contradictory relations of curiosity, ambivalence, responsiveness, and implicatedness (Haraway, 2008; Stewart, 2012). These worlding stories bring attention to both the limiting effects and ethical potentialities of everyday pedagogical encounters, particularly in relation to possibilities for new ethical accountabilities in multispecies relations. These accountabilities are grounded in children's everyday uncertain, embodied, affective, and thoughtful responses that are grounded in "the action of worlding rather than abstract principles" and universalized solutions (Ginn, Beisel, & Barua, 2014, p. 114).

Storying worldings also draws attention to the particularities of the emergent assemblage of children and bumblebees, as well as its multiple and contingent material–discursive relations. As Stewart (2010) notes, "in any worlding we can ask how things come to matter and through what qualities, rhythms, forces, relations and movements" (p. 4). Worlding, then, is a way to see what might be generated by knowledge making that focuses on particular affects, bodily (dis) orientations, and sensory modes of attention in relation to children's and educators' situated encounters with bee life and bee death (Stewart, 2011). In this way, as a micropolitical attunement to everyday affective life, worlding is a mode of being on the lookout for that which eludes easy representation and is not necessarily known in advance of encounter, yet nonetheless has impact and matters. I suggest that these situated, ordinary, and everyday material–discursive encounters matter for the particular modes of livable worlds that they bring into view for children and educators. In other words, in their own small ways, these encounters are world making. Finally, a methodology that attends to worlding situates the researcher as an embedded part of that which is described in relation to children's and educators' encounters, a methodology that itself participates in particular worldings, rather than "standing at a distance and representing the world" (Barad, 2007, p. 49) while claiming innocence.

This chapter draws from pedagogical narrations (see Chapter 1 for details of this research and pedagogical method) and field data in the form of images and written notes gathered from a multi-year multispecies inquiry with young children, educators, and more-than-human co-inhabitants of a child care setting. I present textual and visual worlding stories that connect to children's literal and figurative encounters with bee lifeworlds and precarities. I put these data assemblages to work in a postqualitative approach to analysis that interrupts easy moves to humancentric representations or interpretations of what happened and what it means (Jackson & Mazzei, 2012). Rather than presenting a solely descriptive and singular interpretive account of what happened and was learned by educators and children, the intent is to invite readers to inhabit the intensive affects, effects, and sociomaterialities of these worldings and to ask what they might do toward composing different modes of relating to more-than-human worlds in current times of environmental precarity. I invite readers to consider what new ways of responding, relating, and learning/teaching might be opened up that interrupt the normality of bee death and vulnerability. For example, readers might ask: What do these worlding stories do alongside each other? How do they work? What potentialities, affectivities, and attunements do they provoke as creative and pedagogical interventions? What different kinds of more livable multispecies worldings might come together? How might commodity/capitalist worldings be unsettled? What kinds of pedagogical provocations might emerge in your own early childhood education contexts from attending in your work with young children to affect, human and more-than-human bodies, and ecological vulnerability? Stewart (2008) describes this as a methodology that seeks "to wonder where [analytic subjects-objects] might go and what potential modes of knowing, relating, and attending to things are already somehow present in them as a potential or resonance" (p. 74). For the remainder of the chapter, after contextualizing western bumblebee precarity, I enact this worlding methodology, paying close attention to both already-determined modes of knowledge making and emergent embodied and affective modes of paying attention and responding to bee vulnerabilities.

## Entangled Lives, Entangled Vulnerabilities

The interdependent connections between bees, plant, animal, and human life are multilayered and complex, emerging from bees' symbiotic relationship with flowering plants, a relationship that has been an intrinsic part of coshaping the conditions for planetary human and nonhuman livability for millions of years (Poinar & Danforth, 2006). More recently, bee–plant–human interspecies relationships have also emerged through intentional practices of resource making as western bumblebees and other bee species have been drawn into global capital networks and large-scale agricultural production, where they have been commercially bred as greenhouse crop pollinators.

Current research suggests that the interconnected assemblages of parasitic disease transfer from commercially bred bumblebees; climate change; habitat loss from land development and invasive plants; and neonicotinoid pesticides have come together to place the once-common indigenous western bumblebee (*Bombus occidentalis*), pollinators of both wild and commercially produced flowering plants, in significant decline in southern British Columbia and other parts of the west coast of North America (Cameron et al., 2011; Williams & Osborne, 2009). In addition to being vulnerable to pesticide spray drift, bumblebees, as ground nesters, are thought to be particularly vulnerable to pesticides used on lawns (National Research Council, 2007).

In this particular place on unceded Coast Salish territories, entangled dependent webs of plant, animal, and human life, while already present for millennia, have been made more visible by the anthropogenic decline in indigenous western bumblebees. Beyond the immediate and long-run effects on plant pollination, the multilayered effects of bee decline are not yet fully grasped—though they clearly extend beyond the humancentric focus of many news headlines concerned with agricultural impacts (see, for example, Grossman, 2013). It is amid these messy spaces of entanglement and mutual vulnerability that this chapter is situated in relation to storying how bumblebee death emerged as a matter of concern (Latour, 2004b) for a group of children and educators.

## Learning about Bees

In this preschool-age group care setting in a suburban forest in British Columbia, bees, educators, and children have been in some form of relationship over several years. In previous years, when the center followed a teacher-determined theme-based curriculum, bees were a regular subject in the springtime. In this preset curriculum, bees emerged primarily as a site of scientific knowledge: Children learned about bees through preschool science. Identifying color patterns, counting body parts, distinguishing bees from wasps, and learning about food crop pollination are just a few of the ways bees entered the curriculum. Learning about bees was also engaged through teacher-selected craft projects (see Figure 7.1), typically emerging as a uniform construction of bee-as-craft product. While bumblebees were a presence in the playground, particularly in the spring and summer months, at this time the bee pedagogies did not center on the bees themselves. On the contrary, children were discouraged from engaging with bees, in alignment with already-determined child safety regulations.

While these ways of knowing bees are not necessarily wrong, looking back on them together with educators raised questions for us about the erasure of bee–human–plant relations that exceed commodified pollination networks. From this perspective, scientific knowledge of bees, while necessary and important, was not enough to unsettle children's inheritances of humancentric practices that privilege human mastery or control over more-than-human others (Tsing, 2012b). Unsettling questions also emerged about the ways in which these predetermined pedagogies recirculated the normality of ecologies that remake plant and animal life into resources, often with unintentional eruptions that proliferate unlivable worlds. Anna Tsing (2015) refers to these technologies of replication as a plantation approach to ecology that refigures more-than-human life as a resource. The economies of plantation-style scaled-up bee production have contributed to the current phenomenon of native western bumblebee decline, where, as Jake Kosek (2011) points out, the "changing relationship between bees and humans [has] brought the modern bee into existence in a way that has made it vulnerable to new threats" (p. 227). Indigenous bumblebees are believed to have acquired

**FIGURE 7.1** Bee-as-craft Classroom Assemblage

parasitic diseases from bees bred in Europe and then shipped to North America for crop pollination (Thorp, 2003). These transatlantic events can be seen as colonial worldings (Spivak, 1990). Such worldings reemerge in the Anthropocene as extractive colonial–capitalist relations that continually act to erase Indigenous lifeworlds and normalize conceptions of nature as an uninscribed object of human exploitation (TallBear, 2011).

## Pollination Worldings

Recently, one of the educators noticed that the apple tree in the child care center playground had not flowered and that there were few bumblebees in the playground that spring. The bees they did notice were seen on the ground, either dead or moving slowly. Together with the children, the educator pollinated the apple tree using a paintbrush (see Figure 7.2). Becoming more curious about bee presences and absences, she read with the children a short news article about the decline of the bee population. Troubled by the collapse of bee colonies, the children and educators wonder about its connections with the absence of apple tree pollination.

These small moments of curiosity opened up the beginning of attunements to curiosity—attunements that cannot be captured through a disembodied account of bumblebee decline and children's learning thereof. This type of curiosity was attentive to the particularities of children's immediate worlds, yet was also

**FIGURE 7.2** Paintbrush–Child–Apple-tree Pollination Worldings

imaginative. The responsive collaborations among children, pollen, and apple trees, while an imperfect and partial response to the problem of bee loss, was perhaps the kind of collaborative curiosity that might bring hope amid colonial–capitalist ruins (Tsing, 2015). Paintbrush–apple-tree-pollination–child–bee-absence and more are worlding stories that might be interpreted in multiple ways, rather seeking a singular, smooth narrative, an important orientation in meeting the complexity of current environmental precarity (Rose & van Dooren, 2017). These worlding stories bring questions of response, accountability, and values into early childhood pedagogy in the Anthropocene.

## Learning to be Affected

Over the two years since the apple tree paintbrush pollination first began, the educators in this preschool setting began to engage in ongoing processes of complexifying their practices, such as by working with children on long-term inquiries that nurture educators' and children's curiosities and questions and create movement away from a predetermined theme-based curriculum. An important aspect of this always-in-process rethinking and rearticulation of practice was to consider what it might mean to engage with and respond to more-than-human lifeworlds in ways that unsettle innocent child-in-nature discourses and trouble human/nonhuman, meaning/matter, and nature/culture divisions. Shifting our practices away from these anthropocentric binaries was a necessary yet difficult response to inherited modernist and colonialist dualisms and their attendant environmental vulnerabilities (Plumwood, 2002).

In beginning to experiment with possibilities for unsettling and complicating engagements with nature, educators began to notice, with children, the presences and absences of bees in their immediate surroundings. The educators and children began to notice and become curious about the sluggish, dead, and dying bees they would often encounter outside in their playground and during their walks around the mountain-top university campus where the child care center is situated. Educators and children researched western bumblebees and learned to distinguish and identify the bumblebees by their hair color patterns.

In these encounters, science was an important advisor to, and was intimately entangled with, the children's and educators' affective knowledge making as a part of understanding, relating to, and responding to bee worlds and the particular places they co-inhabit with human and more-than-human life (Tsing, 2015). This bringing together of multiple ways of knowledge making is important since, for the most part, early childhood education has yet to seriously consider what it means to bring, for example, environmental science knowledge into sustained conversation with insights that consider questions of ethics, care, values, more-than-human futurities, and inheritance (Haraway, 2003; Tsing, 2015).

In this inquiry, scientific knowledge making, as an advisor, was more than an accumulation of facts, but rather an important part of coming to know the bees' particular ways of becoming and living in the world. For example, although children and educators were unable to distinguish between indigenous and commercial western bumblebees, they learned that western bumblebees are not generally aggressive unless threatened. As educators and children learned that they could be close to the bees, some became more comfortable learning with bees and attuning to their mutualities. These children learned to practice stillness and slow movement in the presence of bees that still showed signs of life. Here, the affective aspects of children's learning and relating to bees—the multiple ways in which they were moved, became attached, or became detached in bodily ways—were a part of their understandings of bees (Latimer & Miele, 2013).

As bees, children, and educators responded to their mutual presences, children began to make offerings to the bees they encountered crawling on the ground outside. Some children built "homes to try and make the bees feel better," while others kept their distance and watched. Some children picked up some of the still-moving bees and placed them on flowers in the classroom or outside, or tried to find the bees' nesting grounds. Some children also prepared, with educators' help, a sugary water to feed the bees. Occasionally a bee would respond to the offering and then fly away, to the children's delight. Some responded by covering the dead bees with paper "to stop them blowing away" or by building a wood "bridge" so that the bees could "walk" to the flowers. Educators also conducted their own research, such as in reaching out to a western bumblebee researcher at the local university who presented a seminar about the entangled factors that were impacting western bumblebees in British Columbia. While this seminar did not help us ascertain the specific reasons for all of our encounters with dead or dying bumblebees that spring, we gained important insights into the bumblebee crisis impacting our immediate setting.

The children also began to gather and bring the dead bees into the classroom (see Figure 7.3). Fear or alarm did not disappear from these embodied encounters. Children were aware of the threat of a bee sting, and also knew they could easily step on the bees that are sluggishly crawling on the ground. While several children experimented with ways to be in proximity with the bees while keeping fear of being stung at bay, sometimes a bee might come too close for a child's comfort, and they would run away. Some educators voiced their fears of bees even as they encouraged children to learn to be present with the bees. Amid their contradictions, these bodily engagements perhaps held potential for ethically responding to mutual and uneven child–bee vulnerabilities. Following Taylor and Pacini-Ketchabaw (2015), these small moments where children seek closeness to bees might be seen as a form of vulnerability that enacts an embodied learning with and about the precarity of life.

Many dialogues emerged between children and educators about the bumblebees. These conversations grappled with the relationships among bee life, human life, food, and weather. Multiple theories emerged from children's encounters with the bees as they wondered why some bees were not moving or

**FIGURE 7.3** Bee-death Gatherings

flying. Tiredness, hunger, stinging people, and weather emerged as possibilities. For example, some children wondered whether a change in weather ("getting too hot then too cold") was killing the bees, and many postulated that these were not "'normal' deaths" (e.g., "they ate something bad from the flowers"). Children's modes of bearing witness to bee death and caring for bees seemed inseparable from their knowledge making about what was harming the bees.

Children's attunements and orientations toward bee lifeworlds also included theory making in relation to bee–human interdependencies. Children's theories seemed to entangle bees, humans, and more-than-human life. Focusing on attending to what emerges in-between children and bee worlds, rather than solely providing information, educators noticed and documented, using pedagogical narrations, moments where children's theories opened to human/more-than-human entanglements. For example, educators noticed children's dialogues as they tended to the flowers and vegetables planted in the playground to help attract bees. Children discussed relations among soil, bees, leaves, flowers, water, apples, and more as both humans and nonhumans were described by children as growing, becoming strong, eating and drinking. This attention to interconnectedness matters: as Thom van Dooren (2010) says, within "the context of extinctions, this attentiveness to the relationality and interdependence of life is particularly important because the death, and subsequent absence of a whole species, unmakes these relationships on which life depends, often amplifying suffering and death for a whole host of others" (p. 273).

In these moments, new worldings emerged that exceeded our attempts to capture them through description. Perhaps these encounters might be seen as complicated ways of participating in the world, as a practice of responsive witnessing that, as Rose and van Dooren (2017) suggest, "exceeds rational calculation, one that arrives through encounter, recognition and an ongoing curiosity" (p. 124). These worldings brought attention to everyday encounters among children, educators, bumblebees, and bee pedagogies and attendant practices of attachment and detachment. These worldings have micropolitical resonances. While never transcending the vulnerabilities of bumblebees, children's and educators' encounters were experimentations in thinking with, responding to, and becoming more accountable to what Donna Haraway (2008) refers to as "the consequences of nonstop curiosity inside mortal, situated, relentlessly relational worlding" (p. 143).

Entangled within these imperfect worldings are embodied more-than-human caring practices where caring involves affecting and becoming affected, such as through seemingly minor caring practices like the children building bridges and homes for the bees and attempting to nourish them, without necessarily preventing their imminent deaths. As situated and affective doings, I suggest that these modes of caring are the kinds of attunements that are needed in the current time of the Anthropocene, grounded as they are in responding to the situated real-life messiness and uneven inheritances of the places children co-inhabit with bees rather than in universalized or precalculated understandings of what counts as care or of who or what is deserving of care (van Dooren, 2014). While the processes of affective and embodied learning I have described here were uneven, I see them as important beginnings toward pedagogies that immersed children in the lives of bumblebees in ways that were noninnocent, implicated, and foreground mutuality.

## Touching Death

At the child care center, touch and looking emerged as important ways for children to interact with the growing pile of dead bees. Perhaps affective caring bee–child worldings also emerged in the interactions among fingers, fuzzy bee bodies, stiff wings, stiffened legs, and more (see Figure 7.4).

In the encounter shown in Figure 7.4, the child had watched other children picking up and touching the bees, but had not wanted to do so herself. After another child encouraged her, describing the bees' soft "fur" and showing her possibilities for "holding the wing gently," she touched and picked up the bee, looking at it closely and intently for a long time and asking other children and educators why the bees were dead. Rather than sentimentalizing these moments and focusing on the individual child, I point to them as instances of curious attention that cannot be contained within this particular moment, that interrupt anthropocentric viewpoints, and that bring attention to the particularities of bee

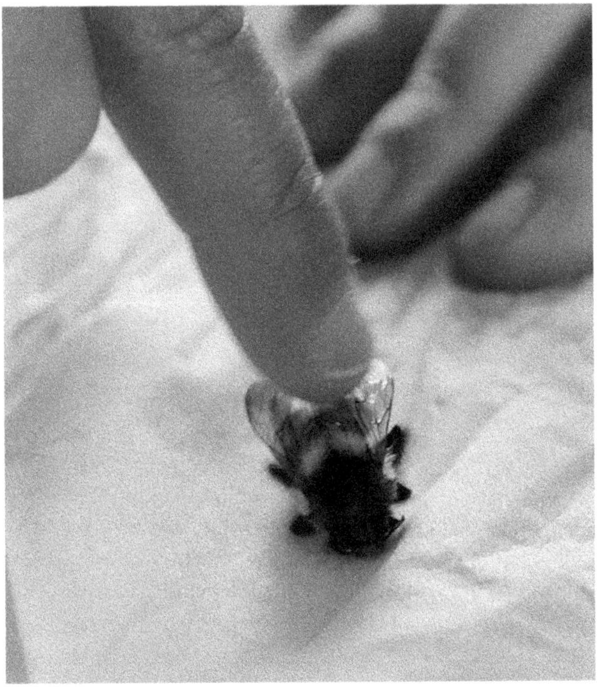

**FIGURE 7.4** Touching Dead Bees

death. While my description describes what children said and did, in these moments the touch, affect, and embodied materiality of bee death all mattered as modes of knowledge making that enacted new worldings of responsive curiosity. As Haraway (2008) notes, "touch does not make one small; it peppers its partners with attachment sites for world making. Touch, regard, looking back, becoming with—all these make us responsible in unpredictable ways for which worlds take shape… Touch and regard have consequences" (p. 36). Following Haraway then, touching dead bees, as world making, immerses children not only in material–discursive worlds of bee death, but also in the plantation worldings of the agriculture industry, pesticides, colonial farming histories, techno-scientific bee breeding, and more. If we consider these complicated and implicated worldings as a part of the seemingly mundane encounters of touching dead bees, it is difficult to contain them within a child-centered discourse of innocent child–bee encounters.

## Conclusions

In this chapter, I have narrated worlding stories of educators' and children's pedagogical, affective, and responsive encounters with dead and dying bees. I have gestured toward their mattering for questions of living and dying in current times of environmental precarity. While I have been working pedagogically with children's inquiries for several years, I have found that shifting from pedagogies that engage more-than-human life as an object of children's learning toward a relational, embodied, responsive, and emergent curriculum—where both affect and scientific learning matter—is not easy; there is no recipe to follow and I am continually challenged to seek ways to describe these pedagogical encounters in ways that center both human and more-than-humans as active participants in learning.

From our inquiries with children and bees, I have discussed how, in this particular place, western bumblebees as a matter of concern materialized through embodied dialogues that entangled children, educators, plants, weather, food, death, pollination… and more in emergent, at times disparate, and relational worldings. Amid these contradictory worldings, bee–child worlds emerged in ways that complicated views of bees as an object of knowledge or resource making. My proposal here is that children's embodied and affective learning with the ways in which, as Anna Tsing (2012b) says, "human nature is an interspecies relationship" (p. 141), matters for learning to live in more ethical ways with more-than-human others, an imperative in current times of anthropogenic change.

Taking seriously the provocation to interrupt grand narratives of progress and heroism in the Anthropocene (Haraway, 2015), this inquiry neither sought nor provided any final resolutions to the troubles of western bumblebee death. With an emergent focus on the potentialities of bee–child affective curiosities and caring responses, these everyday affective worldings are environmentally attuned collective actions that offer different possibilities for inhabiting anthropogenically damaged places. These possibilities include learning to be affected by multispecies loss and engaging with partially recuperative responses. Importantly, these responses, while not ignoring the entanglements of human/more-than-human vulnerability, are not premised on human benefits of child development. These worldings illustrate how responsive bee–child relations and socialities have emerged in ways that trouble anthropocentric ways of learning in early childhood environmental education and in ways that foreground affect as a way of responding to the overwhelming loss in current times.

I take seriously the task of attuning to the pedagogical potentials of children's multispecies relations in ways that interrupt romantic and innocent images of both children and nature that are so prevalent in early childhood education (Taylor, 2013). Perhaps glimpses can be seen in children's close affective encounters with dead and dying bees. Potentials for unsettling the nature/culture divide perhaps also emerged as children theorized bee death and its connections to human and plant life, where children's theorizations seemed to inhabit the messiness of anthropogenic inheritances as a form of situated ethical worldliness.

While bee death might seem minor in relation to the multitudes of human suffering and inequality in current times, I suggest that it matters for responding to anthropogenic times that children learn to be affected by multiple forms of death as a part of being in the world. In other words, it is important to consider what situated childhood pedagogies look like that stay with the difficult questions of what modes of dying are recognized, who recognizes these modes of dying, and which processes of dying are seen as worthy of a response and responsibility (van Dooren, 2010).

Finally, I have considered how pedagogies of relational affect that complicate a dominant focus on "matters of fact" (Latour, 2004b) in young children's learning hold different potentials for encountering the mutual precarities of bee–human lives in current times of anthropogenic change. Importantly these approaches to pedagogy are not presented as exemplars of how young children might be the current or future solution to the crisis of western bumblebee vulnerability, but rather to illustrate possibilities for early childhood pedagogies to enact situated, perspectival, and ethical orientations to the specificities of certain places and possibilities for attending to children's affective responses toward the messy worlds they have inherited.

# 8

# INHABITING A BLACK ANTHROPOCENE

An important thread that runs through the research practices detailed in this book is an attempt to speak back to the absenting of Indigenous and Black onto-epistemologies in pedagogical encounters between young children and settler colonial places. My interest in this chapter is to engage more explicitly with the absences of Black place relations in dominant forms of environmental education for young children, including in the places described in this book. In particular, I want to pick up on the discussions I began in Chapter 6 on the whiteness of current environmental discourses and the urgent need to decolonize the Anthropocene in ways that carefully attend to human exceptionalism, settler colonialism, and anti-blackness. As several scholars have noted, there is a need for attention to be paid to the ways in which environmental precarity (including vulnerability to the impacts of climate change), anti-blackness, and settler colonialism are interconnected (Davis & Todd, 2017; Tuck, Guess, & Sultan, 2014). In this chapter, a key intent is to offer some possibilities for bringing these dialogues into early childhood education with a focus on presencing anti-blackness, including its entanglements with settler colonialism. As Heather Davis and Zoe Todd (2017) note, it is important that dialogues on living in current times of environmental damage "explicitly acknowledge the intertwined and interdependent violences of the Transatlantic slave trade and the genocidal dispossession of Indigenous peoples and territories" (p. 772). This acknowledgment includes paying attention to and responding to the multifarious ways in which these inheritances of the past continue to manifest in current late capitalist conditions of increasing planetary unlivability (Davis & Todd, 2017; Sharpe, 2016; Tsing, 2015). I am particularly interested in possibilities for actively resisting Black erasure in nature education in research and practice in North American contexts. I am also interested in seeking openings for pedagogies that presence Black children's relationships to nature, relationships that disrupt salvation discourses while attending to anti-blackness.

## Unsettling Whiteness: Toward a Black Anthropocene

There is now a significant and growing body of scholarship in early childhood studies that has focused on troubling the dominance of anthropocentric scientific approaches to environmental education for young children, premised, for instance, on the introduction of predetermined science themes that are rarely attuned to the specificities of children's geographies. For example, it is common practice in North American early education contexts for learning about the natural world to be enacted through predetermined topics, such as those relating to the seasons, the daily weather, and plant and animal life cycles (Dove, Everett, & Preece, 1999; Gross, 2012; Havu-Nuutinen, 2005). In complicating these decontextualized anthropocentric approaches, several early childhood education scholars, particularly in the settler colonial contexts of Canada and Australia, have turned to environmental humanities scholarship, as well as to new material feminist perspectives, to decenter the developing, autonomous, universalized, and humanist child as the focus of environmental education (Taylor & Pacini-Ketchabaw, 2017). One approach in this work has been to put new material feminist ontological perspectives to work to bring attention to the agency of the nonhuman world and to the ways in which children are always in situated, entangled, uneven, and fraught relations with the more-than-human world (Malone, 2017; Pacini-Ketchabaw, Taylor, & Blaise, 2016). Another approach has been to bring insights from the environmental humanities to situate children's relations with animals within colonized and ecologically damaged worlds and to take seriously the ethics and politics of settler children's multispecies relations, including moving away from romanticized, child-centered constructions of these relations. Situated predominantly within the settler colonial contexts of Australia and Canada; this work has brought critical attention to fraught cohabitations and relations between settler children and deer, kangaroos, raccoons, bears, and classroom pets, such as stick insects (Pacini-Ketchabaw & Nxumalo, 2015; Pacini-Ketchabaw, di Tomasso, & Nxumalo, 2014; Taylor & Pacini-Ketchabaw, 2017).

Despite this scholarship, there has yet to be a significant shift away from normative, persistently romanticized formations of environmental education for young children. Of particular interest in this chapter are the ways in which contemporary couplings of childhood and nature remain framed by whiteness. These normalized framings can be seen, for instance, in the Google image search results for the term *children and nature*: a plethora of predominantly white cherubic children pictured in pristine nature environments. Clearly, this coupling of children and nature refers to always already racial visions of "perfect innocent children" that need to be returned to certain visions of "perfect natures": visions matched by the whiteness of most of the nature-based early childhood programs that continue to proliferate across North America. These taken-for-granted connections between childhood innocence and perfect nature have been traced back to Romantic-era constructions of childhood (Taylor, 2013). Jean-Jacques Rousseau's conflated and romanticized idealization of childhood and nature, such as in his figure of "nature's child" who learns ideally by freely exploring nature (the ideal teacher) has been particularly influential. Rousseau's work inspired several European early childhood philosophers, including Friedrich Fröebel, Rudolf Steiner, Maria Montessori, and Loris Malaguzzi, whose ideas, in turn, continue to influence the structuring of nature education programs for young children worldwide, including in North America (Taylor, 2013). Just as Rousseau's innocent Romantic-Enlightenment-era nature's child was white, and constructed in direct opposition to his depictions of the so-called uncivilized savage, contemporary couplings of childhood innocence and nature spaces remain framed by whiteness, albeit in more subtle and easily normalized ways.

The Anthropocene is a contested term but is increasingly used to describe the current geological epoch of unprecedented damaging impacts of humans on the environment, including climate change, pollution, extinction, and multiple interconnected effects (Crutzen & Stoermer, 2000; Haraway, 2016; Lewis & Maslin, 2015). Recent critiques of the Anthropocene include the overwhelming whiteness and coloniality of Anthropocene discourses and scholarship, including the ways in which the dominance of scientific perspectives has tended to obscure or minimize the ways in which both the causalities and ongoing uneven vulnerabilities of the Anthropocene are inherently raced and colonial (Davis & Todd, 2017; Parham, 2015; Nxumalo, 2018; Yusoff, 2017). For instance, Françoise Vergès (2017) uses the term *racial Capitalocene* to highlight the need for methodologies that include a "history of the environment that includes slavery, colonialism, imperialism and racial capitalism" (p. 73). Picking up on these critiques to unsettle the overwhelming whiteness of environmental education for young children, I want to foreground Indigenous and Black feminist perspectives that, while not situated within childhood studies or early childhood education, I see as offering transgressive modes of (re)imagining pedagogical places and spaces for young children (Parham, 2015; Sharpe, 2016; Todd, 2016).

In particular, I begin with Christina Sharpe's (2016) profound contention that "the weather is the totality of our environments; the weather is the total climate; and that climate is anti-black" (p. 104). This contention powerfully situates current times of environmental precarity and its unevenly distributed impacts within ongoing conditions of anti-blackness, in marked dissonance with persistent decontextualized approaches to environmental education for young children. Sharpe's (2016) framing of anti-blackness through an all-encompassing climate and the concept of a "Black Anthropocene" (Parham, 2015; Yusoff, 2017) together act as modes of centering the ways in which anti-blackness and settler colonialism are intrinsic to both the beginning of this era of unprecedented human-caused environmental damage and its ongoing unevenly distributed impacts (Davis & Todd, 2017). Brought to North American contexts of early childhood education, the idea of inhabiting a Black Anthropocene underlines the necessity to transform pedagogies on current ecological challenges in ways that do not ignore their underlying anti-Black and settler colonial formations, while simultaneously imagining decolonial and anti-racist possibilities (Nxumalo, 2018; Nxumalo & Cedillo, 2017; Nxumalo & ross, in press). In other words, a necessary part of decolonizing environmental education for young children is finding ways of teaching and encountering "nature" places in ways that resist erasures and deficit constructions of Blackness and erasures of Indigenous dispossession in Anthropocene discourses. So, what might this mean for everyday practice? Without creating prescriptive enclosures around what inhabiting a Black Anthropocene means for environmental early childhood education, I suggest that attuning to the idea of a Black Anthropocene means that, alongside the settler colonial entanglements discussed throughout this book, environmental racism needs to be an intrinsic part of the curriculum for young children. There is already a large body of work in early childhood education that supports young children's capacities for engaging in learning about racialized discourses and materialities in complex ways that go beyond a developmental psychology framing (MacNaughton, 2005; Nxumalo & Adair, 2018). Therefore, I suggest that engaging young Black children with living in a Black Anthropocene needs to include close attention to the particular ways in which anti-Black racism impacts particular environments and the human and more-than-human life therein. One example, which I discuss further later in this chapter, are possibilities for reconceptualizing water pedagogies with ways that bring science into conversation with ongoing environmental racism (Nxumalo, 2018; Nxumalo & ross, in press). Such pedagogies would include modes of witnessing the ways in which Black communities have actively resisted anti-Black formations, such as water-poisoned environments, despite the oppressive containments that structure life in the racial Capitalocene (Vergès, 2017).

An example of how the idea of inhabiting a Black Anthropocene might inspire more politically oriented environmental pedagogies can be found in thinking differently about the weather. I return to Sharpe's (2016) insights that climate and weather, in both literal and figurative senses, are inescapably bound up in anti-Black formations, and that both historically and in the present "weather necessitates changeability and improvisation; it is the atmospheric condition of time and place; it produces new ecologies" (p. 106). Drawing inspiration from these insights can take early childhood environmental education in a multiplicity of directions that disrupt the disembodied ways in which weather is typically learned about in early childhood settings. In particular, it is common, regardless of children's particular geographies and experiences of climate change, for weather in early childhood classrooms to be studied through science lesson plans organized around learning the seasons and identifying the weather of the day (Harlan & Rivkin, 2012; Rooney, 2018).

By bringing weather learning into conversation with anti-Black formations, educators can bring different experiences with and questions about weather and climate to young children, particularly young Black children. Educators can in their own particular contexts consider the ways in which they might expand pedagogical experiences beyond the dominant focus on learning the science of weather and changing climate. I suggest here that for young Black children, who are inordinately denied access to playful outdoor learning experiences, everyday embodied, experiential, and playful encounters with weather are important. However, it is also important that young Black children are provided with opportunities to think with the ways in which weather "produces new ecologies" (Sharpe, 2016, p. 106) in its entanglements with anti-blackness. In other words, environmental education needs to draw attention to the unequal ways in which precarities of climate change are experienced and to the inequitable distribution of the need to respond to the cumulative vulnerabilities of weather changes. Together with children, educators can engage in inquiries about the ways in which Black life and more-than-human life (plants, animals, land, air) in their specific geographies have been impacted by human-caused climate change. Importantly, this learning should also include Black children and educators trying out different ways to respond to that which they witness—where these responses might be imperfect, minor, and small, yet engage children in acts of resistance (Nxumalo, 2018). This is difficult work, particularly within the current contexts of the extreme regulation and surveillance of young Black children beginning in their earliest years of schooling (Dumas & Nelson, 2016). However, perhaps such pedagogies are small but necessary aspects of the experiments in living otherwise that are needed to radically refigure Black life within the brutal enclosures of the Black Anthropocene (Sharpe, 2016).

## Thinking with the Black Outdoors

> Outdoors. The un/homed and unfenced ground of a trespassive imperial desire and its attendant scenes of anti-black subjection. Outdoors. What lingers as ongoing physical potential and a structure of feeling even after "the day of property" offers a momentary stay against eviction.
>
> *(Cervenak & Carter, 2017, p. 46)*

In thinking with what kinds of reimaginings might challenge the erasures of Black places and spaces in environmental education, I am interested in thinking with the Black outdoors as both figurative haunting and material space. As a figurative haunting, I mean that histories of Black relations to land continue to haunt the present in multiple and complex ways, particularly with regard to settler plantation histories and the making of Blackness as property. As Cervenak and Carter (2017) argue, relegating Black people to a literal and figurative outdoors is intrinsic to "ongoing dispossession, rendered as the promiscuous interplay between harvested flesh and land. Un/settled life settled which, in turn, settles and secures stolen land as settled property" (p. 46). This is to say that the Black outdoors then speaks to spaces haunted by pastpresent histories of racial violence, exclusion, and alienation in slavery and its afterlife (Finney, 2014; Hartman, 2016). I suggest here that attunements to these complexities are an important part of creating Black space in environmental education for young children in ways that trouble romanticized notions of nature and child–nature relationships.

Thinking with the Black outdoors expands the borders of what counts as knowledge in environmental education. There are several ways in which the concept of the Black outdoors can be taken up pedagogically with young children. For example, while there is a paucity of Black nature writing that is aimed at young children, a rich archive of Black poetics engages with Black relationships with the outdoors in multiple ways. Alongside bringing attention to the more-than-human world, such as "moss, rivers, trees, dirt, caves, dogs [and] fields" (Dungy, 2009, xxii), Black nature poets also help bring pedagogical attention to the specific cultural and historical legacies of Black nature relations and their accompanying affects of everyday joy, wonder, and warm memory as well as the dampening affects that emerge from dispossession, ambivalence, and trepidation. In moving toward opening up Black space in environmental education, teachers can seek out Black nature writing that does not reproduce the settler colonial "empty wilderness" discourses that thread through many Anglo-American eco-poetic works (Dungy, 2009). They can also encourage young children to create their own poetics of the Black outdoors through multiliteracy pedagogies that include drawing, drama, spoken poems, and storytelling alongside scientific ways of knowing the more-than-human world. Importantly, drawing from Black poetics, educators can also trouble colonial nature/culture divides that would dismiss engagements with Black urban spaces from inclusion in environmental education. That is to say, just as Black poetics highlight the material–discursive complexities of Black relationships to the natural world within both urban and rural places, so can educators engage with Black children's real everyday nature relations; wherever they may be.

## Living Black Feminist Geographies

Black geographies center place and space as key signifiers of materialized and spatialized inequity—bringing into view past, present, and future matterings of Black spaces and places (McKittrick, 2002, 2011; McKittrick & Woods, 2007; Paperson, 2014; Shabazz, 2015). While noting the centrality of racial geographies in Black place relations, Black feminist geographies also bring important complexity to understandings of North American Black relations to place. This includes making visible Black environmental place stories which demonstrate historical in-depth Black knowledge and respect of land, and making visible environmental aspects of prominent civil rights narratives (Glave, 2010). Black geographies also trouble overdetermined representations of Black land relations through labor in plantation landscapes, bringing forth situated examples of non-anthropocentric, generative, and speculative Black relations to space and place beyond the imagery of the Black laboring body (King, 2016). Perspectives from Black feminist geographies bring new possibilities for relating to place, land, and space through what Katherine McKittrick (2013) refers to as "a decolonial poetics that reads black dispossession as a *'question mark'*" (p. 5, emphasis added) and thereby imagines otherwise Black futurities that refuse Black life as ungeographic or placeless. These futures do not aim to erase the endurances and ever-shifting formations of the violences enacted by pastpresent plantation histories, yet inquire into affirmative anticolonial Black futurities through geographies of persistence and inventiveness (McKittrick, 2013). Relations to place and more-than-human lifeworlds within the context of North America are situated in pastpresent geographies of anti-blackness, whether or not these are immediately apparent. These relations include the absence of Black people from certain urban outdoor places, and the hyper-surveilled containment of Black people within places of environmental abandonment and decay (Shabazz, 2015). At the same time, Black feminist geographies teach us that encounters with and experiences with Black geographies are complex and cannot be contained within stories of damaged place relations, surveillance, and absenting (King, 2016; McKittrick, 2011).

Taking up the challenge to bring insights from Black feminist geographies into conversation with place-based and environmental early childhood studies can take this work in a multiplicity of enriching directions in situated time–place–space locations. One such possibility would be to consider, within a particular place, what kinds of pedagogies might trouble "Black narratives of un-belonging" (McKittrick, 2002, p. 28) and erasure in certain places? For example, while it is not within the field of early childhood studies, I am inspired by the work of the Black/Land project which is foregrounding Black relations to land by collecting, (re)remembering, and presencing Black land stories that interrupt views of Black life in North America as ungeographic, while also refusing to dwell only in tales of damage-centered Black relations to land (Tuck et al., 2013). How might such stories be made visible in encounters with particular places with young children? What might emerge from seeking out immigrant and Black land stories with children? For instance, while many stories of Black/land relations in North America are of displacement and destruction—such as Hogan's Alley in what is now Vancouver, Canada (Compton, 2010), and Africville in what is now Nova Scotia, Canada (Nieves, 2007)—within these stories are also stories of survival, reciprocity, community, and refusal.

Alongside presencing situated Black land stories and relations, another possible inspiration for early childhood studies drawn from Black feminist geographies is to seek out and create artistic/creative interventions as another form of (re)storying places in ways that disrupt Black placelessness. For example, educators can draw inspiration from Black speculative fiction and Black poetics in seeking out and cocreating with children place-based and environmentally attuned literary representations that situate Black childhoods in places, including "nature," in ways that unsettle deficit or absented depictions of Black children (see examples in Capshaw, 2014; Grosvenor, 1970; Jordan, 1972). Black feminist geographies politicize, question, and shift what typically counts as knowledge, both in early childhood research and in pedagogical practices. Bringing these perspectives to early childhood studies interrupts the privileged position of Eurocentric theoretical realms and brings complexity to representations of Black environmental experiences. The perspectives on place and place relationalities that have been discussed in this chapter see this work as a necessary intervention of taking seriously the question of how particular places might be known and experienced differently with young children through attention to marginalized stories and relations to place, vibrant more-than-human relationalities of place, and affirmative place relations for those typically seen as not belonging in certain places.

## Testifying-witnessing: Black Children's Lives Matter in the Anthropocene

Black childhoods and Black perspectives in both dominant North American Anthropocene discourses and environmental education for young children are marked predominantly by absence and/or deficit salvation discourses, as well as misrepresentations of Black people as not caring about or as being indifferent to nature (Nxumalo & Cedillo, 2017; Nxumalo & ross, in press). Black feminist theories are invaluable in making sense of the persistence of these discourses in academia, in schooling contexts, and, more broadly, in society and as modes of resisting absence and deficit in thinking with Black childhoods and education in the Anthropocene. Black feminisms bring much-needed attention to the limits of engagements with the Anthropocene that do not also consider Blackness and anti-blackness as necessary parts of the ontological and epistemological constellations that disrupt Euro-Western humanism (Frazier, 2016; King, 2017; Rusert, 2010). Zakiyyah Iman Jackson (2013) eloquently describes the antidote to these erasures of Blackness and anti-blackness as the difficult yet important task of situating "'the human' as an index of a multiplicity of historical and ongoing contestations… rather than tak[ing] 'the human's' colonial imposition as synonymous with all appearances of 'human'" (p. 681). For example, Sylvia Wynter's monumental (1984, 1994, 2003) work has shown the insufficiency of Euro-Western humanism in responding to anthropogenic vulnerability. Her work brings a "both and" orientation that interrupts human exceptionalism while also interrupting a universalized view of the human. Wynter delineates how interrogating humanism and disrupting the colonial human/nonhuman binary requires attention to be paid to how Black people were and continue to be dysselected from belonging within the category of human. Wynter illuminates the problematics of centering more-than-human worlds as a response to the Anthropocene while leaving unexamined differential human vulnerabilities and responsibility in anthropogenic places. These problematics include a lack of attention to the ways in which the entanglements of colonialism, slavery, and advanced racial capitalism continue to create deeply inequitable human effects.

Next, I take inspiration from the teachings of Black feminists to attune to the constitution of the Anthropocene in complex ways that consider anti-blackness, relational Black place making, and practices of resistance. To do this, I return to the articulations of the pastpresent histories of African American testifying and witnessing that I drew on in Chapter 2 to trouble anthropocentric enactments of early childhood education practices. Here I want to draw on testifying-witnessing to disrupt anti-Black dominant salvation discourses about Black children and nature.

Black feminist scholar Patricia Hill Collins (1998) points to testifying as relational practices that include affective responses and are situated within particular Black experiences. She foregrounds testifying as an active naming of multiple and contextualized truths in creative ways. An important effect of the African American testifying tradition is that it not only makes visible difficulties and injustices that might otherwise go unnoticed by the dominant society; it is also a relational affirmation of humanity, strength, resilience, and hope in the face of dehumanizing injustices (Ross, 2003). Therefore, Black feminist practices of what I am calling testifying-witnessing make visible the complexities of Black geographies, beyond stories of damaged place relations, surveillance, and absence (King, 2016; McKittrick, 2011). Put another way, Black life as "an intrinsic part of the world" to quote Tarpley (1995, p. 2), gestures to a refusal of "ungeographic" as a descriptor of Black life (McKittrick, 2006; Tuck et. al., 2013). As McKittrick (2006) states, "space and place give black lives meaning in a world that has, for the most part, incorrectly deemed black populations and their attendant geographies as 'ungeographic'" (p. xiii).

Brought to contexts of environmental and place-based early childhood education, testifying-witnessing can be thought of as modes of revealing the inequitable differentiations of Black children's situatedness within anthropogenic inheritances, while simultaneously affirming Black children's humanity and generative nature relations. These affirmations include, but are not limited to, multiple acts of agency, subversion, and resistance that exceed knowability within the damage-centered anti-Black relations that mark the ongoing wake of slavery (Sharpe, 2016). In thinking with testifying-witnessing as modes of situating North American Black childhoods in the Anthropocene in ways that are affirmative yet also attend to anti-blackness, my underlying questions are these: What are the potentials of practices of testifying-witnessing for making a difference toward situated place inquiry in early childhood education that affirms Black childhoods, affirms Black relations with more-than-human worlds, and is attuned to racialized inequality in the Anthropocene? What might testifying-witnessing as a proposition for changing environmental education look like in curriculum making or pedagogy with young children?

In beginning to engage with these questions, one proposition is to consider testifying-witnessing as an invitation for early childhood educators to seek out a multiplicity of pedagogical encounters—both encounters that witness racialized place-based inequalities and encounters that testify to affirmative possibilities for

Black children's relations to places. A recent children's picture book, *Over and Under the Pond* (Messner, 2017), provides a glimpse into the types of affirmative testifying-witnessing of Black children's relations to the more-than-human world. In this beautifully illustrated book, a young Black boy and his mother are pictured rowing over a pond. The book uses the child's curiosities and wonder about the inhabitants of the pond and its adjacent land to describe the movements, sounds, and doings of a multitude of animal species, including minnows, turtles, larvae, blackbirds, and otters. The animals' doings described in the book pay particular attention to their interconnected worlds, including descriptions of animals hunting and eating other animals. Examples include lively scenes of a heron catching a minnow, a woodpecker digging for ants, and otters digging for mussels. However, there is an absence of Black geographical specificity within the pages of the story. In the author's note, Messner states that the book was inspired by a canoe trip at a pond in the Adirondack Mountains, but the scenes described in the book are not specifically emplaced. The reader also does not learn anything about the mother and child beyond the shared moments of this delightful day-long canoeing journey.

This book could be seen as representing what Affrica Taylor (2013) refers to as romantic, perfect nature for perfect innocent children rather than the reality of anthropogenic landscapes, since all of the animals and plants are situated within a thriving pond ecosystem. Nonetheless, this book can be read as a small example of one kind of testifying-witnessing that is needed to situate Black childhoods in the Anthropocene. This is testifying-witnessing that affirms Black children as *belonging in and curious about* nature and as having affirmative relations with nature. In this example of testifying-witnessing, unsettling deficit depictions of Black childhoods also includes drawing on child–nature couplings that counter images of Black children as not belonging in or as absent from "nature" environments, including in ways that reclaim the innocence of Black childhoods. Testifying-witnessing framed as situating Black childhoods in nature considers that, while coupling privileged white settler children with romantic "pure" natures can reaffirm colonialisms (Taylor, 2013), for Black children, similar images can enact anticolonial and anti-racist orientations. These contradictions point to the complexities of unsettling racialized nature/culture and human/more-than-human divides in educational contexts (Nxumalo & Cedillo, 2017).

## Resisting Discourses of Black Un-belonging

Finding children's books that witness Black childhoods and nature in affirmative ways while highlighting relationality and belonging is not an easy task. In seeking out depictions of Black children's relationships to nature in several children's books, it has been challenging to find stories that are not linked to oppression and displacement. While the intent is not to ignore these stories, an ethos of testifying-witnessing points to the need for different kinds of stories for young children.

These are stories that unsettle deficit or absented depictions, stories that, in the vein of Black speculative fictions, testify to and witness generative Black place relations and Black futurities. How might such stories be made visible in encounters with particular places with young children? What might emerge from seeking out Black land stories with children?

In seeking to further resist what McKittrick calls "Black narratives of unbelonging" (2002, p. 28), and amid the lack of diverse children's literature that reflects the complexities of Black children's relations to nature, including land, I suggest that Black speculative fiction provides an ethos that might be brought to early childhood education as a creative and interruptive mode of testifying-witnessing. Black speculative fiction has a long history of theorizing about Black life in utopic and dystopic geographies—radically imagining Black futurities and reimagining past Black life (Benjamin, 2016; Imarisha & brown, 2015). The work of Octavia Butler is seminal in this area in creatively bringing together science fiction, environmental issues, and new imaginaries for Black life (Butler, 1988, 1995). What I am proposing is that, in addition to real-world encounters, educators can draw inspiration from Black speculative fiction in seeking out and cocreating with children place-based and environmentally attuned creative inventions that situate Black childhoods in places, including "nature," in ways that unsettle deficit or absented depictions of Black children and that imagine new kinds of Black childhood–nature worldings (Nxumalo & ross, in press). Jackson (2016) describes such interventions as enacting "speculation as an intervention into and as theory, intensifying speculation's performance as theory and theory's performance by blackness" (p. 5). While there is a paucity of speculative Black fiction written specifically for young children, there is a rich body of work for adults and young adults that can provide inspiration (Nxumalo & Cedillo, 2017). One example is the comic book *Niobe: She is Life*, named after its Black, half-elf warrior heroine who navigates good and evil in a fantasy world alongside fantastical creatures, a subversion of images of Black children as out of place in nature (Jones & Stenberg, 2015). While the inhabited worlds in Black speculative fiction works are often far from utopian, they offer what Chelsea Frazier (2016) refers to as powerful "transgressive visions that center black female subjectivity, challenge the (dis)connections between human and nonhuman entities, and initiate alternative notions of environmental/ecological ethics" (p. 46). These strategic forms of representation can be seen as resistant and performative worldings that simultaneously make visible the workings of anti-Black representation and perform otherwise possibilities.

As mentioned previously, alongside an ethic of resistance and an affirmation of Black humanity, African American traditions of testifying bear witness to injustices that might otherwise go without care and response by the dominant society (Tarpley, 1995). In bringing these Black feminist onto-epistemologies to early childhood education, I am interested in possibilities for enacting testifying-witnessing in ways that pay attention to anti-blackness and its entanglements with anthropogenic damage. One illustrative example is young children's pedagogical experiences with water. Water, either in surplus or in scarcity, is at the forefront of the environmental challenges brought by climate change (United States Environmental Protection Agency, 2016). Feminist environmental humanities scholars have pointed to the need for ethical water relations that recognize our implication in water-related inequities at local, regional, and global scales (Andrijasevic & Khalili, 2013; Chen, MacLeod, & Neimanis, 2013). Water is a ubiquitous material in North American early childhood settings; it is a foundational exploration, play, and learning material in both indoor and outdoor environments (Pacini-Ketchabaw & Clark, 2016) Regardless of context, water is typically viewed as a resource for young children's physical/sensory, socio-emotional, and cognitive development (Gallagher, 2005; Waller et al., 2017). This learning typically takes the form of a scientific and mathematical approach, such as "what sinks or floats" learning activities and the use of containers and tools to control and measure water. Water is rarely linked to climate change science and issues of the Anthropocene, such as floods, drought, and water pollution in children's immediate environments (Dove et al., 1999; Gross, 2012; Havu-Nuutinen, 2005). Water, then, holds the potential for the creation of different kinds of pedagogies that are attuned to environmental justice, as well as to more relational and less objectifying ways of being-with water in early education contexts.

One potentiality for restorying water in ways that testify to racial and classed inequalities is found in the story of the poisoning of Flint, Michigan's water supply. Laura Pulido (2016) describes the case of Flint's water as a story of structural environmental racism and its entanglements with racial capitalism. This story is told by lead-leached water, Legionnaire's disease-causing bacteria, myriad health problems and fatalities faced by the predominantly Black and poor residents of Flint, lead-poisoned bodies of Black children, decaying infrastructure, necropolitical governmental practices of neglect and abandonment, the accumulation of plastic water bottles, and Mari Copeny, also known as Little Miss Flint, a 10-year-old Black girl from Flint whose activism has become a symbol for the community's resistance and fight for clean water (Latty, Scribe, Peters, & Morgan, 2016; Pulido, 2016). Flint water pedagogies as testifying-witnessing can help to activate different kinds of water relations. Such relations unsettle the romance of water–child couplings in early childhood education by attending to specific Black childhoods impacted by anthropogenic waterways. Importantly, pedagogies that are attuned to stories of watery environmental damage and racial inequality do not preclude attention to science. It is possible, for example, to consider how teachings of Flint lead-water-pipe–water–illness–Blackness might emerge alongside science, ethics, and environmental racism learning.

These are not easy pedagogies to enact; there is a risk of environmental racism pedagogies promulgating damage-centered stories of Black communities and activating pity (Tuck, 2009). In this particular example, the story of Little Miss Flint's activism is one antidote against this risk that can be brought to children.

Testifying-witnessing to the complexities of water and water–child relations could include seeking out particular anthropogenic water stories in children's local environments, paying attention to how differently raced, classed, gendered, and colonized bodies are affected in different ways by water in current times of environmental precarity.

## Tending to Black and Indigenous Relations

> What if we thought about territory in terms of all of its multiple scales and engaged protocols to include the manifestations of radical inclusion, *radical relationality*, and the building of creative intimacies as our (re)worlding project of love?
>
> *(Recollet, 2016, p. 101, emphasis added)*

Inhabiting a Black Anthropocene also means drawing pedagogical attention to the entanglements of settler colonialism and anti-blackness. As Indigenous and Black feminisms continue to teach me, connectedness to land in settler colonial contexts always takes place within the entangled yet different cartographies of Black and Indigenous land dispossession (King, 2016; Tuck & Guess, 2017). Thinking with a Black Anthropocene, then, requires, as Eve Tuck (2016) suggests, a "generosity in attending to relationships on selfsame land… [including] productive affective approaches [that] prioritize generosity" (n.p.) with respect to Indigenous and Black life on Turtle Island. Following up this invitation toward generosity, I want to bring forward an Indigenous ethos of *radical relationality* (Recollet, 2016) that enacts reciprocity and mutual obligation. I propose that this ethos has much to teach about learning to live in respectful, reparative, regenerative, and recuperative Black and Indigenous relations on selfsame land (TallBear, 2013, 2016; Todd, 2017; Tuck, 2016).

Indigenous conceptions of relationality have never bifurcated humans from the more-than-human world, and have always taken seriously the agency and sociality of the more-than-human world. Many diversely situated Indigenous knowledges foreground the relatedness of human and more-than-human worlds, emphasizing reciprocity, care, accountability, and interdependency (Cajete, 2017; Todd, 2017). Indigenous onto-epistemologies of relationality encompass connectedness and kinship with ancestors, future generations, spiritual beings, waterways, skyways, and animal and plant life (Martin, 2008; Tuck, McKenzie, & McCoy, 2014). Dakota scholar Kim TallBear (2016) refers to this as Indigenous people's "co-constitut[ion] in relation to [specific] lands and waters and skies" (para. 10). The human/more-than-human relational entanglements recognized for millennia by Indigenous worldviews include their multiple articulations through place-specific creation stories, protocols, teachings, and Indigenous science (Whyte, 2017). In these understandings, human life involves an ongoing immersion in different expressions and experiences of reciprocal relatedness expressed in multiple, specific, pedagogical, sacred, and ecological ways (Tuck, McKenzie, & McCoy, 2014).

Connecting these ways of knowing and being toward Indigenous and Black relations brings considerations of possibilities for the ways in which both Black and Indigenous children might learn to relate to each other and to more-than-human life in particular places and spaces in decolonizing ways—particularly in ways that center "inextricable relationships between land, bodies, time, and stories" (Todd, 2016, para. 3). Importantly, an ethos of radical relationality is not the same as romanticizing the more-than-human world; nor does it mean romanticizing Indigenous and Black relations. Indigenous relationships to the more-than-human world are not romantic: Reciprocal relations include ethical, practical, systematic, adaptive ways of flourishing together and dying well together with more-than-human relatives (Whyte, 2017). In addition, a call to center relationships between Indigenous and Black children is not a call to return to tropes of child innocence that gloss over the difficult work needed toward renewal and recuperation of damaged and estranged relations (Todd, 2016).

While Indigenous onto-epistemologies of relationality have yet to see significant engagement in non-Indigenous environmental educational contexts, they create movements toward what Cree scholar Karyn Recollet (2015) refers to as the "radical turn towards relationality, difference and interdependence" (p. 132) that is needed, not only to decolonize early childhood education, but to create nourishing pedagogical connections between Indigenous and Black children. I am interested in imagining educational possibilities that bring together young Black and Indigenous children to encounter "natural" places and their more-than-human inhabitants in ways that resist deficit constructions of Black–nature relationships and erasures of Indigenous land and life. As the pedagogies described in this book demonstrate, in normative environmental pedagogies, Canada's so-called pure nature awaits settler children's learning and discoveries, reenacting colonialism's terra nullius through love for the "empty wilderness." Settler colonialism, then, is perpetuated through the persistent erasure of Indigenous land and life in settler children's pedagogical encounters with outdoor places alongside persistent idealized, romanticized, and human-centered couplings of children and nature.

My suggestion is that there is a need for educational places and spaces where both Black and Indigenous children's relations with the natural world and outdoor places are affirmed—without a reliance on the always already racialized trope of romantic childhood innocence that dominates child–nature discourses in mainstream early childhood education—where Black and Indigenous land relationships and knowledges are affirmed and tended to without ignoring the structural violences of Indigenous land dispossession and environmental racism, and where the environmental learning of Black and Indigenous children is not premised on inclusion into so-called inclusive Eurocentric developmental trajectories that rely on locating deficits in individual children. Such reconceptualized Black and Indigenous spaces in environmental education can be seen as both departure and refuge from the ongoing violences of the afterlife of school segregation (Dumas & ross, 2016; Nxumalo & ross, in press).

Materializing Black and Indigenous children's pedagogical collaborations inspired by radical relationality brings difficult yet important questions: How might Black children's place-based and environmental education avoid assimilating them into the settler colonial nation-building project as currently perpetuated by dominant forest school pedagogies? What kinds of pedagogies might be enacted that create attunement to ways of practicing, noticing, and nurturing reciprocal Black and Indigenous relations toward each other and with more-than-human others (Nxumalo & Cedillo, 2017)? For example, what might it look like for educators of Black and Indigenous children to take seriously the contention that relationality with more-than-human others is foundational for learning to create and sustain decolonized worlds? What might it mean pedagogically for early childhood teachers of young Black and Indigenous children to take seriously the idea that the natural world exerts agency and participates in sociocultural worlds in multiple ways, many of which are beyond human influence and knowledge? How might these ways of relating inspire Black and Indigenous childhood relations, while staying away from appropriative and consumptive engagements with Indigenous knowledges? There are no simple and generalized answers to these questions, and I remain skeptical about whether these different pedagogies can take place within current formations of public schooling.

Nonetheless, I return to the possibilities of water pedagogies as an example of propositional encounters that could engage a politics of radical relationality between young Indigenous and Black children and the damaged places and spaces they have inherited. In particular, I focus on these pedagogical encounters as engaging radical relationality inspired by Indigenous knowledges in ways that unsettle child-centered pedagogies, resist the erasure of Indigenous land onto-epistemologies in early childhood education, and situate Indigenous and Black childhoods within the Anthropocene in generative ways. In reimagining water pedagogies through pedagogies of radical relationality, several stories can be brought to children (e.g., the story of the Ojibwe grandmother Josephine Mandamin and her sacred walks for the water of the Great Lakes) as enactments of radical relationality. In Mandamin's (2014) words:

> Water has to live, it can hear, it can sense what we're saying, it can really, really, speak to us. Some songs come to us through the water. We have to understand that water is very precious. (n.p.)

This story has been recently captured in the children's book *The Water Walker* by Joanne Robertson (2017). Josephine Mandamin's teachings and actions can bring radical relationality with water to life for young Black and Indigenous children. I have also written about how young Black and Indigenous children can learn from the events of Standing Rock, particularly efforts to halt the Dakota Access Pipeline and protect the waters of Lake Oahe, Lake Sakakawea, and the Missouri and Mississippi rivers (NYC Stands with Standing Rock Collective, 2016). Standing

Rock offers profound lessons about the impacts of Indigenous dispossession and settler colonial anthropogenic extraction that can be brought to young Black and Indigenous children (Grande, 2017). The protectors of Standing Rock enacted radical relationality with water in ways that disrupt normative water pedagogies in early childhood education (Grande, 2017).

By bringing together Black and Indigenous stories such as the water stories I have briefly discussed in this chapter, it is not difficult to imagine how educators can begin to make connections with young children on the entangled impacts of anti-Black environmental racism and Indigenous dispossession. Importantly, while these water stories do not necessarily have neatly resolved endings, they nonetheless enact hopeful Black and Indigenous futurities—futurities of resistance, survivance, and living in good relations with more-than-human life.

There is no prescriptive how-to for enacting environmental pedagogies for young Black and Indigenous children that foreground radical relationality—either between Black and Indigenous children or between these children and more-than-human life. However, I see these pedagogies as necessary moves in re(imagining) Black and Indigenous life in ways that affirm Black and Indigenous childhoods, while also taking seriously the ways in which settler colonialism and anti-blackness are always already imbrigated in the asymmetric impacts of current times of environmental precarity.

# MOVING FORWARD

## Toward Decolonial Place Encounters in Early Childhood Education

This book has gestured toward what I see as possibilities of a decolonizing orientation toward nature education in both research and practice in settler colonial contexts. I have pointed to the necessity of politicizing place relations within children's inheritances of neocolonial relations and ecologically damaged places. I see this work as a minor contribution toward unsettling taken-for-granted nature pedagogies for young children learning and living within current conditions of settler colonialism, anti-blackness, and environmental damage. I have highlighted how refiguring presences, as an onto-epistemologically situated approach, might disrupt, destabilize, and subvert taken-for-granted master narratives and settler colonial logics of knowing particular places in environmental education for young children. My intent is to underline that a decolonizing ethos in environmental early years education necessitates political choices, such as which stories, encounters, and histories to make visible, what knowledge counts in the making of a place, and which pastpresent inhabitants of place matter.

I have aimed to bring attention to the need to reconceptualize environmental and place-based education by crafting and enacting a situated methodological and research approach of refiguring presences that brings into conversation, seeks intersections, and highlights tensions between child–educator "natural" place encounters, Indigenous knowledges, and anti-blackness. My intent has been to bring forward possibilities for apprehending and refiguring what is considered present within the complexities of everyday settler colonial and anti-Black formations in early childhood place encounters.

Importantly, while I have not suggested prescriptive "how-tos" in relation to nature pedagogies in early childhood, I have brought forward pedagogical possibilities that are intended to create openings for educators to have difficult conversations. Perhaps educators in their particular contexts might ask what it might mean to attend to their accountabilities to decolonization and anti-racism in ways that attend to both human and more-than-human relations. Such an orientation includes putting into practice an ethos that encounters more-than-human others through radical relationality, rather than simply as objects of scientific discovery, learning, and naming. This is also a provocation to educators to trace some of the ways in which colonization and anti-blackness come to matter in the early childhood places in which they work. My suggestion here is that these tracings also include attending to the ways in which specific more-than-human others as active witnesses might interrupt obscurances and omissions of settler colonialism and anti-blackness. Attending to the more-than-human as active witnesses means that educators should seek out and collaboratively create place-based stories in place encounters where neither the stories nor the storytellers are limited to the human. I invite educators to consider the ways in which, in their particular contexts, they might (re)story young children's place encounters in ways that disrupt, destabilize, and subvert taken-for-granted settler colonial narratives of "knowing" a place.

I believe that the provocations I have offered here for educators bring possibilities for being on the lookout for more ethical relationalities in early childhood pedagogies. Here an immanent ethics centers responsibility and accountability for multiple relations within which educators and children are always already entangled. The provocations I have offered also do not present educators with already-determined "solutions" or the possibility of transcendental positions. Instead, the place encounters described in this book suggest that educators might consider ethical practices as situated "doings," enacted through specific pedagogies, such as those emerging from situated practices of testifying-witnessing and presencing. Such practices grapple with the tenuous knots that connect encounters to settler colonialism and anti-blackness. An ethos of accountability and responsibility toward multiple relations might be seen as enacted through early childhood practices that open to both decolonial and nonanthropocentric perspectives.

Decolonizing placed-based pedagogies might be seen as becoming ethical through particular acts—acts that involve deciding which stories/encounters/histories to make visible and questioning whose knowledge counts and which past and present inhabitants of place matter. I view all of the research and pedagogical orientations and questions that this book has generated as having cumulative decolonizing resonances. That is to say, (re)storying place encounters through human/more-than-human relations, settler colonial histories, Indigenous knowledges, and the Black Anthropocene enacts a micropolitics of decolonial resonances.

In closing, I want to emphasize that this work is not intended to enact a "metaphorization of decolonization" (Tuck & Yang, 2012, p. 1). Decolonization requires and is led by Indigenous peoples, knowledges, and ontologies (Smith, 2013). I also resonate with the perspectives of Indigenous scholars who state that decolonization is not possible amid ongoing settler colonial formations that continue to dispossess Indigenous peoples (see, for example, Byrd, 2011; Simpson,

2011; Tuck & Yang, 2012). Such displacements remain in place in the Coast Salish territories where my research was conducted, where, at the time this research was conducted, there were no Indigenous educators or children in the specific settings in which I worked. While underlining these important limitations, I take seriously the contention that inheriting settler colonial histories is a task that demands accountable responses from all, including responding to the ways in which these inheritances connect to anthropogenic damage and anti-blackness. The writing I have undertaken here is but one such micropolitical response toward situating early childhood education within these pastpresent histories and unsettling settler colonial relations and anti-blackness in early childhood pedagogies.

# APPENDIX

A selection of readings that educators engaged with in the research project.

## Decolonizing Perspectives

Ritchie, J. (2012). Early childhood education as a site of ecocentric counter-colonial endeavour in Aotearoa New Zealand. *Contemporary Issues in Early Childhood*, 13(2), 86–98.

## Environmental Humanities

Tsing, A. (2012). Unruly Edges: Mushrooms as companion species. *Environmental Humanities*, 1, 141–154.

van Dooren, T. (2014). Care: Living lexicon for the environmental humanities. *Environmental Humanities*, 5, 291–294.

## Indigenous Feminisms

Kimmerer, R. W. (2003). Gathering moss: A natural and cultural history of mosses. Corvallis, OR: OSU Press.

Watts, V. (2013). Indigenous place-thought and agency amongst humans and nonhumans. *First Woman and Sky Woman go on a European world tour! Decolonization*, 2(1), 20–34.

## Postcolonial & Anti-racist Feminisms

Pacini-Ketchabaw, V., Berikoff, A., Elliot, E., & Tucker, A. (2007). Anti-racism and postcolonialism in early childhood education. *The Early Childhood Educator*, 22(2), 30–33.

Viruru, R. (2005). The impact of postcolonial theory on early childhood education. *Journal of Education*, 35, 7–29.

## Posthumanist & New Material Feminisms

Lenz Taguchi, H. (2011). Investigating learning, participation and becoming in early childhood practices with a relational materialist approach. *Global Studies of Childhood*, 1 (1), 36–50.

Puig de la Bellacasa, M. (2012). "Nothing comes without its world": Thinking with care. *The Sociological Review*, 60(2), 197–216.

## Poststructural Feminist

Mac Naughton, G. (2005). Doing Foucault in early childhood: Applying poststructural ideas to early childhood. London, UK: Routledge.

Ryan, S., & Grieshaber, S. (2005). Shifting from developmental to postmodern practices in early childhood teacher education. *Journal of Teacher Education*, 56(1), 34–45.

Taylor, A., & Richardson, C. (2005). Queering home corner. *Contemporary Issues in Early Childhood*, 6(2), 163–173.

# REFERENCES


Addison, J. A. (2009). Distribution and impacts of invasive earthworms in Canadian forest ecosystems. *Biological Invasions*, 11, 59–79.

Ahmed, S. (2004). *The cultural politics of emotion*. New York, NY: Routledge.

Ahmed, S. (2010). Orientations matter. In D. Coole & S. Frost (Eds.), *New materialisms: Ontology, agency, and politics* (pp. 234–257). Durham, NC: Duke University Press.

Ahmed, S. (2014). Mixed orientations. *Subjectivity*, 7, 92–109. doi:10.1057/sub.2013.22

Alaimo, S. (2010). Material engagements: Science studies and the environmental humanities. *Ecozon@: European Journal of Literature, Culture, and Environment*, 1(1), 69–74.

Alfred, T., & Corntassel, J. (2005). Being Indigenous: Resurgences against contemporary colonialism. *Government & Opposition*, 40(4), 597–614.

Anderson, J. (2012). Relational places: The surfed wave as assemblage and convergence. *Environment & Planning D: Society & Space*, 30, 570–587.

Anderson, K. (2007). *Race and the crisis of humanism*. London, UK: Routledge.

Andrijasevic, R., & Khalili, L. (2013). Water. *Feminist Review*, 103, 1–4.

Armstrong, J. E. (1990). *Vancouver geology*. Vancouver, BC: Geological Association of Canada.

Badger, G. (2013, February 4). *Unsettled objects: The alchemy of dispossession and display* [blog post]. Retrieved from http://thepowerplant.org/SwitchOn/Features/February-2013/Unsettled-Objects-%28The-Alchemy-of-Dispossession-an.aspx

Baldwin, W. A. (2013). Racialisation and the figure of the climate-change migrant. *Environment and Planning A: Economy and Space*, 45, 1474–1490.

Bang, M., & Marin, A. (2015). Nature–culture constructs in science learning: Human/non-human agency and intentionality. *Journal of Research in Science Teaching*, 52(4), 530–544.

Bang, M., & Medin, D. (2010). Cultural processes in science education: Supporting the navigation of multiple epistemologies. *Science Education*, 94(6), 1008–1026.

Barad, K. (2003). Posthumanist performativity: Toward an understanding of how matter comes to matter. *SIGNS: Journal of Women in Culture and Society*, 28(30), 801–829.

Barad, K. (2007). *Meeting the universe halfway: Quantum physics and the entanglement of matter and meaning*. Durham, NC: Duke University Press.

Barad, K. (2011). Nature's queer performativity. *Qui Parle: Critical Humanities and Social Sciences*, 19(2), 121–158.

Barad, K. (2012). On touching: The inhuman that therefore I am. *Differences: A Journal of Feminist Cultural Studies*, 23(3), 206–223.

Barajas-López, F., & Bang, M. (2018). Claywork in an Indigenous STEAM Program. *Equity & Excellence in Education*, 51(1), 7–20.

Barker, A. J. (2009). The contemporary reality of Canadian imperialism: Settler colonialism and the hybrid colonial state. *The American Indian Quarterly*, 33(3), 325–351.

Barman, J. (2006). *Stanley Park's secret: The forgotten families of Whoi Whoi, Kanaka Ranch, and Brockton Point*. Vancouver, BC: Harbour Publishing.

Barney, M. W. (1919). *Follow the Pied Piper join the United States School Garden-Army* [poster]. Retrieved from https://archive.org/details/CAT31125191. Credit: United States Department of Agriculture Poster Collection.

Battiste, M., & Henderson, J. S. Y. (2000). *Protecting Indigenous knowledge and heritage: A global challenge*. Saskatoon, SK: Purich.

Battiste, M., Bell, M., Findlay, I., Findlay, L., & Henderson, J. S. Y. (2005). Thinking place: Animating the Indigenous humanities in education. *Australian Journal of Indigenous Education*, 34, 7–19.

Benjamin, R. (2016). Racial fictions, biological facts: Expanding the sociological imagination through speculative methods. *Catalyst: Feminism, Theory, Technoscience*, 2(2), 1–28.

Bennett, J. (2004). The force of things: Steps toward an ecology of matter. *Political Theory*, 32, 347–372.

Bennett, J. (2010). *Vibrant matter: A political ecology of things*. Durham, NC: Duke University Press.

Berger, I. (2010). Extending the notion of pedagogical narration through Hannah Arendt's political thought. In V. Pacini-Ketchabaw (Ed.), *Flows, rhythms, and intensities of early childhood education curriculum* (pp. 57–76). New York, NY: Peter Lang.

Berlant, L. (2008). Thinking about feeling historical. *Emotion, Space, and Society*, 1(1), 4–9.

Bertoni, F. (2012). Charming worms: Crawling between natures. *The Cambridge Journal of Anthropology*, 30(2), 65–81.

Blaise, M. (2013). Activating micropolitical practices in the early years: (Re)assembling bodies and participant observations. In R. Coleman & J. Ringrose (Eds.), *Deleuze and research methodologies* (pp. 184–200). Edinburgh, UK: Edinburgh University Press.

Blaser, M. (2014). Ontology and indigeneity: On the political ontology of heterogeneous assemblages. *Cultural Geographies*, 21(1), 49–58.

Borkwood, M. E. (1980). *A study of environments and vegetation on the Simon Fraser University campus* (Unpublished master's thesis). Simon Fraser University, Burnaby, BC.

Braches, F. (2009). Chile, Peru, and the early lumber exports of BC. *BC History*, 42(2) (Summer), 2–7.

Braidotti, R. (2018). A theoretical framework for the critical posthumanities. *Theory, Culture & Society*, 1–31. Advance Online at: doi:10.1177/0263276418771486

Braun, B. (2000). Producing vertical territory: Geology and governmentality in late Victorian Canada. *Ecumene*, 7(1), 7–46.

Braun, B. (2002). Colonialism's afterlife: Vision and visuality on the Northwest Coast. *Cultural Geographies*, 9, 202–247.

British Columbia Ministry of Education. (2008). *British Columbia Early Learning Framework*. Victoria, BC: Ministry of Education, Ministry of Health, Ministry of Children and Family Development, & Early Advisory Group.

Burgmann, T. (2014, November 21). First Nations vow to stand in unity with protesters as Kinder Morgan survey work begins. *Vancouver Sun*. Retrieved from www.vancouversun.com/news/First+Nations+stand+unity+with+protesters+Kinder+Morgan+survey+work+begins/10403505/story.html

Buswell, S. (1980). Victory gardens: The garden warriors of 1942. *City Farmer*, 3(2). Retrieved from www.cityfarmer.org/victgarA57.html

Butler, J. (2004). *Precarious life: The powers of mourning and violence*. London, UK: Verso.

Butler, O. (1988). *Dawn*. New York, NY: Warner Books.

Butler, O. (1995) *Parable of the sower*. New York, NY: Time Warner Books.

Byrd, J. A. (2011). *The transit of empire: Indigenous critiques of colonialism*. Minneapolis, MN: University of Minnesota Press.

Byrd, J. A., & Rothberg, M. (2011). Between subalternity and indigeneity. *Interventions*, 13 (1), 1–12. doi:10.1080/1369801X.2011.545574

Cajete, G. (2017). Children, myth, and storytelling: An Indigenous perspective. *Global Studies of Childhood*, 7(2), 113–130.

Calderón, D. (2014). Speaking back to manifest destinies: A land education based approach to critical curriculum inquiry. *Environmental Education Research*, 20(1), 24–36. doi:10.1080/13504622.2013.865114

Cameron, E. (2008). Indigenous spectrality and the politics of postcolonial ghost stories. *Cultural Geographies*, 15(3), 383–393.

Cameron, E. (2011). Copper stories: Imaginative geographies and material orderings of the central Canadian Arctic. In A. Baldwin, L. Cameron, & A. Kobayashi (Eds.), *Rethinking the great white North: Race, nature, and the historical geographies of whiteness in Canada* (pp. 169–190). Vancouver, BC: UBC Press.

Cameron, E. (2012). New geographies of story and storytelling. *Progress in Human Geography*, 36(5), 572–591.

Cameron, S. A., Lozier, J. D., Strange, J. P., et al. (2011). Patterns of widespread decline in North American bumble bees. *Proceedings of the National Academy of Sciences*, 108, 662–667.

Camosun Bog Restoration Group. (n.d.). Camosun Bog. Retrieved from http://camosunbog.ca/

Capshaw, K. (2014). *Civil rights childhood: Picturing liberation in African American photobooks*. Minneapolis, MN: University of Minnesota Press.

Carlson, K. T. (2009). *Mountains that see, and that need to be seen: Aboriginal perspectives on degraded visibility associated with air pollution in the BC Lower Mainland and Fraser Valley*. Retrieved from www.clearairbc.ca/visibility/Documents/Aboriginalperspectives.pdf

Cassidy, R. (2007). Introduction: Domestication reconsidered. In R. Cassidy & M. Mullin (Eds.), *Where the wild things are now: Domestication reconsidered* (pp. 1–27). Oxford, UK: Berg.

Casteel, S. P. (2003). New world pastoral: The Caribbean garden and emplacement in Gisele Pineau and Shani Mootoo. *Interventions: International Journal of Postcolonial Studies*, 5(1), 12–28.

Casteel, S. P. (2007). *Second arrivals: Landscape and belonging in contemporary writing of the Americas*. Charlottesville, VA: University of Virginia Press.

Cattelino, J. R. (2011). Thoughts on the U.S. as a settler society. *North American Dialogue: Newsletter of the Society for the Anthropology of North America*, 14(1), 1–6.

Cattelino, J. R. (2013). Settler colonial nature in the Everglades. Retrieved from www.aaanet.org/sections/ae/index.php/settler-colonial-nature-in-the-everglades/

Cervenak, S. J., & Carter, J. K. (2017). Untitled and outdoors: Thinking with Saidiya Hartman. *Women & Performance: A Journal of Feminist Theory*, 27(1), 45–55.

Chen, C. (2011). Mapping watery relations at the La Chine Rapids. *Alternatives Journal*, 37 (1), 20–21.

Chen, C. (2013). Mapping waters: Thinking with watery places. In C. Chen, J. McLeod, & A. Neimanis (Eds.), *Thinking with water* (pp. 274–298). Montreal, QC: McGill-Queen's University Press.

Chen, C., MacLeod, J., & Neimanis, A. (2013). *Thinking with water*. Montreal, Q.C.: McGill-Queen's University Press.

Chilisa, B. (2012). *Indigenous research methodologies*. London, UK: SAGE.

Chilisa, B., & Ntseane, G. (2010). Resisting dominant discourses: Implications of Indigenous African feminist theory and methods for gender and education research. *Gender and Education*, 22(6), 617–632.

City of Burnaby. (2000). Burnaby Mountain Conservation Area management plan. Retrieved from http://scec.ca/publications/mng-plan/

City of Burnaby. (2013a). Wildlife. Retrieved from www.burnaby.ca/About-Burnaby/About/Green-Burnaby/Wildlife.html

City of Burnaby. (2013b). *Burnaby Mountain Conservation Area*. Retrieved from www.burnaby.ca/Assets/New+Things+To+Do/Explore+The+Outdoors/Parks/Burnaby+Mountain+-+Conservation+Brochure+-+English.pdf

Clare, S. D. (2011). *Earthly encounters: Readings in feminist theory, poststructuralism, and Canadian settler colonialism* (Doctoral dissertation). Retrieved from https://rucore.libraries.rutgers.edu/rutgers-lib/35936/PDF/1/play/

Clark, V., Pacini-Ketchabaw, V., & Hodgins, D. (2015). Thinking with paint: Troubling settler colonialisms through early childhood art pedagogies. *International Journal of Child, Youth, and Family Studies*, 5(4.2), 751–781.

Cockle, K. L., Martin, K., & Wesołowski, T. (2011). Woodpeckers, decay, and the future of cavity-nesting vertebrate communities worldwide. *Frontiers in Ecology and the Environment*, 9(7), 377–382.

Cole, P. (2006). *Coyote and raven go canoeing: Coming home to the village*. Montreal, QC: McGill-Queen's University Press.

Cole, T. (1842). *The voyage of life: Childhood* [painting]. National Gallery of Art, Washington, DC. Retrieved from www.nga.gov/content/ngaweb/Collection/art-object-page.52450.html

Collard, R.-C., Dempsey, J., & Sundberg, J. (2015a). A manifesto for abundant futures. *Annals of the Association of American Geographers*, 105(2), 322–330.

Collard, R.-C., Dempsey, J., & Sundberg, J. (2015b). The moderns' amnesia in two registers. *Environmental Humanities*, 7, 227–232. Retrieved from http://environmentalhumanities.org/arch/vol7/7.13.pdf

Collins, P. H. (1998). *Fighting words: Black women and the search for justice*. Minneapolis, MN: University of Minnesota.

Compton, W. (2010). *After Canaan: Essays on race, writing, and region*. Vancouver, BC: Arsenal Pulp Press.

Corntassel, J., & Bryce, C. (2012). Practicing sustainable self-determination: Indigenous approaches to cultural restoration and revitalization. *The Brown Journal of World Affairs*, 18(2), 151–162.

Crampton, C. B. (1980). *Natural science studies of Burnaby and Belcarra mountains*. Discussion Paper No. 8. Burnaby, BC: Simon Fraser University.

Crawford, T. (2014, November 29). Kinder Morgan stops drilling, begins moving equipment from Burnaby Mountain. *Vancouver Sun*. Retrieved from www.vancouversun.

com/news/Kinder+Morgan+stops+drilling+begins+moving+equipment+from+Burna by+Mountain/10423297/story.html
Crutzen, P. (2006). The Anthropocene. In E. Ehlers & T. Krafft (Eds.), *Earth system science in the Anthropocene* (pp. 13–18). Berlin, Germany: Springer [e-book].
Crutzen, P., & Stoermer, E. (2000). The "Anthropocene." *IGBP Newsletter*, 41, 17–18.
CTV News. (2011, October 30). Vancouver's huge hollow tree stands tall once again. Retrieved from www.ctvnews.ca/vancouver-s-huge-hollow-tree-stands-tall-once-aga in-1.718714#ixzz2Q6NgKnc4
Dahlberg, G., Moss, P., & Pence, A. (2013). *Beyond quality in early childhood education and care: Languages of evaluation* (3rd ed.). London, UK: Routledge.
David Suzuki Foundation. (2012, December 10). *Camosun Bog: Member of the Musqueam Nation (Larry Grant)* [video]. Retrieved from www.youtube.com/watch?v=v6K7jASVzl8
Davis, H., & Todd, Z. (2017). On the importance of a date, or, decolonizing the Anthropocene. *ACME: An International Journal for Critical Geographies*, 16(4), 761–780. Retrieved from www.acme-journal.org/index.php/acme/article/view/1539
de Finney, S. (2010). "We just don't know each other": Racialised girls negotiate mediated multiculturalism in a less diverse Canadian city. *Journal of Intercultural Studies*, 31(5), 471–487.
Dei, G. J. S. (2002). Spirituality in African education. *International Journal of Children's Spirituality*, 7(1), 37–56.
Deleuze, G. (2009). Deleuze on assemblages. Retrieved from http://larvalsubjects.wordp ress.com/2009/10/08/deleuze-on-assemblages/
Deleuze, G., & Guattari, F. (1986). *Kafka: Toward a minor literature* (D. Polan, Trans.). Minneapolis, MN: University of Minnesota Press.
Deleuze, G., & Guattari, F. (1987). *A thousand plateaus: Capitalism and schizophrenia* (B. Massumi, Trans.). Minneapolis, MN: University of Minnesota Press.
Deleuze, G., & Guattari, F. (1994). *What is philosophy?* (H. Tomlinson & G. Burchill, Trans.). London, UK: Verso.
Derrida, J. (1992). *The other heading* (P.-A. Brault & M. B. Naas, Trans.). Bloomington, IN: Indiana University Press.
Deur, D., & Turner, N. J. (Eds.). (2005). *Keeping it living: Traditions of plant use and cultivation on the northwest coast of North America.* Seattle, WA: University of Washington Press.
Dickinson, E. (2013). The misdiagnosis: Rethinking "nature-deficit disorder." *Environmental Communication: A Journal of Nature and Culture*, 7(3), 315–335. doi:10.1080/17524032.2013.802704
Dove, J., Everett, L., & Preece, P. (1999). Exploring a hydrological concept through children's drawings. *International Journal of Science Education*, 21(5), 485–497.
Driskill, Q.-L., Finley, C., Gilley, B. J., & Morgensen, S. L. (2011). Introduction. In Q.-L. Driskill, C. Finley, B. J. Gilley, & S. L. Morgensen (Eds.), *Queer Indigenous studies: Critical interventions in theory, politics, and literature* (pp. 1–28). Tucson, AZ: University of Arizona Press.
Duhn, I. (2012). Places for pedagogies: Pedagogies for places. *Contemporary Issues in Early Childhood*, 13(2), 99–106.
Dumas, M. J., & Nelson, J. D. (2016). (Re)Imagining Black boyhood: Toward a critical framework for educational research. *Harvard Educational Review*, 86(1), 27–47.
Dumas, M. J., & ross, k. m. (2016). "Be real Black for me": Imagining BlackCrit in education. *Urban Education*, 51, 415–442.
Dungy, C. T. (Ed.). (2009). *Black nature: Four centuries of African American nature poetry.* Athens, GA: University of Georgia Press

Elabor-Idemudia, P. (2002). Participatory research: A tool in the production of knowledge. In K. Saunders (Ed.), *Feminist post-development thought* (pp. 227–242). London and New York: Zed Books.

Fawaz, R. (2012). Settling scores: Claiming ground for native and Indigenous critique in the Americas. *Anthropological Quarterly*, 85(1), 257–272.

Finney, C. (2014). *Black faces, white spaces: Reimagining the relationship of African Americans to the great outdoors*. Chapel Hill, NC: University of North Carolina Press.

Four Arrows, F. A., Jacobs, J. L., & Ryan, S. (2010). Anthropocentrism's antidote: Reclaiming our Indigenous orientation to non-human teachers. *Critical Education*, 1(3), 1–20.

Frazier, C. M. (2016). Troubling ecology: Wangechi Mutu, Octavia Butler, and Black feminist interventions in environmentalism. *Critical Ethnic Studies*, 2(1), 40–72.

French, C. (2008). *Social production of community garden space: Case studies of Boston, Massachusetts, and Havana, Cuba*. Ann Arbor, MI: Proquest UMI.

Frost, J. L. (2009). *A history of children's play and play environments: Toward a contemporary child saving movement*. New York, NY: Routledge.

Gallagher, K. C. (2005). Brain research and early childhood development: A primer for developmentally appropriate practice. *Young Children*, 60(4), 12–18.

Garibaldi, A., & Turner, N. (2004). Cultural keystone species: Implications for ecological conservation and restoration. *Ecology and Society*, 9(3), 1–18. Retrieved from www.ecologyandsociety.org/vol9/iss3/art1/

Ginn, F. (2008). Extension, subversion, containment: Eco-nationalism and (post)colonial nature in Aotearoa New Zealand. *Transactions of the Institute of British Geographers*, 33, 335–353.

Ginn, F. (2009). Colonial transformations: Nature, progress, and science in the Christchurch Botanic Gardens. *New Zealand Geographer*, 65, 35–47.

Ginn, F. (2012). Dig for victory! New histories of wartime gardening in Britain. *Journal of Historical Geography*, 38(3), 294–305.

Ginn, F. (2014). Sticky lives: Slugs, detachment, and more-than-human ethics in the garden. *Transactions of the Institute of British Geographers*, 39(4), 532–544.

Ginn, F., Beisel, U., & Barua, M. (2014). Flourishing with awkward creatures: Togetherness, vulnerability, killing. *Environmental Humanities*, 4, 113–123.

Glave, D. (2010) *Rooted in the earth: Reclaiming the African American environmental heritage*. Chicago, IL: Lawrence Hill Books.

Goeman, M. (2008). (Re)Mapping Indigenous presence on the land in Native women's literature. *American Quarterly*, 60(2), 295–302.

Grande, S. (2017, July 4). The future of US education is Standing Rock [op-ed]. *Truthout*. Retrieved from www.truth-out.org/opinion/item/41146-the-future-of-us-education-is-standing-rock

Grant, L. (2012, December). *Camosun bog: Member of the Musqueam Nation*. Retrieved from www.youtube.com/watch?v=v6K7jASVzl8

Green, G. (1947). *History of Burnaby and vicinity*. Vancouver, BC: Shoemaker, McLean, & Veitch.

Gross, C. (2012). Science concepts young children learn through water play. *Dimensions of Early Childhood*, 40(2), 3–11.

Grossman, E. (2013, April 30). Declining bee populations pose a threat to global agriculture. *Yale Environment 360*. Retrieved from http://e360.yale.edu/feature/declining_bee_populations_pose_a_threat_to_global_agriculture/2645/

Grosvenor, K. (1970). *Poems by Kali*. New York, NY: Doubleday.

Guhn, M., Janus, M., & Hertzman, C. (2007). The early development instrument: Translating school readiness assessment into community actions and policy planning. *Early Education and Development*, 18(3), 369–374.

Haraway, D. (1985). Manifesto for cyborgs: Science, technology, and socialist feminism in the 1980s. *Socialist Review*, 80, 66–108.

Haraway, D. (1988). Situated knowledges: The science question in feminism and the privilege of partial perspective. *Feminist Studies*, 14(3), 575–599.

Haraway, D. (1991). *Simians, cyborgs, and women: The reinvention of nature*. New York, NY: Routledge.

Haraway, D. (1992). The promises of monsters: A regenerative politics for inappropriate/d others. In L. Grossberg, C. Nelson, & P. A. Treichler (Eds.), *Cultural studies* (pp. 295–337). New York, NY: Routledge.

Haraway, D. (1994). A game of cat's cradle: Science studies, feminist theory, cultural studies. *Configurations*, 2(1), 59–71.

Haraway, D. (1997). *Modest_witness@second_millenium. FemaleMan©_meets_OncoMouse TM: Feminism and technoscience*. London, UK: Routledge.

Haraway, D. (2003). *A companion species manifesto: Dogs, people, and significant otherness*. Chicago, IL: Prickly Paradigm.

Haraway, D. (2006). When we have never been human, what is to be done? An interview by N. Gane. *Theory, Culture & Society*, 23(7–8),135–158.

Haraway, D. (2008). *When species meet*. Minneapolis, MN: University of Minnesota Press.

Haraway, D. (2011). *Playing cat's cradle with companion species: The Wellek lectures*. Retrieved from http://people.ucsc.edu/~haraway/

Haraway, D. (2012). Awash in urine: DES and Premarin® in multispecies response-ability. *WSQ: Women's Studies Quarterly*, 40(1–2), 301–316.

Haraway, D. (2014a, May 9). *Anthropocene, Capitalocene, Chthulucene: Staying with the trouble* [public lecture]. Retrieved from https://vimeo.com/97663518

Haraway, D. (2014b). *Flight ways (review)* [blog post]. Retrieved from http://thomvandooren.org/publications/flight-ways/

Haraway, D. (2015, June 25). Tunneling in the Chthulucene: Stories for resurgence on a damaged planet. Keynote presentation, 11th biennial Association for the Study of Literature and Environment conference, University of Idaho, Moscow. Retrieved from www.youtube.com/watch?v=FkZSh8Wb-t8

Haraway, D. (2016). *Staying with the trouble: Making kin in the Chthulucene*. Durham, NC: Duke University Press.

Harlan, J. D., & Rivkin, M. S. (2012). *Science experiences for the early childhood years: An integrated affective approach*. Boston, MA: Pearson.

Hartman, S. V. (2016). *The Black outdoors: Fred Moten and Saidiya Hartman at Duke University* [video file]. Retrieved from https://fhi.duke.edu/videos/black-outdoors-fred-moten-saidiya-hartman

Havu-Nuutinen, S. (2005). Examining young children's conceptual change process in floating and sinking from a social constructivist perspective. *International Journal of Science Education*, 25, 259–279.

Head, L., & Muir, P. (2006). Suburban life and the boundaries of nature: Resilience and rupture in Australian backyard gardens. *Transactions of the Institute of British Geographers*, 31(4), 505–524.

Henry, G. (1994). *The light people*. Norman, OK: University of Oklahoma Press.

Heritage Burnaby. (2013). Research. Retrieved from https://heritageburnaby.ca/research/

Highlights for the armchair gardener. (2002). *The Globe and Mail* (1936–Current), p. L5.

Hird, M. J. (2014, April 11). *Landscapes of terminal capitalism, aporias of responsibility: Lifeworlds inherited, inhabited, and bequeathed* [public lecture]. Retrieved from http://c21uwm.com/anthropocene/conference-videos

Hodgins, B. D. (2012). Pedagogical narrations' potentiality as a methodology for child studies research. *Canadian Children*, 37(1), 4–11.

Hodgins, D. (2015). Wanderings with waste: Pedagogical wonderings about intergenerational ecological justice-to-come. *Canadian Children*, 40(2), 89–101.

Holbraad, M., Pedersen, M. A., & Viveiros de Castro, E. (2014, January 13). The politics of ontology: Anthropological positions. *Cultural Anthropology* website. Retrieved from http://culanth.org/fieldsights/462-the-politics-of-ontology-anthropological-positions

Holmes, R. (2012). A fantastic decomposition: Unsettling the fury of having to wait. *Qualitative Inquiry*, 18(7), 544–556.

Horton, J., & Kraftl, P. (2006). What else? Some more ways of thinking and doing "children's geographies." *Children's Geographies*, 4(1), 69–95.

Hultman, K. (2009). A posthumanist deconstruction of gendered mathematical subjectivities. *International Journal of Equity and Innovation in Early Childhood*, 7(2), 16–27.

Hultman, K., & Lenz Taguchi, H. (2010). Challenging anthropocentric analysis of visual data: A relational materialist methodological approach to educational research. *International Journal of Qualitative Studies in Education*, 23(5), 525–542.

Hunt, S. (2014a). Ontologies of indigeneity: The politics of embodying a concept. *Cultural Geographies*, 21, 27–32.

Hunt, S. (2014b). *Witnessing the colonialscape: Lighting the intimate fires of Indigenous legal pluralism* (Doctoral dissertation). Simon Fraser University, BC, Canada. Retrieved from http://summit.sfu.ca/item/14145#310

Imarisha, W., & brown, a. m. (2015). (Eds.). *Octavia's brood: Science fiction stories from social justice movements*. Chico, CA: AK Press.

Instone, L. (1998). The coyote's at the door: Revisioning human-environment relations in the Australian context. *Cultural Geographies*, 5(4), 452–467.

Instone, L. (2004). Situating nature: On doing cultural geographies of Australian nature. *Australian Geographer*, 35, 131–140.

Instone, L. (2010a). Walking towards Woomera: Touring the boundaries of "unAustralian geographies." *Cultural Geographies*, 17, 359–378.

Instone, L. (2010b). Encountering native grasslands: Matters of concern in an urban park. *Australian Humanities Review*, 49, 91–117.

Instone, L. (2014). Unruly grasses: Affective attunements in the ecological restoration of urban native grasslands in Australia. *Emotion, Space, and Society*, 10, 79–86.

Jackson, A. Y. (2013). Posthumanist data analysis of mangling practices. *International Journal of Qualitative Studies in Education*, 26(6), 741–748.

Jackson, A. Y., & Mazzei, L. A. (2012). *Thinking with theory in qualitative research: Viewing data across multiple perspectives*. New York, NY: Routledge.

Jackson, Z. I. (2013). Animal: New directions in the theorization of race and posthumanism. *Feminist Studies*, 39(3), 669–685.

Jackson, Z. I. (2016). Sense of things. *Catalyst: Feminism, Theory, Technoscience*, 2(2), 1–48.

Jaworski, A., & ThurlowC. (2010). Introducing semiotic landscapes. In A. Jaworski & C. Thurlow (Eds.), *Semiotic landscapes: Language, image, space* (pp. 1–40). London, UK: Continuum.

Jones, S. A., & Stenberg, A. (2015). *Niobe: She is life*. Los Angeles, CA: Stranger Comics.

Jordan, J. (1972). *Dry victories*. New York, NY: Holt, Rinehart, & Winston.
Kheraj, S. (2007). Restoring nature: Ecology, memory, and the storm history of Vancouver's Stanley Park. *Canadian Historical Review*, 88(4), 577–612.
Kimmerer, R. W. (2003). *Gathering moss: A natural and cultural history of mosses*. Corvallis, OR: Oregon State University Press.
Kind, S. (2010). Art encounters: Movements in the visual arts and early childhood education. In V. Pacini-Ketchabaw (Ed.), *Flows, rhythms, and intensities of early childhood education curriculum* (pp. 113–132). New York, NY: Peter Lang.
King, T. L. (2016). The labor of (re)reading plantation landscapes fungible(ly). *Antipode*, 48, 1022–1039.
King, T. L. (2017). Humans involved: Lurking in the lines of posthumanist flight. *Critical Ethnic Studies*, 3(1), 162–185.
Kirksey, E. (2012). Living with parasites in Palo Verde National Park. *Environmental Humanities*, 1(1), 23–55.
Kirksey, E., & Helmreich, S. (2010). The emergence of multispecies ethnography. *Cultural Anthropology*, 25(4), 545–576.
Klein, N. (2014). *This changes everything: Capitalism vs. the climate*. New York, NY: Simon & Schuster.
Korteweg, L., & Russell, C. (2012). Decolonizing + indigenizing = moving environmental education towards reconciliation [editorial]. *Canadian Journal of Environmental Education*, 17, 5–14.
Kosek, J. (2011). The natures of the beast: On the new uses of the honey bee. In R. Peet, P. Robbins, & M. Watts (Eds.), *Global political ecology* (pp. 227–253). London, UK: Routledge.
Kothari, U., & Wilkinson, R. (2010). Colonial imaginaries and postcolonial transformations: Exiles, bases, beaches. *Third World Quarterly*, 31(8), 1395–1412.
Kwiáht. (2014). Ancient gardens. Retrieved from www.kwiaht.org
Langford, S. (2012). *Six gardening trends to watch and try in 2012*. Retrieved from www.canadiangardening.com/how-to/gardening-basics/six-gardening-trends-to-watch-and-try-in-2012/a/38632
Lather, P. (2013). Methodology-21: What do we do in the afterward? *International Journal of Qualitative Studies in Education*, 26(6), 634–645.
Latimer, J., & Miele, M. (2013). Naturecultures? Science, affect, and the non-human. *Theory, Culture, & Society*, 30(7–8),5–31.
Latour, B. (1993). *We have never been modern*. London, UK: Harvester Wheatsheaf.
Latour, B. (2004a). *Politics of nature: How to bring the sciences into democracy*. Cambridge, MA: Harvard University Press.
Latour, B. (2004b). Why has critique run out of steam? From matters of fact to matters of concern. *Critical Inquiry*, 30, 225–248.
Latty, S., Scribe, M., Peters, M., & Morgan, A. (2016). Not enough human: At the scenes of Indigenous and Black dispossession. *Critical Ethnic Studies*, 2(2), 129–158.
Law, J. (2004). *After method: Mess in social science research*. Abingdon, UK: Routledge.
Law, J. (2011). *What's wrong with a one-world world*. Retrieved from www.heterogeneities.net/publications/Law2011WhatsWrongWithAOneWorldWorld.pdf
Lawson, L. (2005). *City bountiful: A century of community gardening in America*. Berkeley, CA: University of California Press.
Le Grange, L. (2009). Participation and participatory action research (PAR) in environmental education processes: For what are people empowered? *Australian Journal of Environmental Education*, 25, 3–14.

Le Grange, L. (2012a). Ubuntu, ukama, environment, and moral education. *Journal of Moral Education*, 41(3), 329–340. doi:10.1080/03057240.2012.691631

Le Grange, L. (2012b). Ubuntu, ukama, and the healing of nature, self, and society. *Educational Philosophy and Theory*, 44(S2), 56–67.

Lee, D. (2011, August 30). *Dibaajimowinan: Four stories of resurgence in Michi Saagiig Nishnaabeg territory* [blog post]. Retrieved from http://dibaajimowin.wordpress.com

Lewis, S. L., & Maslin, M. A. (2015). A transparent framework for defining the Anthropocene epoch. *The Anthropocene Review*, 2(2), 128–146.

Lloro-Bidart, T. (2015). A political ecology of education in/for the Anthropocene. *Environment and Society: Advances in Research*, 6, 128–148.

Longhurst, R. (2006). Plots, plants, and paradoxes: Contemporary domestic gardens in Aotearoa New Zealand. *Social & Cultural Geography*, 7(4), 581–593. doi:10.1080/14649360600825729

Lorimer, J. (2012). Multinatural geographies for the Anthropocene. *Progress in Human Geography*, 36, 593–612.

Louv, R. (2008). *Last child in the woods: Saving our children from nature-deficit disorder* (2nd ed.). Chapel Hill, NC: Algonquin Books of Chapel Hill.

MacDonald, M. (2007). Toward formative assessment: The use of pedagogical documentation in early elementary classrooms. *Early Childhood Research Quarterly*, 22(2), 232–242.

MacLure, M. (2011). Qualitative inquiry: Where are the ruins? *Qualitative Inquiry*, 17, 997–1005.

MacNaughton, G. (2005). *Doing Foucault in early childhood studies: Applying poststructural ideas*. New York, NY: Routledge.

Malone, K. (2017). Ecological posthumanist theorising: Grappling with child–dog-bodies. In K. Malone, S. Truong, & T. Gray (Eds.), *Reimagining sustainability in precarious times* (pp. 161–172). Singapore: Springer.

Mandamin, J. (2014, September 25). Meet Josephine Mandamin (Anishinaabekwe), the "water walker" [interview]. Retrieved from http://indigenousrising.org/josephine-mandamin/

Marshall, V. G., & Fender, W. M. (1998). Native earthworms of British Columbia forests. *Northwest Science*, 72(2), 101–102.

Marshall, V. G., & Fender, W. M. (2007). Native and introduced earthworms (Oligochaeta) of British Columbia, Canada. *Megadrilogica*, 11(4), 29–52.

Martin, K. (2007). "Here we go 'round the broomie tree": Aboriginal early childhood realities and experiences in early childhood services. In J. Ailwood (Ed.), *Early childhood in Australia: Historical and comparative contexts* (pp. 18–34). Frenchs Forest, Australia: Pearson Education.

Martin, K. (2008). *Aboriginal worldview, knowledge, and relatedness theory: A framework for pedagogy and praxis and the teaching-learning interface with Aboriginal students*. Paper presented at AIATSIS seminar series, Canberra, Australia.

Massey, D. (2005). *For space*. London, UK: SAGE.

Mbembe, A. (2002). African modes of self-writing. *Public Culture*, 14(1), 239–273.

McKittrick, K. (2002). Their blood is there, and they can't throw it out: Honouring Black Canadian geographies. *Topia: Canadian Journal of Cultural Studies*, 7, 27–37.

McKittrick, K. (2006). *Demonic grounds: Black women and the cartographies of struggle*. Minneapolis, MN: University of Minnesota Press.

McKittrick, K. (2011). On plantations, prisons, and a black sense of place. *Social & Cultural Geography*, 12(8), 947–963.

McKittrick, K. (2013). Plantation futures. *Small Axe: A Caribbean Platform for Criticism*, 3 (42), 1–15.

McKittrick, K., & Woods, C. (2007). (Eds.) *Black geographies and the politics of place*. New York, NY: Between the Lines Press.

McLellan, S. (2010). Pedagogical documentation as research in early mathematics. *Alberta Journal of Educational Research*, 56(1), 99–101.

Messner, K. (2017). *Over and under the pond*. San Francisco, CA: Chronicle Books.

Mignolo, W. (2002). The geopolitics of knowledge and the colonial difference. *The South Atlantic Quarterly*, 101(1), 57–96.

Ministry of Community Development & Union of British Columbia Municipalities. (2009). *Dig it! How local governments can support community gardens*. Victoria, BC: Author. Retrieved from www.toolkit.bc.ca/resource/dig-it-community-garden-guide-how-local-governments-can-support-community-gardens

Mohanty, C. (2003). *Feminism without borders: Decolonizing theory, practicing solidarity*. Durham, NC: Duke University Press.

Mol, A. (2002). *The body multiple: Ontology in medical practice*. Durham, NC: Duke University Press.

Mol, A. (2014, January 13). Other words: Stories from the social studies of science, technology, and medicine. *Cultural Anthropology Online*. Retrieved from http://culanth.org/fieldsights/472-other-words-stories-from-the-social-studies-of-science-technology-and-medicine

Morgensen, S. L. (2011). The biopolitics of settler colonialism: Right here, right now. *Settler Colonial Studies*, 1, 52–76.

Moss, P., & Dahlberg, G. (2008). Beyond quality in early childhood education and care: Languages of evaluation. *New Zealand Journal of Teachers' Work*, 5(1), 3–12.

Murris, K., Reynolds, R-A., & Peers, J. (2018). Reggio Emilia inspired philosophical teacher education in the Anthropocene: Posthuman child and the family (tree). *Journal of Childhood Studies*, 43(1), 15–29.

National Research Council. (2007). *Status of pollinators in North America*. Washington, DC: National Academies Press.

Nelson, N., Pacini-Ketchabaw, V., & Nxumalo, F. (2018). Rethinking nature-based approaches in early childhood: Common worlding practices. *Journal of Childhood Studies*, 43(1), 4–14.

Nieves, A. D. (2007). Memories of Africville: A case study of urban renewal: The struggle for reparations and the Africadian diaspora. In K. McKittrick & C. Woods (Eds.), *Black geographies and the politics of place* (pp. 82–96). New York, NY: Between the Lines Press.

Nxumalo, F. (2015). Forest stories: Restorying encounters with "natural" places in early childhood education. In V. Pacini-Ketchabaw & A. Taylor (Eds.), *Unsettling the colonial places and spaces of early childhood education* (pp. 21–42). New York, NY: Routledge.

Nxumalo, F. (2016a). Storying practices of witnessing: Refiguring quality in everyday pedagogical encounters. *Contemporary Issues in Early Childhood*, 17(1), 39–53.

Nxumalo, F. (2016b). Towards "refiguring presences" as an anti-colonial orientation to research in early childhood studies. *International Journal of Qualitative Studies in Education*, 29(5), 640–654.

Nxumalo, F. (2016c). Touching place in childhood studies: Situated encounters with a community garden. In H. Skott-Myhre, V. Pacini-Ketchabaw, & K. Skott-Myhre (Eds.), *Youth work, early education, and psychology: Liminal encounters* (pp. 131–158). New York, NY: Palgrave Macmillan.

Nxumalo, F. (2017a). Geotheorizing mountain–child relations within anthropogenic inheritances. *Children's Geographies*, 15(5), 558–569.

Nxumalo, F. (2017b). Stories for living on a damaged planet: Environmental education in a preschool classroom. *Journal of Early Childhood Research*. doi:10.1177/1476718X17715499

Nxumalo, F., & Cedillo, S. (2017). Decolonizing "place" in early childhood studies: Thinking with Indigenous onto-epistemologies and Black feminist geographies. *Global Studies of Childhood*, 7(2), 99–112.

Nxumalo, F. (2018). Situating Indigenous and Black childhoods in the Anthropocene. In A. Cutter-Mackenzie, K. Malone, & E. Barratt Hacking (Eds.), *International research handbook on childhood nature: Assemblages of childhood and nature* (pp. 1–22). New York, NY: Springer. doi:10.1007/978-3-319-51949-4_37-2

Nxumalo, F., & Adair, J. (2018). Social justice and equity in early childhood education. In C. P. Brown, M. McMullen, & N. File (Eds.), *Handbook of early childhood care and education* (pp. 1–22). Hoboken, NJ: Wiley Blackwell. doi:10.1007/978-3-319-51949-4_37-2

Nxumalo, F., & Cedillo, S. (2017). Decolonizing "place" in early childhood studies: Thinking with Indigenous onto-epistemologies and Black feminist geographies. *Global Studies of Childhood*, 7(2), 99–112.

Nxumalo, F., & ross, k. m. (in press). Envisioning Black space in environmental education for young children. *Race, Ethnicity, & Education*.

Nxumalo, F., & Rubin, J. C. (2018). Encountering waste landscapes: More-than-human place literacies in early childhood education. In C. R. Kuby, K. Spector, & J. Johnson Thiel (Eds.), *Posthumanism and literacy education: Knowing/being/doing literacies*. New York, NY: Routledge.

Nxumalo, F., Delgado, C., & Nelson, N. (2018). Pedagogical gatherings in early childhood education: Mapping interferences in emergent curriculum. *Curriculum Inquiry*, 48 (4), 433-453.

Nxumalo, F., Oh, S., Hughes, J., & Bhanji, S. (2015). Entangled dialogues on learning how to inherit in colonized and damaged lifeworlds. *Canadian Children*, 40(2), 82–88.

Nxumalo, F., Pacini-Ketchabaw, V., & Rowan, C. (2011). Lunch time at the child care centre: Neoliberal assemblages in early childhood education. *Journal of Pedagogy*, 2(2), 195–223.

NYC Stands with Standing Rock Collective. (2016). #StandingRockSyllabus. Retrieved from https://nycstandswithstandingrock.wordpress.com/standingrocksyllabus/

Oliver, J. (2007). Beyond the water's edge: Towards a social archaeology of landscape on the Northwest Coast. *Canadian Journal of Archaeology*, 31(1), 1–27.

Oliver, J. (2010). *Landscapes and social transformations on the Northwest Coast: Colonial encounters in the Fraser Valley*. Vancouver, BC: UBC Press.

Ontario Ministry of Education. (2014). *How does learning happen? Ontario's pedagogy for the early years: A resource about learning through relationships for those who work with young children and their families*. Toronto, Canada: Ontario Ministry of Education.

Opondo, S. O. (2008). Genre and the African city: The politics and poetics of urban rhythms. *Journal for Cultural Research*, 12(1), 59–79.

Osgood, J., & Giugni, M. (2015). Reconfiguring "quality": Beyond discourses and subjectivities to matter, bodies, and becomings in early childhood education. In G. S. Cannella, M. Salazar Perez, & I. Lee. (Eds.), *Critical examinations of quality in childhood education and care: Regulation, disqualification, and erasure* (pp. 50–70). New York, NY: Peter Lang.

Pacini-Ketchabaw, V. (2008). Perspectives on child and adolescent development: Challenges and possibilities for teaching. *Relational Child and Youth Care Practice*, 21(3), 39–42.

Pacini-Ketchabaw, V. (2012). Postcolonial entanglements: Unruling stories. *Child & Youth Services*, 33(3–4), 303–316. doi:10.1080/0145935X.2012.745790

Pacini-Ketchabaw, V. (2013). Frictions in forest pedagogies: Common worlds in settler colonial spaces. *Global Studies of Childhood*, 3(4), 355–365.

Pacini-Ketchabaw, V. (Ed.). (2010). *Flows, rhythms, and intensities of early childhood education curriculum*. New York, NY: Peter Lang.

Pacini-Ketchabaw, V., & Clark, V. (2016). Following watery relations in early childhood pedagogies. *Journal of Early Childhood Research*, 14, 98–111.

Pacini-Ketchabaw, V., & Nxumalo, F. (2010). A curriculum for social change: Experimenting with politics of action or imperceptibility. In V. Pacini-Ketchabaw (Ed.), *Flows, rhythms, and intensities of early childhood education curriculum* (pp. 133–154). New York, NY: Peter Lang.

Pacini-Ketchabaw, V., & Nxumalo, F. (2012). Unpacking racialization through pedagogical documentation: Exploring nomadic practices. In A. Fleet, C. Patterson, & J. Robertson (Eds.), *Conversations about Pedagogical Documentation* (pp. 259–272). Castle Hill, N.S.W.: Pademelon Press.

Pacini-Ketchabaw, V., & Nxumalo, F. (2013). Re-generating research partnerships in early childhood education: A non-idealized vision. In J. Duncan & L. Conner (Eds.), *Research partnerships in early childhood education: Teachers and researchers in collaboration* (pp. 11–26). New York, NY: Palgrave Macmillan.

Pacini-Ketchabaw, V., & Nxumalo, F. (2015). Unruly raccoons and troubled educators: Nature/culture divides in a childcare centre. *Environmental Humanities*, 7, 151–168.

Pacini-Ketchabaw, V., & Pence, A. (2011). The postmodern curriculum: Making space for historically and politically situated understandings. *Australasian Journal of Early Childhood*, 36(1), 4–8.

Pacini-Ketchabaw, V., & Taylor, A. (2013). *Learning to inherit and respond to the challenges of the Anthropocene: Toward an early years multispecies pedagogy*. Paper delivered at the 7th World Environmental Education Congress, June 9–14, 2013, Marrakech, Morocco.

Pacini-Ketchabaw, V., di Tomasso, L., & Nxumalo, F. (2014). Bear–child stories in late liberal colonialist spaces of childhood. *Canadian Children*, 38(3), 26–55.

Pacini-Ketchabaw, V., Nxumalo, F., & Rowan, C. (2014). Researching neoliberal and neocolonial assemblages in early childhood education. *International Review of Qualitative Research*, 7(1), 39–57.

Pacini-Ketchabaw, V., Nxumalo, F., Kocher, L., Elliot, E., & Sanchez, A. (2014). *Journeys: Reconceptualizing early childhood practices through pedagogical narration*. Toronto, ON: University of Toronto Press.

Pacini-Ketchabaw, V., Taylor, A., & Blaise, M. (2016). Decentring the human in multispecies ethnographies. In C. Taylor & C. Hughes (Eds.), *Posthuman research practices in education* (pp. 149–167). London, UK: Palgrave Macmillan.

Paperson, L. (2014). A ghetto land pedagogy: An antidote for settler environmentalism. *Environmental Education Research*, 20(1), 115–130.

Parham, M. (2015). *Still life in digital: Black life, trauma, and social media*. Mellon Mays Lecture presented at the University of Texas at Austin, September 30, 2015.

Pelo, A. (2013). *The goodness of rain: Developing an ecological identity in young children*. Redmond, WA: Exchange Press.

Peng, M. S., & Thompson, W. T. (2003). Some aspects of the effect of surface friction on flows over mountains. *Quarterly Journal of the Royal Meteorological Society*, 129(593), 2527–2557.

Pérez, M. S., & Saavedra, C. M. (2017). A call for onto-epistemological diversity in early childhood education and care: Centering global south conceptualizations of childhood/s. *Review of Research in Education*, 41(1), 1–29.

Pinter, N., & Brandon, M. T. (1997). How erosion builds mountains. *Scientific American*, 276, 74–79.

Plant a victory garden: A garden will make your rations go further [poster]. (1944–1945). Library and Archives Canada, Acc. No. 1981-32-22. Retrieved from www.collectionscanada.gc.ca/

Plumwood, V. (1993). *Feminism and the mastery of nature*. New York, NY: Routledge.

Plumwood, V. (2002). *Environmental culture: The ecological crisis of reason*. New York, NY: Routledge.

Plumwood, V. (2005). Decolonising Australian gardens: Gardening and the ethics of place. *Eco-humanities Corner*, 36(2). Retrieved from http://australianhumanitiesreview.org/2005/07/01/decolonising-australian-gardens-gardening-and-the-ethics-of-place/

Poinar, G. O., Jr., & Danforth, B. N. (2006). A fossil bee from Early Cretaceous Burmese amber. *Science*, 314(5799), 614. doi:10.1126/science.1134103

Point, R. (2012). *Susan's video* [film]. Retrieved from http://susanpoint.com/media/

Potter, E., & Hawkins, G. (2009, May). Naturecultures: Introduction. *Australian Humanities Review*, 46. Retrieved from http://australianhumanitiesreview.org/2009/05/01/naturecultures-introduction/

Povinelli, E. A. (2011). The governance of the prior. *Interventions: International Journal of Postcolonial Studies*, 13(1), 13–30. doi:10.1080/1369801X.2011.545575

Povinelli, E. A. (2012a). A conversation with Elizabeth Povinelli by K. T. DiFruscia. *Transcripts*, 2, 76–89.

Povinelli, E. A. (2012b). Beyond the names of the people. *Cultural Studies*, 26(2–3), 370–390. doi:10.1080/09502386.2011.636206

Povinelli, E. A. (2013, August 30). *Geontologies: Being, belonging, and obligating as forms of truth making*. Presentation at "Knowledge, Governance, and Organization Management Through Objects" symposium. Charles Darwin University. Retrieved from www.youtube.com/watch?v=oRcEydtnM3w

Povinelli, E. A. (2014a, January 13). Geontologies of the otherwise. *Cultural Anthropology Online*. Retrieved from http://culanth.org/fieldsights/465-geontologies-of-the-otherwise

Povinelli, E. A. (2014b, March 6). *Interview with Elizabeth Povinelli by Mat Coleman and Kathryn Yusoff*. Retrieved from http://societyandspace.com/2014/03/06/interview-with-elizabeth-povinelli-with-mat-coleman-and-kathryn-yusoff/

Povinelli, E. A., Coleman, M., & Yusoff, K. (2017). An interview with Elizabeth Povinelli: Geontopower, biopolitics and the Anthropocene. *Theory, Culture & Society*, 34 (2–3), 169–185. doi:10.1177/0263276417689900

Pratt, M. L. (1992). *Imperial eyes: Travel writing and transculturation*. London, UK: Routledge.

Prystupa, M. (2015, October 27). Tsleil-Waututh Nation take NEB to court to stop Kinder Morgan hearing. *National Observer*. Retrieved from www.nationalobserver.com/2015/10/27/news/tsleil-waututh-nation-take-neb-court-stop-kinder-morgan-hearing

Puig de la Bellacasa, M. (2009). Touching technologies, touching visions. *Subjectivity*, 28 (1), 297–315.

Puig de la Bellacasa, M. (2011). Matters of care in technoscience: Assembling neglected things. *Social Studies of Science*, 41(1), 85–106.

Pulido, L. (2016). Flint, environmental racism, and racial capitalism. *Capitalism, Nature, Socialism*, 27(3), 1–16.

Rautio, P. (2013). Children who carry stones in their pockets: On autotelic material practices in everyday life. *Children's Geographies*, 11, 394–408.

Recollet, K. (2015). Glyphing decolonial love through urban flash mobbing and Walking with our Sisters. *Curriculum Inquiry*, 45(1), 129–145.

Recollet, K. (2016). Gesturing Indigenous futurities through the remix. *Dance Research Journal*, 48(1), 91–105.

Rinaldi, C. (2006). *In dialogue with Reggio Emilia*. New York, NY: Routledge.

Ritchie, J. (2012). Early childhood education as a site of ecocentric counter-colonial endeavour in Aotearoa New Zealand. *Contemporary Issues in Early Childhood*, 13(2), 86–98.

Ritskes, E. (2012). "A great tree has fallen": Community, spiritual ecology, and African education. *African Journal of Teacher Education*, 2(1), 1–21.

Robertson, J. (2017). *The water walker*. Toronto, ON: Second Story Press.

Rooney, T. (2018). Weather worlding: Learning with the elements in early childhood. *Environmental Education Research*, 24(1), 1–12.

Rose, D. B. (2004). *Reports from a wild country: Ethics for decolonization*. Sydney, Australia: University of New South Wales Press.

Rose, D. B. (2014, May 17). *Arts of living on a damaged planet* [blog post]. Retrieved from http://deborahbirdrose.com/tag/symbiotic-mutualism/

Rose, D. B., & van Dooren, T. (2011). Introduction to unloved others: Death of the disregarded in the time of extinctions. *Australian Humanities Review*, 50, 1–4.

Rose, D. B., & van Dooren, T. (2017). Encountering a more-than-human world: Ethos and the arts of witness. In U. Heise, J. Cristensen, & M. Niemann (Eds.), *Routledge companion to the environmental humanities* (pp. 120–128). London, UK: Routledge.

Rose, D. B., van Dooren, T., Chrulew, M., Cooke, S., Kearnes, M., & O'Gormand, E. (2012). Thinking through the environment, unsettling the humanities. *Environmental Humanities*, 1, 1–5.

Ross, R. E. (2003). *Witnessing and testifying: Black women, religion, and civil rights*. Minneapolis, MN: Fortress Press.

Rusert, B. M. (2010). Black nature: The question of race in the age of ecology. *Polygraph*, 22, 149–166.

Saguaro, S. (2006). *Garden plots: The politics and poetics of gardens*. Aldershot, UK: Ashgate.

Said, E. (1978) *Orientalism*. London, UK: Penguin.

Saldanha, A. (2006). Reontologising race: The machinic geography of phenotype. *Environment and Planning D*, 24(1), 9–24.

Shabazz, R. (2015). *Spatializing Blackness: Architectures of confinement and Black masculinity in Chicago*. Chicago, IL: University of Illinois Press.

Sharpe, C. (2016). *In the wake: On blackness and being*. Durham, NC: Duke University Press.

Simpson, L. (2011). *Dancing on our turtle's back: Stories of Nishnaabeg re-creation, resurgence, and a new emergence*. Winnipeg, MB: Arbeiter Ring.

Simpson, L. (2013a, March 5). Dancing the world into being: A conversation with Idle No More's Leanne Simpson (by Naomi Klein). *Yes Magazine*. Retrieved from www.yesmagazine.org/peace-justice/dancing-the-world-into-being-a-conversation-with-idle-no-more-leanne-simpson

Simpson, L. (2013b). Leaks. *Decolonization: Indigeneity, Education, & Society*, 2(1), 131–132.

Smith, L. T. (2012). *Decolonizing methodologies: Research and Indigenous peoples* (2nd ed.). London, UK: Zed Books.

Smithsonian Environmental Research Center. (2013). Earthworm invaders. Retrieved from http://ecosystems.serc.si.edu/earthworm-invaders/

Somerville, M. (2006). *An enabling place pedagogy for new teachers*. Paper presented at the Australian Association for Research in Education 2006 international educational research conference, Adelaide, Australia. Retrieved from www.aare.edu.au/data/publications/2006/som06819.pdf

Somerville, M. (2013). The nature/cultures of children's place learning maps. *Global Studies of Childhood*, 3(4), 407–417. doi:10.2304/gsch.2013.3.4.407

Spivak, G. (1990). *The post-colonial critic: Interviews, strategies, dialogues* (S. Harasym, Ed.). New York, NY: Routledge.

Spivak, G. (2000). Translation as culture. *Parallax: A Journal of Metadiscursive Theory and Cultural Practices*, 14, 13–34.

Spivak, G. (2010). Can the subaltern speak? In R. Morris (Ed.), *Can the subaltern speak? Reflections on the history of an idea* (pp. 21–80). New York, NY: Columbia University Press.

St. Pierre, E. (2011). Post-qualitative research: The critique and the coming after. In N. Denzin & Y. Lincoln (Eds.), *The handbook of qualitative research* (4th ed.; pp. 611–635). Thousand Oaks, CA: SAGE.

St. Pierre, E. A. (1997). An introduction to figurations: A poststructural practice of inquiry. *International Journal of Qualitative Studies in Education*, 10(3), 279–274.

St. Pierre, E., & Jackson, A. (2014). Qualitative data analysis after coding. *Qualitative Inquiry*, 20(6), 715–719. doi:10.1177/1077800414532435

Stewart, H. (1995). *Cedar: Tree of life to the Northwest Coast Indians*. Vancouver, BC: Douglas & McIntyre.

Stewart, K. (2007). *Ordinary affects*. Durham, NC: Duke University Press.

Stewart, K. (2008). Weak theory in an unfinished world. *Journal of Folklore Research*, 45(1), 71–82.

Stewart, K. (2010). Atmospheric attunements. *Rubric*, 1, 1–14.

Stewart, K. (2011). Atmospheric attunements. *Environment and Planning D*, 29(3), 445–453.

Stewart, K. (2012). Precarity's forms. *Cultural Anthropology*, 27(3), 518–525. https://doi.org/10.1111/j.1548-1360.2012.01157.x

Stewart, K. (2014). Road registers. *Cultural Geographies*, 21(4), 549–563.

Stó:lō Nation Lalems ye Stó:lō Si:ya:m. (2003). *Stó:lō heritage policy manual: Xólhmet te mekw'stám ít kwelát: We have to look after everything that belongs to us*. Retrieved from www.srmcentre.com/media_pdf/StoloHeritagePolicyManual.pdf

Stoler, A. L. (2008). Imperial debris: Reflections on ruins and ruination. *Cultural Anthropology*, 23(2), 191–219.

Sundberg, J. (2014). Decolonizing posthumanist geographies. *Cultural Geographies*, 21, 33–47. doi:10.1177/1474474013486067

TallBear, K. (2011). Why interspecies thinking needs Indigenous standpoints. *Cultural Anthropology*. Retrieved from https://culanth.org/fieldsights/why-interspecies-thinking-needs-indigenous-standpoints

TallBear, K. (2013). *Beyond life/not life: A feminist-Indigenous reading of cryopreservation, interspecies thinking, and the new materialisms*. Lecture presented at University of California, Los Angeles, Center for the Study of Women. Retrieved from www.youtube.com/watch?v=TkUeHCUrQ6E

TallBear, K. (2015). An Indigenous reflection on working beyond the human/not human. *GLQ: A Journal of Lesbian and Gay Studies*, 21(2–3), 230–235.

TallBear, K. (2016). *Failed settler kinship, truth and reconciliation, and science*. Presentation at "Courage and Social Justice in Our Time" panel, University of Alberta, Edmonton, March 14, 2016. Retrieved from http://indigenoussts.com/failed-settler-kinship-truth-and-reconciliation-and-science/

Tarpley, N. (Ed.). (1995). *Testimony: Young African-Americans on self-discovery and black identity*. Boston, MA: Beacon Press.

Taylor, A. (2011). Reconceptualizing the nature of childhood. *Childhood*, 18(4), 420–433. doi:10.1177/0907568211404951

Taylor, A. (2013). *Reconfiguring the natures of childhood*. New York, NY: Routledge.

Taylor, A., & Giugni, M. (2012). Common worlds: Reconceptualising inclusion in early childhood communities. *Contemporary Issues in Early Childhood Education*, 13(2), 108–120.

Taylor, A., & Pacini-Ketchabaw, V. (2015). Learning with children, ants, and worms in the Anthropocene: Towards a common world pedagogy of multispecies vulnerability. *Pedagogy, Culture, & Society*, 23(4), 507–529.

Taylor, A., & Pacini-Ketchabaw, V. (2017). Kids, raccoons, and roos: Awkward encounters and mixed affects. *Children's Geographies*, 15(2), 131–145.

Thobani, S. (2007). *Exalted subjects: Studies in the making of race and nation in Canada*. Toronto, ON: University of Toronto Press.

Thompson, D. (2010). A story to unsettle assumptions about critical reflection in practice. In V. Pacini-Ketchabaw (Ed.), *Flows, rhythms, & intensities of early childhood education curriculum* (pp. 77–94). New York, NY: Peter Lang Publishing.

Thorp, R. W. (2003). Bumble bees (Hymenoptea: Apidae): Commercial use and environmental concerns. In K. Strickler & J. H. Cane (Eds.), *For nonnative crops, whence pollinators of the future?* (pp. 21–40). Lanham, MD: Thomas Say Publications in Entomology.

Timeto, F. (2011). Diffracting the rays of technoscience: A situated critique of representation. *Poiesis and Praxis*, 8(2–3),151–167.

Todd, Z. (2015). Indigenizing the Anthropocene. In H. Davis & E. Turpin (Eds.), *Art in the Anthropocene: Encounters among aesthetics, politics, environment, and epistemology* (pp. 241–254). London, UK: Open Humanities Press.

Todd, Z. (2016). Relationships. *Cultural Anthropology* website. Retrieved from https://culanth.org/fieldsights/relationships

Todd, Z. (2017). *Commentary: The environmental anthropology of settler colonialism*, Part I. Environment and Anthropology Society Engagement blog. Retrieved from https://aesengagement.wordpress.com/2017/04/11/commentary-the-environmental-anthropology-of-settler-colonialism-part-i/

Tourism Burnaby. (2013). *Discover Burnaby's parks and trails*. Retrieved from www.tourismburnaby.com/upload/editor/File/Burnaby%20Parks%20&%20Trails%20Guide.pdf

Tsing, A. (2011). Arts of inclusion, or, how to love a mushroom. *Australian Humanities Review*, 50, 5–21.

Tsing, A. L. (2005). *Friction: An ethnography of global connection*. Princeton, NJ: Princeton University Press.

Tsing, A. L. (2012a). On nonscalability: The living world is not amenable to precision-nested scales. *Common Knowledge*, 18(3), 505–524.

Tsing, A. L. (2012b). Unruly edges: Mushrooms as companion species. *Environmental Humanities*, 1, 141–154. Retrieved from https://environmentalhumanities.org/arch/vol1/EH1.9.pdf

Tsing, A. L. (2013). More than human sociality: A call for critical description. In K. Hastrup (Ed.), *Anthropology and nature* (pp. 27–42). New York, NY: Routledge.

Tsing, A. L. (2015, November 10). *A feminist approach to the Anthropocene: Earth stalked by man*. Helen Pond McIntyre '48 lecture, Barnard College, New York, NY. Retrieved from http://bcrw.barnard.edu/videos/anna-lowenhaupt-tsing-a-feminist-approach-to-the-anthropocene-earth-stalked-by-man/

Tsleil-Waututh Sacred Trust. (2016). Assessment of the Trans Mountain Pipeline and tanker expansion proposal. Retrieved from http://twnsacredtrust.ca/

Tuck, E. (2009). Suspending damage: A letter to communities. *Harvard Educational Review*, 79(5), 409–427.

Tuck, E. (2014, April). *A turn to where we already were? Settler inquiry, Indigenous philosophy, and the ontological turn*. Paper presented at American Educational Research Association (AERA) conference, Philadelphia, PA.

Tuck, E. (2016, November 5). Keynote lecture. "Race, Anti-Racism and Indigeneity: Anti-Colonial Resurgence and Decolonial Resistance" conference, Ontario Institute for Studies in Education, Toronto. Retrieved from www.youtube.com/watch?v=1kqbywXKEyA

Tuck, E., & Gaztambide-Fernández, R. (2013). Curriculum, replacement, and settler futurity. *Journal of Curriculum Theorizing*, 29(1), 72–89.

Tuck, E., & Guess, A. (2017). Collaborating on selfsame land. In N. Ares, E. Buendía, & R. Helfenbein (Eds.), *Deterritorializing/reterritorializing. Breakthroughs in the sociology of education* (pp. 45–56). Rotterdam, The Netherlands: Sense.

Tuck, E., & McKenzie, M. (2014). *Place in research: Theory, methodology, and methods*. New York, NY: Routledge.

Tuck, E., & McKenzie, M. (2015). Relational validity and the "where" of inquiry: Place and land in qualitative research. *Qualitative Inquiry*, 21(7), 633–638.

Tuck, E., & Yang, K. W. (2012). Decolonization is not a metaphor. *Decolonization: Indigeneity, Education, & Society*, 1(1), 1–40.

Tuck, E., & Yang, K. W. (2014). Unbecoming claims: Pedagogies of refusal in qualitative research. *Qualitative Inquiry*, 20(6), 811–818. doi:10.1177/1077800414530265

Tuck, E., Guess, A., & Sultan, H. (2014, June 26). Not nowhere: Collaborating on selfsame land. *Decolonization: Indigeneity, Education, & Society* [journal blog]. Retrieved from https://decolonization.wordpress.com/2014/06/26/not-nowhere-collaborating-on-self same-land/

Tuck, E., McKenzie, M., & McCoy, K. (2014). Land education: Indigenous, post-colonial, and decolonizing perspectives on place and environmental education research. *Environmental Education Research*, 20(1), 1–23.

Tuck, E., Smith, M., Guess, A. M., Benjamin, T., & Jones, B. K. (2013). Geotheorizing black/land: Contestations and contingent collaborations. *Departures in Critical Qualitative Research*, 3(1), 52–74.

United States Environmental Protection Agency. (2016). Water resources. Retrieved from www.epa.gov/learn-issues/learn-about-water

van Dooren, T. (2010). Pain of extinction: The death of a vulture. *Cultural Studies Review*, 16(2), 271–289.

van Dooren, T. (2014). *Flight ways: Life and loss at the edge of extinction*. New York, NY: Columbia University Press.

van Dooren, T., & Rose, D. B. (2012). Storied places in a multispecies city. *Humanimalia: A Journal of Human/Animal Interface Studies*, 3(2), 1–27.

Vergès, R. (2017). Racial Capitalocene. In G. T. Johnson & A. Lubin (Eds.), *Futures of Black radicalism* (pp. 72–82). Brooklyn, NY: Verso Books.

Waller, T., Ärlemalm-Hagsér, E., Hansen Sandseter, E. B., Lee-Hammond, L., Lekies, K. S., & Wyver, S. (2017). (Eds.). *SAGE handbook of outdoor play and learning*. London, U. K: SAGE.

Warner, S. B. (1987). *To dwell is to garden: A history of Boston's community gardens*. Boston, MA: Northeastern University Press.

Watts, V. (2013). Indigenous place-thought and agency amongst humans and non-humans (First Woman and Sky Woman go on a European world tour!). *Decolonization: Indigeneity, Education, & Society*, 2(1), 20–34.

Weakland, J. P. (2012). Queering ecology: Interrogating "seductions to organic wholeness" in popular environmental rhetoric. In A. E. J. Wals & P. B. Corcoran (Eds.), *Learning for sustainability in times of accelerating change* (pp. 121–132). Wageningen, The Netherlands: Wageningen Academic Publishers.

Whatmore, S. (2006). Materialist returns: Practicing cultural geography in and for a more than-human world. *Cultural Geographies*, 13(4), 600–609.

Whyte, K. (2017). Indigenous climate change studies: Indigenizing futures, decolonizing the Anthropocene. *English Language Notes*, 55(1–2),153–162.

Willems-Braun, B. (1997). Buried epistemologies: The politics of nature in (post)colonial British Columbia. *Annals of the Association of American Geographers*, 87(1), 3–31.

Williams, P. H., & Osborne, J. L. (2009). Bumblebee vulnerability and conservation world-wide. *Apidologie*, 40, 367–387.

Williamson, E. A. (2002). A deeper ecology: Community gardens in the urban environment. Retrieved from www.cityfarmer.org/erin.html

Wolfe, P. (2006). Settler colonialism and the elimination of the native. *Journal of Genocide Research*, 8(4), 387–409.

Wolfenden, M. (2000). *Dictionary of Canadian biography: Robert Burnaby*. Retrieved from www.biographi.ca/009004-119.01-e.php?&id_nbr=4869

Wong, R. (2011). *Downstream: Reimagining water* [website]. Retrieved from http://downstream.ecuad.ca/

Wynter, S. (1984). The ceremony must be found: After humanism. *Boundary*, 2, 19–70.

Wynter, S. (1994). No humans involved: An open letter to my colleagues. *Forum N.H.I.: Knowledge for the 21st Century*, 1(1), 42–73.

Wynter, S. (2003). Unsettling the coloniality of being/power/truth/freedom: Towards the human, after man, its overrepresentation—An argument. *New Centennial Review*, 3(3), 257–337.

Yusoff, K. (2013). Geologic life: Prehistory, climate, futures in the Anthropocene. *Environment and Planning D: Society and Space*, 31(5), 779–795.

Yusoff, K. (2015). Geologic subjects: Nonhuman origins, geomorphic aesthetics, and the art of becoming inhuman. *Cultural Geographies*, 22, 383–407.

Yusoff, K. (2017, June). *Towards a thousand Black Anthropocenes*. Keynote lecture presented at UNESCO conference "The Ethics of Decolonizing Nature and Culture," Maison de l'UNESCO, Paris, France.

Yuxweluptun, L. P. (1995). *Usufruct* [image]. Retrieved from http://lawrencepaulyuxweluptun.com/

Yuxweluptun, L. P. (1997). *Burying another face of racism on First Nations soil* [image]. Retrieved from http://lawrencepaulyuxweluptun.com/

Yuxweluptun, L. P. (n.d.) *Introductory video* [Artist statement video file]. Retrieved from http://lawrencepaulyuxweluptun.com/

# INDEX

Page numbers in *italics* denote figures.

Milton Keynes UK
Ingram Content Group UK Ltd.
UKHW052018170624
444208UK00027B/758